Lessons in Persuasion

Lessons in Persuasion

Creative Nonfiction / Pittsburgh Connections

edited by Lee Gutkind

University of Pittsburgh Press

Issue 15 of *Creative Nonfiction*

Published by the University of Pittsburgh Press, Pittsburgh, Pa. 15261

Copyright © 2000 by the Creative Nonfiction Foundation

All rights reserved

Reproduction, whether in whole or in part, without permission is strictly prohibited

Manufactured in the United States of America

Printed on acid-free paper

10 9 8 7 6 5 4 3 2 1

Library of Congress Cataloging-in-Publication Data

Lessons in persuasion : creative nonfiction/Pittsburgh Connections /
edited by Lee Gutkind.
    p. cm.
    ISBN 0-8229-5715-9 (alk. paper)
    I. Gutkind, Lee. 1. Pittsburgh (Pa.)—Biography. 2. Pittsburgh (Pa.)—Description
and travel. 3. Pittsburgh (Pa.)—Social life and customs.
    F159.P653 A256 1999
    974.8'8604'0922—dc21   99-006834

Special thanks to the Vira I. Heinz Endowment, the Grable Foundation, and the Buhl Foundation for their generous support of this issue of Creative Nonfiction.

The Creative Nonfiction Foundation also gratefully acknowledges the Juliet Lea Hillman Simonds Foundation, Inc., Goucher College's Center for Graduate and Continuing Studies, and the Pennsylvania Council on the Arts for their ongoing support.

Special thanks to the editorial board of Creative Nonfiction, *Lea Simonds, Laurie Graham, and Patricia Park, managing editor Leslie Boltax Aizenman, and editorial assistant Jane Liddle.*

Contents

LEE GUTKIND	From the Editor: Leaving Home? 1
ANNIE DILLARD	Notes for Young Writers 8
ELISSA WALD	Notes from the Catwalk 15
STEWART O'NAN	*My* Mysteries of Pittsburgh: An Alphabet 31
OMARI C. DANIEL AND JACK L. DANIEL	We Fish 45
LESTER GORAN	The Conjurer's Profession 71
LESLIE RUBINKOWSKI	In the Woods 91
CHUCK KINDER	That Sweet Anarchy We Call Youth 102
HILARY MASTERS	Passing Through Pittsburgh 122
KATHLEEN VESLANY	Lessons in Persuasion 132
NATALIE L. M. PETESCH	Who Am I to Speak? 144
LEA SIMONDS	A Way to Make Some Money 157

DIANE ACKERMAN	Language at Play	175
MEGAN FOSS	Skin Deep	187
MALCOLM CASH	The Preacher Says	217
PETER S. BEAGLE	The Poor People's Campaign	236
KEELY BOWERS	How Butterflies Grew Wings	260
RICHARD F. PETERSON	As I Was Walking Down Carson Street: A South Side Childhood	279
JAN BEATTY	Ghost Story	294

Lessons in Persuasion

From the Editor

Leaving Home?

LEE GUTKIND

When I graduated high school at eighteen, I told anyone who would listen that I intended to leave Pittsburgh and never come back. I succeeded only in part.

I skipped the college route most of my classmates followed and went directly into the military. After my discharge, I worked a variety of jobs, including truck driver, traveling salesman, shoe clerk, and, sometime later, an account executive for advertising and public relations agencies. I traveled widely for these jobs from one coast to the other. Eventually I became enamored with motorcycles. I resigned from all gainful employment in order to connect the corners of the country on two wheels.

My motorcycle excursions led to my first book; my second book permitted me to travel from ballpark to ballpark with a crew of National League baseball umpires and immerse myself in their lives. My third book took me into the backwoods of West Virginia and Pennsylvania, where I observed, close up, rattlesnake sackers, a one-armed blacksmith, a cooper, and a marijuana farmer. For other books, I have immersed myself in the lives of pediatricians, veterinarians, organ-transplant surgeons, and psychiatrists. For all of these books and a number of other adventures, I left Pittsburgh frequently and traveled widely. But eventually, I always returned to the city of my bad dreams.

I wasn't plagued with nightmares, but memories of my hometown were pretty negative. I was an outcast and a loner as far back as I could remember. My high school, Taylor Allderdice, was located in the prominently Jewish upper-middle-class area called Squirrel Hill. I was Jewish, but lived in a working-class section adjacent to Squirrel Hill, a blue-collar, heavily Catholic neighborhood called Greenfield.

Neighborhoods in Pittsburgh, then and now, are the anchors of urban life. When you meet Pittsburghers, they might mention the Pirates, the Steelers, or the Penguins—but not before they mention where they come from—Point Breeze (Annie Dillard's childhood home), the Hill District (of *Hill Street Blues* TV fame), Garfield, the West End, the North Side. Every neighborhood has an identity and meaning: Fox Chapel means you are wealthy and perhaps somewhat aristocratic, while Homewood, where John Edgar Wideman grew up, is mostly African American. Bloomfield is Pittsburgh's little Italy, and "Souside," as Pittsburghers call the South Side, has become an upscale center for antiques, art galleries, blues joints—and big-ticket brasseries.

My parents always claimed we were from Squirrel Hill—not Greenfield—because technically we shared the same zip code (15217). But I didn't buy it, nor did my classmates, who made it clear that I was not a desirable mate by choosing not to include me in most of their social or athletic activities. I wasn't even significant enough to be taunted or criticized or ridiculed. I was ignored. Erased. I didn't exist. Teachers, students, from Greenfield or Squirrel Hill, paid little attention—until I decided to make a spectacle of myself by acting out in class or causing trouble in the neighborhood. I did things that I never really intended to do (throw chalk, place thumbtacks on other people's chairs, wisecrack and shout, fight, break windows), just so I would be noticed, if only for an instant.

The other thing going on in my life growing up in Pittsburgh was more personal and damaging: My father and I were locked in an ongoing battle of wills. My first memory of my father is the day he slapped me on the hand for taking something he said didn't belong to me. I was maybe three years old. From that moment, our battles escalated, with many horrendous confrontations and consequences for every member of my immediate family.

The simple fact that I was expected to follow his bidding upon command, or face a beating with a leather strap if I didn't, frightened and angered me. I refused to bend to his power. I confronted him continually, matching my will against his. In school, my personal problems simmered inside of me with no teachers, neighbors, relatives, or friends to talk to or share my entrapment and distress.

There were others in my school and neighborhood who felt similarly alienated and desperate, I suspect. And the story I am telling has little to do with Pittsburgh, actually, or Squirrel Hill, or school. Isolation, loneliness, and alienation occur everywhere, and often to people who seem on the surface to be intimately engaged with that "in" crowd. Two very popular boys around my same age, whom I admired, were to take their own lives not long after high school. One, a prominent community leader, left a young family behind. I remember my shock and surprise when I learned about their self-inflicted deaths. As battered and demoralized as I was, I would have never considered such a destructive action as suicide. I wanted a way out of my depression and alienation, not by ending my life but by finding a new and better one. <u>This was my motivation for wanting to leave home. Life had to be better elsewhere, I thought.</u> And at least I would be ignored by people who didn't know me—rather than people I had come into contact with all my life.

So why then did I stay in Pittsburgh? At least two reasons: First there was tenure at the University of Pittsburgh—that blessed privilege of academia that, at its best, frees an artist or scholar of the burden of worrying about job security and allows us to research, write, paint—think and speak out. The year I earned my undergraduate degree (I had been taking college classes at night) I published my first book and was subsequently invited to teach in the creative writing program in Pitt's English Department. I've been there since, working my way up the academic ladder. To my knowledge, I'm the only tenured full professor in the entire university without an advanced degree.

My other reason for not leaving Pittsburgh had something to do with what journalists call the five Ws—the who, what, when, where, and why I would be leaving. I have realized recently that I could not have permitted myself to leave Pittsburgh until I confronted the people who had made me uncomfortable in the city through most of my life. So I stayed. I got married, bought a house, amassed possessions, got divorced, and entered into psychotherapy for nine years, all the while writing and publishing and living in but apart—emotionally distanced—from my hometown.

A few years after I remarried, I did something I thought I would never do: I moved back to Squirrel Hill. I shouldn't say "back" to Squirrel Hill, but rather into Squirrel Hill for the first time, in an exclusive area Pittsburghers refer to as "north of Forbes"—Forbes being the avenue that divides the ordinary middle class in the neighborhood from the wealthy elite.

As I began attempting to become a part of the neighborhood, I saw many familiar faces—people with whom I had grown up, my former teachers, merchants on the street with whom I or my parents had done business. There was Little's Shoe Store, Forbes Hardware, Franks' Men's Store, Kards Plus. At first, the sight of these people, old and gray (and fat), freaked me out. And I braced myself each time I walked up Forbes or Murray, the other main street, waiting for some big insult to my character, personality, my clothes, wife, or child. It never happened. In fact, nothing happened. I met very few people in the four years I lived there, engaged in remarkably few conversations either with old acquaintances or new. This was just like high school, except that now I was an adult, a writer, and teacher—a man who had been shrunk for nine years and who now possessed a strong sense of the five Ws—the who, where, when, why, and what I was.

Leaving Home?

When I was a kid, watching that community from a point of total isolation, I desperately wanted to be accepted by somebody. But, jealous and intimidated, I couldn't seem to make any significant social headway. Now, however, I had a life, a family of which I was proud, students who liked me. I didn't need to be a part of someone else's world. I was a part of my own world. I was to leave Squirrel Hill and move into nearby Shadyside a couple of years later, a necessity of my second divorce. But I would have left anyway, divorce or not; I didn't belong there, and that realization made me feel free.

As I said, I went into therapy after my first divorce. My memories were dark, desperate, and seemingly never-ending. You'd think that a grown man—I was in my thirties—could walk away from something that had happened when he was in his teens, but I couldn't put it behind me without reliving it—repeatedly going over every incident having to do with the circumstances that led up to my confrontations with my father. I analyzed everything, including my mother's manipulations of the confrontations, the impact of my father's parents on his rough parenting skills. My talking, complaining, reliving the past went on and on. After a long time, I realized that although I couldn't completely forgive, I could put my past behind me and attempt to forge a new relationship with him.

My own son has been the glue to that relationship. My father has become an active presence in his life. Sam adores his grandfather; they play together frequently. I don't know what demons prevented my dad from being the same active, positive presence in my life, but it truly no longer matters to me. My son is what matters—and my own feelings about myself as a human being. The fact that the isolation, alienation, and anger I felt as a child toward my parents has now become an increasingly distant memory is the signal I have been awaiting ever since my high school graduation and my pronouncement that I wanted to blow this pop stand—leave Pittsburgh and never come back. All those years since high school, the demons from my childhood kept me prisoner. It has taken many decades to tame them. Now I feel released. For the first time in my life I am ready to leave Pittsburgh. I can finally turn my back on my hometown and walk away without leaving any baggage behind.

And because there is little baggage remaining, I find I can also choose to stay. Sam likes it here. He lives with me, but his mother and his grandparents are very close, and he loves his school, which, ironically, is located in Squirrel Hill. The University of Pittsburgh where I work has supplanted the steel industry as the area's leading employer. The neighborhoods are still strong; my house in Shadyside is comfortable. There are three large parks in running or walking distance of my home. Two new stadiums for the Pirates and Steelers respectively will be constructed in the next few years. My students are bright and for the most part appreciative. I recently purchased a house in a beach town to live in in the summer. I no longer walk the streets in Pittsburgh experiencing the simmering heat of my bad dreams.

I don't know the direction I will choose next, but that state of paralysis of wanting to leave and being unable to actually take the steps necessary to make my departure a reality is now gone. This is a fact of my life that provides a feeling of tremendous relief and freedom. Knowing that I am free to leave this city and never come back or stay and anchor myself and Sam as true citizens of the "Burgh" is exhilarating and liberating. For the first time, I am analyzing my hometown with objective eyes.

Like me, all of the writers in *Lessons in Persuasion* have roots in or connections to Pittsburgh. The majority of the contributors have lived here for varied periods of time—and then moved on. The lessons in this collection can be gentle or jarring, but are always eclectic and persuasive. Elissa Wald finds stripping less degrading and more lucrative than waitressing or working as an office temp, while Diane Ackerman defines the nature of poetry through the eyes of her students as a game—"a ritual dance with words." Jan Beatty employs poetry—as a way to understand her adoption. Annie Dillard also speaks to students and writers, endorsing the basics of writing (learn grammar and punctuation)—and life. Chuck Kinder profiles Sid Hatfield, a key figure in West Virginia's famed Matewan shootout. Lester Goran recreates the Atlantic City boardwalk before blackjack and Donald Trump. Wald, Kinder, and Goran are novelists, as are contributors Stewart O'Nan and Hilary Masters—crossing genres into creative nonfiction—and Pittsburghers, which is the glue that binds this collection.

Pittsburgh is not the subject of all of the essays, but each work shares the connective blood and fiber of a writer anchored there. In addition to these well-known Pittsburghers, a number of new writers are being introduced: Kathleen Veslany (whose essay serves as title for the collection), Megan Foss (a recent winner of the Rona Jaffe Foundation Women's Writers' Award), Keely Bowers, Leslie Rubinkowski, Richard Peterson, Malcolm Cash, and the father-son duo of Jack and Omari Daniel. Also featured is a photo and prose retrospective of the work of the African-American Pittsburgh photographer Teenie Harris by Lea Simonds, who also serves on the editorial board of *Creative Nonfiction*. Simonds poured through the vast Teenie Harris collection, many thousands of images, to choose the thirteen included here as representative of Harris's extensive photographic accomplishments.

Notes for Young Writers

ANNIE DILLARD

Dedicate (donate, give all) your life to something larger than yourself and pleasure—to the largest thing you can: to God, to relieving suffering, to contributing to knowledge, to adding to literature, or something else. Happiness lies this way, and it beats pleasure hollow.

A great physicist taught at the Massachusetts Institute of Technology. He published many important books and papers. Often he had an idea in the middle of the night. He rose from his bed, took a shower, washed his hair, and shaved. He dressed completely, in a clean shirt, in polished shoes, a jacket and tie. Then he sat at his desk and wrote down his idea. A friend of mine asked him why he put himself through all that rigamarole. "Why," he said, surprised at the question, "in honor of physics!"

If you have a choice, live at least a year in very different parts of the country.

Never, ever, get yourself into a situation where you have nothing to do but write and read. You'll go into a depression. You have to be doing something good for the world, something undeniably useful; you need exercise, too, and people.

Read for pleasure. If you like Tolstoy, read Tolstoy; if you like Dostoevsky, read Dostoevsky. Push it a little, but don't read something totally alien to your nature and then say, "I'll never be able to write like that." Of course you won't. Read books you'd like to write. If you want to write literature, read literature. Write books you'd like to read. Follow your own weirdness.

You'll have time to read after college.

Don't worry about what you do the first year after college. It's not what you'll be doing for the rest of your life.

People in the arts, I read once, take about eight years just to figure out which art they're in! Notify your parents.

MFA and MA writing programs are great fun, and many are cheap or free.

Learn grammar. Get a grammar book and read it two or three times a year. (Strunk and White is classic.)

Learn punctuation; it is your little drum set, one of the few tools you have to signal the reader where the beats and emphases go. (If you get it wrong, any least thing, the editor will throw your manuscript out.) Punctuation is not like musical notation; it doesn't indicate the length of pauses, but instead signifies logical relations. There are all sorts of people out there who know these things very well. You have to be among them even to begin.

Check the spelling; proofread. Get someone else to proofread, too.

Don't use passive verb constructions. You can rewrite any sentence.

Annie Dillard

Don't misspell dialect. Let the syntax and words suggest the pronunciation.

Don't use any word for "walk" or "say" except "walk" or "say." I know your sixth-grade teacher told you otherwise. She told me otherwise, too, and is still telling her sixth graders otherwise.

Always locate the reader in time and space—again and again. Beginning writers rush in to feelings, to interior lives. Instead, stick to surface appearances; hit the five senses; give the history of the person and the place, and the look of the person and the place. Use first and last names. As you write, stick everything in a place and a time.

Don't describe feelings.

The way to a reader's emotions is, oddly enough, through the senses.

If something in your narrative or poem is important, give it proportional space. I mean, actual inches. The reader has to spend time with a subject to care about it. Don't shy away from your big scenes; stretch them out.

Writing in scenes doesn't mean in television scenes. No dull dialogue: "Honey, I'm home! Where's the beer?" "In the refrigerator!" (I think most fiction contains far too much dialogue.)

Capturing the typical isn't a virtue. Only making something new and interesting is. If you find life dull and people hateful, keep thinking until you can see it another way. Why would any reader pick up a book to read a detailed description of all that is most annoying in his daily life?

Don't use any extra words. A sentence is a machine; it has a job to do. An extra word in a sentence is like a sock in a machine.

Buy hardback fiction and poetry. Request hardback fiction and poetry as gifts from everyone you know. Give hardback fiction and poetry as gifts to everyone. No shirt or sweater ever changed a life. Never complain about publishing if you don't buy hardcover fiction and poetry regularly.

Buy books from independent booksellers, not chain stores. For complicated reasons, chain stores are helping stamp out literary publishing.

(Similarly, register and vote. If you don't vote, don't complain.)

Write for readers. Ask yourself how every sentence and every line will strike the reader. That way you can see if you're misleading, or boring, the readers. Of course it's hard to read your work when you've just written it; it all seems clear and powerful. Put it away and rewrite it later. Don't keep reading it over, or you'll have to wait longer to see it afresh.

Don't write about yourself. Think of books you like. Isn't it their subjects you like best? Boring people talk about themselves.

The work's unity is more important than anything else about it. Those digressions that were so much fun to write must go.

Usually you will have to rewrite the beginning—the first quarter or third of whatever it is. Don't waste much time polishing this; you'll just have to take a deep breath and throw it away anyway, once you finish the work and have a clearer sense of what it is about. Tear up the runway; it helped you take off, and you don't need it now. This is why some writers say it takes "courage" to write. It does. Over and over you must choose the book over your own wishes and feelings.

Ignore your feelings about your work. These are an occupational hazard. If you are writing a book, keep working at it, deeper and deeper, when you feel it is awful; keep revising and improving it when you feel it is wonderful. When you are young and starting out, often it is better, however, to write something else than to labor over something that was a bad idea in the first place. Write something else; then write something else; then write something else. No matter how experienced you are, there is no correlation, either direct or inverse, between your immediate feelings about your work's quality and its actual quality. All you can do is ignore your feelings altogether. It's hard to do, but you can learn to do it.

When you are writing full-time (three to four hours a day), go in the room with the book every day, regardless of your feelings. If you skip a day it will take three painful days to get to believing in the work again. Have a place where you can leave the work out and open, so you don't have to get it all out and spread before you can start again.

The more you read, the more you will write. The better the stuff you read, the better the stuff you will write. You have many years. You can develop a taste for good literature gradually. Keep a list of books you want to read. You soon learn that "classics" are books that are endlessly interesting—almost all of them. You can keep rereading them all your life—about every ten years—and various ones light up for you at different stages of your life.

Don't find an interesting true story—a life, say, or a historical incident—and decide to turn it into a novel instead of a biography or a historical account. The novel based on fact is a muddy hybrid; readers can't tell what's true. Publishers won't touch these. Write it as nonfiction if you want to write it.

If you want to write novels (and if you buy hardcover novels regularly), go ahead and write novels. Publishing has changed, however, and novels are very difficult to publish. If you want to improve the odds that people will read what you write, write nonfiction narrative.

For fiction, poetry, or nonfiction, the more research you do, the more materials you will have to play with. You are writing for readers—a very educated bunch in this country. It's hard and interesting to tell them something they don't know. The more you read, the better you will know what they know.

No one can help you if you're stuck in a work. Only you can figure a way out, because only you see the work's possibilities. In every work, there's an inherent impossibility which you discover sooner or later—some intrinsic reason why this will never be able to proceed. You can figure out ways around it. Often the way around it is to throw out, painfully, the one idea you started with.

Publication is not a gauge of excellence. This is harder to learn than anything about publishing, and very important. Formerly, if a manuscript was "good," it "merited" publication. This has not been true for at least twenty years, but the news hasn't filtered out to change the belief. People say, "Why, Faulkner couldn't get published today!" as if exaggerating. In fact, Faulkner certainly couldn't, and publishers don't deny it. The market for hardback fiction is rich married or widowed women over fifty (until you all start buying hardback books). The junior editors who choose new work are New York women in their twenties, who are interested in what is chic in New York that week, and who have become experts in what the older women will buy in hardcover. Eight books of nonfiction appear for every book of fiction. The

Annie Dillard

chance of any manuscript coming into a publishing house and getting published is 1 in 3,000. (Agents send in most of these manuscripts. Most agents won't touch fiction.)

When a magazine rejects your story or poem, it doesn't mean it wasn't "good" enough. It means that magazine thought its particular readers didn't need that exact story or poem. Editors think of readers: what's in it for the reader? There is a cult of celebrity, too, in this country, and many magazines publish only famous people, and reject better work by unknown people.

You need to know these things somewhere in the back of your mind, and you need to forget them and write whatever you're going to write.

Annie Dillard is the author of eleven books, mostly nonfiction narrative. At the moment, she doesn't know where she lives.

Notes from the Catwalk

ELISSA WALD

I have worked as a stripper off and on for the last four years, mostly off for the last two, but recently I've returned. This latest stint began in December, and I told myself it would end with 1997—four weeks max, in and out; I would get that fast-flowing holiday cash and get out. New Year's came and New Year's went, and I'm still at it, an admission that brings me as much perverse pride as shame. Each return inspires a barnyard chorus of friends and family, people who care about me: "This is b-a-a-a-d." I don't disagree with them, but it's not that simple. I believe that most of us have our "netherlands"—subterranean places we visit to tap into our own pathology, resilience, and despair. The strip joint is an arena where I confront much of my own. I hope it will soon exhaust what it has to show me, but it hasn't yet.

I return during low points of my life, drawn like a child to what glitters instead of holding out for the warm and solid gold. I need the attention, the affection, the adulation. And the objectification and brutality just underneath? The strip joint is a sadomasochistic place, and sadomasochism is at the core of all my writing; it's the lens through which I see the world. For this reason, the job is endlessly interesting to me.

There is an immediate change in lifestyle. I spend money: on gourmet coffee, luxurious bath products, taxis, takeout deliveries, a new coat. Walking past storefront windows, I feel as if the world has opened back up to me. If I'm at the grocery store, I don't have to agonize over whether I can afford the imported tomatoes. If I'm going to a party, I bring a bottle of good liquor and a dozen roses for the hostess.

I sleep a good part of the day and stay up all night, often well beyond the end of the night's work. My shift ends at four in the morning, and why stop there? I'll go to The Hellfire Club—an after-hours S&M establishment—for a free and thorough foot massage, and then to breakfast with strangers. There is a heightened sense of adventure, abandon, unreality. Day turns into night turns into next day. . . . I crash and then it's time to do it again.

I work in a club I'll call The Catwalk. It's in midtown, a few blocks northwest of Times Square. Sometimes on my way to work I imagine I'm an actress, or maybe a real dancer, who's gone too long between successful auditions. I walk past 42nd Street, under the big-time billboards, past the Broadway shows, then the off-Broadway shows, and finally into the strip club.

There is a bodily consolation in the entrance, that blast of heat as I come in from the cold (as Stephen Dunn put it, "What fools the body more than warmth?"). Too, the music at the door is like a wave that flattens all thought, washes it away. I am never without gratitude for its mindless, insistent rhythm; I become part of its pulse almost instantly. It pulls me out of myself and into Jo-Jo, my stripping persona.

The strip joint has a carnival atmosphere: seedy, raucous, lusty. The D.J. natters on like a barker all night long, calling girls to the stage, pushing the Champagne Lounge, casually insulting the customers ("Hey guys, do you remember your first blow job? How did it taste? Har!"). There is even a freak-show element: the feature performers with their engorged silicone breasts, boasting measurements like 101, 24, 36, who dance with snakes, fellate foot-long sausages, and the like.

Notes from the Catwalk

A few words about how the place works:

The club does not pay the dancers to work there. The dancers pay the club: thirty dollars to the house, a ten-dollar minimum tip-out to the D.J. (double that if you want to be on his good side—and believe me, you do), and at least seven dollars to the housemother. All in all, including the taxi home, girls drop an average of seventy-five dollars a night to work in a club like The Catwalk, relying solely on the customers to make it back and more.

Dancers rotate on stage as called by the D.J. Each stage set is three songs; girls strip down to a g-string and heels by the end of the first. Between stage sets, the dancers circulate on the floor and attempt to sell private dances to customers at $10 a song. The girls are topless during these private dances, which consist mostly of teasing a man into a frenzy. At the height of frustration, some men will elect to visit the Champagne Lounge, a room upstairs where a customer can take his favorite girl. The Champagne Lounge is the ultimate scam. The hourly rate starts at $300, and this entitles the patron to exclusive time with the dancer of his choice and a bottle of champagne. Nothing special happens in there, though many customers imagine otherwise. I don't pretend to understand why anyone pays for it when they can open the Yellow Pages and find an escort for half the price. But dozens of men put their hundreds down every night and it's not unusual for them to buy more hours when the first one is up.

The Champagne Lounge is the strangest aspect of a very strange place. Here is a man I don't know, and I'm climbing into his lap, and he's cradling me. Sometimes this is all they want, and once in a while when I'm in the midst of such an encounter, everything falls away and I no longer remember how I got there. Only: he's hurting and I'm hurting and we're clinging to each other for this hour out of life. His arms are around me, strong male arms. My cheek is resting against the starched whiteness of his shirt. He rocks me, croons to me. This happens. I close my eyes and I am held. This is all I know; at this moment, all I need to know. All I need.

Each shift is something like an egg hunt. We're turned loose for the night at 8:00, and we convene in the dressing room again at 4:00 A.M., each girl with a different amount of money, bounty, depending on her calculations and effort and luck. The money is not discussed except in the vaguest of terms:
"How'd you do tonight?"
"Oh, I did all right. You?"

Strip-joint managers run a tight ship. The dress code is nonnegotiable. G-strings must be opaque, heels a minimum of four inches high. The only agony to match dancing in those stilettos for eight hours is the moment they come off: the effort to readjust to being flat-footed. (In this respect, they resemble tit clamps—the hot insistent bite while they're on; the excruciating rush of blood back into the nipple when they're removed.)

Tattoos must be covered; bodily piercings stripped of all jewelry; legs, armpits, and the bikini area kept clean-shaven or waxed. Garters are required, and each girl is expected to have several different costumes.

Dancers are not allowed to talk to each other while on stage. ("And I don't care what you're talkin' about. Just don't do it. Even if you're just tellin' another girl her tampon string's hangin' out. I don't know what you're talkin' about, and I'll make sure you get a five-song set.") Five-song sets are one way to torture a dancer. The stage is intended as a showcase, and the time spent up there is generally compensated with only single-dollar tips. The real money comes from working the floor, so extra time on stage is to be avoided at all costs.

More serious infractions are fined: $25 if your stockings have a run, $50 for lateness, $100 for missing a night of work regardless of the reason, $500 for missing work on a holiday, like Christmas Eve. Payment is exacted for absences without exception. Illnesses, a death in the family, emergencies of any kind cut no ice with the management. In this respect, the job is like the military. There is only one acceptable response after going AWOL: *No excuse, sir, there is no excuse.*

As a result, dancers drag themselves to work even when they're very sick. Recently I worked with the flu. My throat was sore, my voice nearly gone. To be heard at the club you have to shout above the music, and since I didn't want to do that, I had an inspiration: I would pretend to be mute. All night I indicated with hand signals, to men I hadn't met before, that I couldn't speak. Afterward, when I got home, I realized I'd made more money than ever before.

The Catwalk is a place where I can go up to a man I've never seen or spoken to, take his face in my hands, and say, "How beautiful you are." It's a place one can touch and be touched. There is an easy physical intimacy between strangers, an immediacy to each encounter. I trace scars, asking, "What happened here?" I smooth hair back from foreheads and loosen ties. I knead muscles, telling every single customer: "You work too hard."

"I know," they respond, to a man.

The strip joint is supposed to be about fantasy, but sometimes it seems to be about the bare bones of reality. The veil that hangs between the sexes on the outside—the guarded gaze, the pretended disinterest—is lifted; the men in their naked desire often seem more exposed than the women. Once I was in conversation with a customer whose friends were impatient to leave. We were seated at a table and his companions kept glancing pointedly at their watches. He ignored them. Finally one of them tugged at his sleeve.

"Tom, come on, look at the time. We gotta *go,* man."

He barely looked up. "Go ahead without me."

"What! You're not coming? You can't be serious."

Finally he turned to his friend with an incredulous glare, as if he couldn't believe he was being interrupted. "Come on, man, what's with you? *Can't you see I'm talking to a female?*"

I was on the side stage the other night—a little caged-in platform by the bar—when a kid of about twenty-five came up to me.

"Do you remember me?" he asked. "It's Frank, from The Dollhouse."

The Dollhouse was the first place I ever danced. I hadn't seen him in years, since the beginning of my go-go career, and while he did look vaguely familiar, I wouldn't have been able to recall his name.

"Frank!" I said. "Great to see you. It's been a long time! What are you doing these days?"

Sometimes I am still overcome by the surreal nature of such a situation: I am nearly naked, in a cage, striking up casual conversation with a fully clothed boy just beyond the bars.

"I'm a cop now," he told me.

"A cop?"

"Yeah."

"In the N.Y.P.D.?"

"Yeah."

"Really," I said. "Are you packing tonight?"

He nodded, then offered shyly, "Want to feel my gun?"

Of course I did. It was at the small of his back and I reached around and stroked it. It was an arousing moment, seeming as primal, as quintessential a male-female exchange as the rest of what goes on in there. We might have been a small boy and girl in that age-old transaction: "I'll show you mine if . . ."

Just minutes ago, I'd asked a guy in a cowboy hat, "Are you a cowboy?"

"No," he answered.

"An outlaw?"

He shook his head.

"What then?"

"A photographer," he told me.

"Well, I was warm," I said. "Think about it: a cowboy, an outlaw, and a photographer. What do all of you have in common? You all shoot!"

He answered, "I think all men have that in common."
He was much cleverer than I was, and he wasn't even trying.

I'd rather strip than waitress, or temp, or work as a receptionist. I've done all of the above and found them equally degrading, far less lucrative, and not nearly as interesting. Stripping brings me into contact with women and men from all walks of life. Some of the dancers are single mothers. Some are putting themselves through school or pursuing an artistic career. Others are just indulging expensive habits and a few are hustlers and junkies. The men are equally diverse. Stockbrokers come in and so do construction workers. There are the stereotypical dirty old men, and there are fresh-faced boys in for bachelor parties. I have dozens of conversations a night. It is unusual for an hour to go by in which I don't learn something new.

The stage names the girls choose for themselves have such fire and color, such a poignant and hopeful poetry: *Ambrosia. Blaze. Clementine. Delicia. Electra. Fantasia. Gypsy. Harlowe. Isis. Jade. Keiko. Lolita. Magdalene. Nikki. Odessa. Precious. Queenie. Ruby. Sapphire. Tabitha. Una. Vixen. Wanda. Xiola. Yasmine. Zora.*

The job allows me to wear costumes and accoutrements I would seldom have a chance to indulge in otherwise: elbow-length gloves, thigh-high boots, feather boas, sequins, long velvet gowns that lace up the front. It is the stuff of old-time movies, of vaudeville. I even went through a phase where I wore a pair of angel's wings.

I dress like a sanitation worker much of the time when I'm not at work. I go out in shapeless, oversized clothing, hair pulled back into a slovenly knot, little or no makeup. Part of it is exhaustion, the desire to be comfortable and warm after so many hours in spiked heels and a thong. Part of it is wanting a respite from male appraisal.

I like dancing for the customers most of the other girls are afraid to approach: dwarves, amputees, men in wheelchairs. When they come into the club, I'm across the room like a shot. Once I danced for a guy with a very unfortunate birthmark: a dark splotch, almost perfectly round, directly in the middle of his face like a bull's eye. To me, he automatically had an edge on everyone else, the power that would come from walking around thus marked all his life. He had endured and by now, I could only assume, had the strength and stamina only such a person could possess. I wanted to rub up against him, in the hope that some of it would rub off on me.

The girls take care of each other. An outsider might imagine that the strip joint is an atmosphere that fosters competition, jealousy, backstabbing. But every dancer I've encountered seems to share the conviction that it's Us against Them. It's a tight sisterhood, and all of us call the housemother—the woman who oversees the dressing room, who provides aspirin and tampons and will fix a torn piece of clothing in a pinch—"Mom."

The other night while I was on stage, I had some words with a customer. He took a deep drag on his cigarette and blew the smoke directly in my face. I countered by spitting into his. The roar that went up from the sidelines was like the sound in a stadium when the home team scores. All the girls in the house, it seemed, had erupted in savage joy: "Yeah, Jo-Jo! You go, girl!" My immediate rush of pleasure was soon replaced by fear as I waited for him to report me to the management. He left instead, slunk out the door, and I realized it was the reaction of the girls that had most likely saved me. He must have perceived the atmosphere as too hostile to stay another minute.

Another illustration: one recent night after work there were no cabs outside the club. I began trudging toward the nearest avenue—Ninth—but when I got there no cars were in sight. It was 4:15 in the morning, sleet was coming down hard, and I was alone in the middle of midtown with all that money. Somewhat anxious now, I began straining for a lit storefront, an open bodega to wait by, when a cab came around the corner and stopped. The back door opened and a female voice summoned me from the interior. "Jo-Jo! What are you doing out here alone? Get in!"

I approached the car and saw Serena, one of the other dancers, in the backseat. "Oh, Serena, hi," I said. I was slightly bewildered. "I live down on Avenue D, do we . . . do we live in the same direction?"

"It doesn't matter," she said. "Just get in."

One night I was dancing for a guy right next to the stage, and the girl who was on it leaned toward me. We kissed wordlessly above the man's head, as if by some prearranged choreography. I'd never seen her before, didn't know even her stage name; in fact, I still don't.

When you're out in the daytime and you see another dancer on the street, you don't always acknowledge each other. Your eyes will meet, and often there will be an almost imperceptible shake of the head, an indication that you shouldn't approach. Maybe she's with family, or a guy who doesn't know what she does. And even if she can think fast enough to invent another context for knowing you, the two of you probably don't know each other's real names. You don't want to unthinkingly say, "Hey, Bambi," or "Amber" or "Gemini" or "Venus." So it's best to not even speak to each other; you'll see her later, maybe even tonight. Still, there's an excitement in this silent communiqué, a sense of two spies exchanging signals in enemy territory.

A variation on this theme takes place when the Gaiety boys come into the club. The Gaiety is a gay male strip bar just a block and a half away, and a lot of the male dancers there are straight. They come to The Catwalk between their own stage sets as an antidote to the predatory male energy directed at them all night. The Gaiety boys are as good as it gets, as far as Catwalk clientele: they're clean, smooth, gorgeous, muscle-bound, and loaded. The condescension so prevalent in most of the customers is wholly absent in them. Their attitude is: *We* know exactly what you're dealing with in here; you are our sisters in slavery; let's just help each other through it in any way we can. They pay $20 to $50 for a dance. They come back at 4:00 A.M. to take you to breakfast. You compare notes over eggs and toast. They understand every single thing you say.

When I'm not having breakfast with a male counterpart, or any of the other girls, I often go alone. As a rule I don't eat for several hours before work, and then I dance for eight hours straight. At 4:00 A.M. I'm wired and ravenous, and there's an all-night diner around the corner. At that time it's nearly deserted, and arriving there is like walking into an Edward Hopper painting. There is something satisfying in the wan quiet. I have a sense of a lull in the action, of a space between the night's work and the average person's morning. It's an empty pocket and I'm in it, bone-tired and anonymous and cozy. I feel all alone in the world but right now it feels good instead of bad. I scribble notes on the napkins and paper placemats. I order comfort food: a baked potato, a cup of soup.

A customer—I'll call him Al—taught me one of the most important lessons of my life. I'd danced for him several times when he invited me to come to the restaurant he owned, an upscale grill in SoHo. Several weeks later, I did go in there, and while my friend and I waited to be seated, Al walked by several different times. He kept glancing at me with a puzzled expression, as if to say, "I know I've seen you before, but where?" I thought it better not to enlighten him, surrounded as he was by his staff, and the evening passed without a word exchanged between us.

About a week later, he was back in The Catwalk. I went over to him.

"Hey, Al," I said. "I took you up on your invitation and came into the restaurant last week. But I guess you didn't recognize me with clothes on."

"That was *you!*" he exclaimed. "That was driving me crazy, I *knew* I knew you, but for the life of me I couldn't place you."

"Yeah, well, I could see that," I said. "But of course I didn't want to say anything in front of your employees."

"Why not?" he wanted to know.

"Oh," I said, startled. "You mean, it would have been okay?"

"Well, I'm here . . . right?" he said, ". . . so it has to be okay."

Said so simply, yet it struck like lightning, left me open-mouthed in amazement. *I'm doing it, so it has to be all right.* I never lied about my job again.

The manager can walk into the girls' locker room at any time without knocking. The Champagne Lounge host, the D.J., and the janitor have to knock, and will wait outside until everyone is "decent." The half-nakedness outside in the club—exhibited from the stage, revealed by degrees, washed in neon and bared against music—acquires the siren pull of eroticism; whereas our total nudity in the dressing room, under the cheap fluorescent-tube lighting, is no more exciting than the bodies of livestock in a pen.

A scene from my second year in the business:

It was fifteen minutes before the night shift would begin, and there were perhaps two dozen girls in the locker room when Randall, the manager, strode in, dragging Maggie by the upper arm. Maggie worked the middle shift, from 5:00 P.M. till 1:00 in the morning. She was a rail-thin, statuesque blonde, on this evening decidedly glaze-eyed. Randall was in a barely contained rage.

"Maggie, you're gone. Get dressed and get out."

"Randall!" she said wildly. "What did I do?!"

"If you're not out of here of your own accord in exactly ten minutes, I'm throwing your ass in the street, and I don't care if you're butt naked. If you don't believe that, keep trying to talk to me."

Maggie was crying now, her tears mascara-black. She moved, sniffling and unsteady, to her locker and began to get dressed.

Randall addressed the rest of us. "For the information of everyone else, Maggie has just been fired for doing cocaine in this club. You just have to look at her to see she's fucked up. She wasn't fucked up when she got here at five o'clock. But she's fucked up now. What does that mean? It means she's fucking up on my time. In my space!"

Maggie tried to cut in. "Randall, I'm —"

"Eight minutes and counting, Maggie." He paused. "You girls have tried my patience to the limit. Every night I reiterate my warnings about the plainclothes pigs crawling all over this place. If you think I'm going to get closed down because of your indiscretion, you'd better think again." He opened the door of the dressing room and called out to George, the janitor. "George! Come in here."

George entered.

"George, the girls are at the nose candy again," Randall told him. "They have to be sniffing their lines in the bathroom, because those are the only closed doors they have to hide behind. So I want you to go get your crowbar and take the bathroom doors off their hinges."

"Yes, sir," George said. He went out again.

There was a stunned silence in the dressing room. Finally Diamond broke it. "The bathroom doors are coming off? Permanently?"

"You heard right."

"Then I'm quitting," she said. "I'm sorry, I can't deal with that."

"Good-bye," Randall said. He looked around. "Anyone else who shares Diamond's point of view is free to check out of this job right now."

"I'm with her," Mercedes said. "This is supposed to be a club, not a prison."

"Nice knowing you," Randall said. "Anyone else?"

Silence.

"The rest of you, be ready to start at eight as usual."

The atmosphere in the dressing room had been altered. There was a general air of resignation and defeat. Above the lowered heads and averted eyes, I met Randall's gaze. I stared at him in a kind of daze and as he stared straight back at me I felt the heat rushing to my face. His recognition of my arousal intensified it, made it almost painful. The music from outside the door seemed to become more audible as we locked eyes.

There were a handful of such moments while Randall was the manager, unsettling moments: the slow burn, some unspeakable exchange that never even attempted to find words, a secret betrayal of my rightful allegiances. Another one came a few weeks later. I was working the room, circulating on the main floor, and as I walked by the leather sofas that line the back wall, a man touched my arm. "You. Are you available for a private dance?"

"Of course I am." I smiled. "I'm Jo-Jo. And you are?"

"Jo-Jo, I'm John. And this," he indicated the kid beside him, a boy of about 18, "is my young friend Ben. I'm kind of showing him the ropes." He winked at me as he took $20 from his wallet and slid it into my garter. "So I'd like you to dance for him."

"John, it would be my pleasure," I said. I moved to the boy, invaded the space between his knees, and began slowly stripping off my dress.

"Touch her," John said to him.

Ben shot his older friend a nervous glance. His hands stayed at his sides.

"Go on," John repeated. "Touch her."

"I thought the guys aren't allowed to touch the dancers," Ben said.

John reached out and ran a possessive hand up my flank. I closed my eyes.

"Look at her," I heard John say. "Is she all upset? Is she yelling for a bouncer?" He caressed me further, moving his hand to the inside of my thigh. I felt my breathing become rapid and shallow.

"See?" John went on. "She wants it. She wants you to touch her. She's a woman, she needs it. Go ahead. Put your hands on her."

Ben tentatively put his hand on my other leg. The two men

stroked me simultaneously: John as an owner would stroke a pet, Ben with tremulous disbelief. I shivered in a genuine response. Suddenly Jimmy, the bouncer, materialized. He grabbed John's wrist in his formidable grip. Ben snatched his hand away.

"What the fuck do you think you're doing?" Jimmy growled. He squeezed the other man's wrist in his fist.

"Ah—don't—" John gasped.

"You picked the wrong girl, scumbag. Naw, scratch that; you ain't allowed to touch *any* of the girls. But especially not Randall's girl."

This was the first time I heard someone articulate what I thought was my own private knowledge, the most subtle understanding.

Jimmy gave the man's wrist a vicious twist before releasing it. "Now you got thirty seconds to get the fuck out of here."

John and Ben scrambled up and scurried out of the club. I pulled my dress back on, not looking at Jimmy. My face was burning, my body too.

"Jo-Jo," Jimmy said. "Whaddaya doin'? Whaddaya fuckin' thinkin'?"

I couldn't look at him.

"Randall wants to talk to you," Jimmy said. "He said to send you to his office."

Randall's office was in the basement. He was behind his desk when I entered. He indicated that I should sit across from him and he passed one hand wearily over his eyes before speaking.

"What are you trying to do, Jo-Jo?" he asked. "I don't believe what I just saw with my own eyes." He paused. "The middle of the floor! *Two* scumbags! Their paws all over you! And you panting and squirming like a bitch in heat."

"I'm sorry, Randall."

"You think this is a joke? Think I'm playing with you?"

"No..."

"You think I won't fire you?"

I was silent, staring at the cluttered surface of the desk. But I thought, *Yes. Yes, I do think you won't fire me.*

"This is my last warning to you," he said finally. "If you provoke me one more time, you're out of here."

"I won't," I said. "I'm sorry. Thank you."

Did I love Randall? I did love him a little. It pains me to admit this.

Randall was a long time ago. After he left, Richie became the manager, and after Richie it was Johnny, and now it's Anthony. I never felt anything for any of the others. I don't know where Randall is now.

The terrible and redemptive aspects of the business will balance each other out for some time before the whole proposition begins to turn like milk. Sooner or later, for every dancer, the time comes when you can't swallow it anymore. Looking back on all the times I've left, I can't really pinpoint what in particular, if anything, finally made me walk. Maybe it was the sight of Angel, a feverish dancer trying to sleep between stage sets, curled by the locker-room radiator in her pink bikini, lying on the bare linoleum. Maybe it was the man who threw his single dollar bills one by one onto the stage floor, so we would have to bend over to get them.

As for this time around, not long ago I went to work a few hours after putting my cat to sleep. The cat was old and very sick, but I was heartbroken and unable to check my grief at the door.

"Whatsa matter, Jo-Jo," the Champagne Lounge host wanted to know. "Why such a sad face?"

"My cat died this afternoon," I told him.

Incredibly, his doughy face creased into a grin. "Aw look, honey, don't take it too hard," he guffawed. "As long as your other pussy's holding up."

Yes, the job can make you hate men.

"Laying and paying," is a phrase you hear repeated like a mantra in the locker room. "That's all they're good for. Laying. And paying."

As if it's a point of pride that the exploitation is mutual.

Yes, the job can make you hate yourself. Because you're holding up the other half of that transaction, perpetuating it night after night after night of your life.

There are tell-tale signs of when a dancer is on her way out: arriving at work five minutes prior to the beginning of a shift, instead of the half-hour needed to get ready; drinking too early; passing most of the night at the bar; crying on stage. For myself, I know the jig is almost up when I come out of the dressing room and instead of trying to identify the man most likely to spend a lot of money, I look for someone I think I can stand to talk to. This is the wrong attitude.

Last night the ache was upon me and I kept searching for, seizing upon, any man who might alleviate some small part of it. I walked around the club in several desperate circles, scanning the crowd for someone who seemed strong, smart, competent, gentle, kind. There was no one like that anywhere.

Once again, it's almost time to go.

Elissa Wald is a writer, ex-stripper, and long-distance runner living in New York City. She is the author of the collection **Meeting the Master** *(Grove Press, 1996) and the forthcoming novel* **Holding Fire.**

My *Mysteries of Pittsburgh*
An Alphabet

STEWART O'NAN

I grew up in Pittsburgh, in Point Breeze, between John Edgar Wideman's Homewood and Michael Chabon's Squirrel Hill. It was the '60s, just late enough to miss Annie Dillard's *American Childhood*, though later (I think) I delivered their *Post-Gazette*. I also claim to have delivered David McCullough's morning paper, but that, like many of my memories, may be untrue.

Like a people, a city grows its own legends, passes its lore down to younger generations. Sometimes, as in the case of Michael Chabon, an outsider arrives and adds to that lore, though mostly the job (and privilege) of telling a city's stories falls to those who were born and raised there, as in the case of John Edgar Wideman.

I've written very little about Pittsburgh. Not the fictional Pittsburgh which, like any good writer, I could cobble together from deeply felt characters' lives and realistic details, but the real Steel City, the city that's shared imaginatively by all long-term Pittsburghers. A popular, common, yet ultimately hidden culture. People and things we as Pittsburghers know, whether they're true or not. Stories, I guess. History. Here's just a sampling.

A

For *Adventure Time*, a children's show in the '60s whose host Paul Shannon raised his magic sword and brought the curtain down in front of a bleacherful of Cub Scouts so he could show the next cartoon. At home, we envied the kids on TV, even in their weenie uniforms. We wondered how we could get on short of joining the Cub Scouts and envisioned our faces—our very particles—beamed out across all of Pittsburgh from the WTAE studios our parents sometimes drove us by on the way to Monroeville. TV was like family. We all knew the local anchors—Paul Long, Bill Burns and his daughter Patti, Ray Tannehill, and of course Chilly Billy Cardille, who hosted Friday night's *Chiller Theater* on WIIC. When these people talked to us, we listened, because we knew them. There was an intimacy that, as children, we didn't know was manufactured. It still obtains today, despite our hard-won cynicism. When I see Lori Cardille in *Day of the Dead*, I'm inexplicably happy, connected again to people I've never met.

B

For the Bridge to Nowhere, actually, an on-ramp of the Fort Duquesne Bridge, a span across the Allegheny that took forever to build, whether for lack of funds or some other political issue. For years the on-ramp arched inconclusively over the river, leading from the North Side into thin air, blocked off by a fence of striped Department of Transportation barricades. Legend is—fact is—one night in 1964 a twenty-one-year-old chemistry major from Pitt went flying up the ramp, through the signs, and launched his Chrysler station wagon off it like Evel Knievel. This was before my time, because they say his car landed in the mud, half in the water and half on shore, and there's no mud there anymore, just a stone lip. The guy wasn't even hurt, according to the story, just embarrassed. He refused to discuss what happened, but we all thought: what was it like, that first second when he knew something was wrong? The tires must have stopped making noise, and then it was just freefall, darkness, like drifting in space. And then the water, freezing even in spring.

C

For Connie Hawkins, who they say was the greatest playground ace roundball has ever seen. The Hawk played briefly for the ABA Pipers as well as a number of NBA clubs, but was supposed to haunt the courts of the Hill District and both Westinghouse and Mellon Parks, taking on all comers, drawing crowds with ridiculous skywalking jams. Maybe the best ever, people said, in an age when Dr. J was just showing us the dunk, but everyone knew he had some trouble with drugs. Scag, or boy it was called then. A waste, people said, a shame, but the fatal flaw only deepened the legend. Did he play for money, laying down his Jackson on the baseline so he could cop later on, or was it sheer love of the game? It was all just rumors, pickup games long before the age of videotape. You'll find men who played against him. They just shake their heads. Couldn't stop him, couldn't even foul him. He was just playing with us.

D

For the Duke Beer clock across the Mon, visible when you were driving in on the Parkway or the Boulevard of the Allies. It sat on top of the Duquesne Brewery, its giant hands letting you know you were on time for work. But then the brewery faltered in the '70s, like the rest of the economy, and they sold the plant and moved to Cleveland, of all places. For a while the clock sat there, stopped. Then it was taken over by Stroh's Beer (from Detroit, which we held no grudge against, even though it was the U.S. auto industry who basically sealed our fate), and then, mercifully, by Iron City. The building's changed hands since then, and is no longer making beer, but the clock remains, stopped again, stuck at 5:30 until a summer tornado reset it to 6:35. Not like the reliable Alcoa clock across from Three Rivers Stadium (now the

Bayer clock, I'm told), which still lights up the hillside with digital precision. A good lesson, I suppose, in capitalization. I remember being puzzled that an entire company, massive brewery vats and all, could suddenly disappear. I wasn't puzzled long.

E

For Ernie "Arrowhead" Holmes, defensive tackle beside Mean Joe Greene in the Steelers' vaunted Steel Curtain. Named Arrowhead for shaving his skull and leaving a forward-pointing arrow that ended in his widow's peak to indicate the direction he was going through the opposing offensive line. In an incident never publicly resolved (at least in the Pittsburgh papers), Ernie Holmes was driving on the interstate in Ohio when he stopped his car, got out, and began firing at a police helicopter with a rifle. Motives? Left wide open. Why was the helicopter there? Erratic driving, I think Paul Long said, but more likely he was simply Driving While Black. He rejoined the Steelers. They won.

Also for Doc Ellis, who in his memoir ghosted by the poet Donald Hall claims to have thrown his no-hitter against the Padres while tripping. A claim that paradoxically only makes sense when *you* are tripping.

F

For Forbes Field, home of the Pirates and earlier the Steelers when they were named the Pirates. Razed in 1970 to make room for a new law building at Pitt. Honus Wagner and Cool Papa Bell played here, Ralph Kiner and Roberto Clemente. In the '30s Joe Louis beat Max Baer under the lights behind second base, and of course Bill Mazeroski hit his series-winning home run here, over Yogi Berra's head (why Yogi with his catcher's duckpin legs was playing left is anyone's guess). That part of the left-field wall (brick with ivy) still stands, beyond it a Little League field named after Maz. My brother and I went to the last two games at Forbes Field, a doubleheader against the Cubs which the Bucs swept. It was standing room only, and after the last out people whipped out their pliers and screwdrivers, unbolted whole rows of seats and walked them out the centerfield gate and away. A decade later you'd see the seats on people's porches, the blue and gray paint flaking off year after year.

G

For Gertrude Stein, rarely associated with Pittsburgh, but born on the North Side, then called Allegheny, P-A. How she became the Stein we associate with Paris and the avant-garde is all properly documented, but what must she have thought of her hometown? Certainly she fled it, but can we ascribe some of her love of plain speech and regular people to being nursed here, the cadences heard in the cradle? And I think she'd get a kick out of our other great expatriate, Andy Warhol, having his own museum right here on the North Side, where you couldn't have paid him to set foot again. All the same, he's partly ours. New York may claim him, or that nebulous world of Art and Fashion, but somehow—yes, that's what's hard to figure out—somehow Pittsburgh is a big ingredient in him as well.

H

For Heinz 57, the massive factory along the Allegheny we were marched through as schoolchildren (Andy Warhol too?), the teachers fretfully counting heads as we clattered along the catwalk over the open vats of ketchup and vegetable soup. Steam roiled up from the floor, and the stench of vinegar had us holding our noses. This was definitely not Willie Wonka, though we could see how easily other stuff could get into our food—like the plastic shower-capped workers, bending perilously over the soup with long steel paddles. At the end of the tour we all got a small box of Heinz products and a pickle-shaped pin, and spent most of the bus ride home imagining horrible industrial accidents. "You want ketchup on that?" my father said over dinner. "No," I said, "I'm okay."

Also for Homewood Cemetery, our favorite playground. In winter the ponds were perfect for hockey, and year-round we could find open ground to play football or just kill-the-man. The muddy backhoes that rolled through didn't intimidate us, and the famous dead were industrialists, completely boring. The only thing that worried us was the German shepherd the caretaker let run free inside the high, spiked fence. And the crematorium, maybe, its chimney leaking a thin wisp of smoke, even on weekends. "They roast them slow," my friend Mark said, "so all that's left is the teeth." Can't teeth burn? I didn't know, so I didn't argue with him.

And also for Highland Park, where, when my father was a child, a bear got loose from the zoo and eluded the police for three days, then supposedly escaped by swimming the Allegheny River across to Aspinwall. This last part I don't believe at all, but the start of the story is good: my father and his friends stayed home from school for three days, and my grandmother kept a shotgun with her in the kitchen.

I

For Isaly's, an ice cream company with a chain of neighborhood restaurants with soda fountains that have pretty much disappeared. Their specialties were distinctly Pittsburgh—chip-chopped ham and whitehouse ice cream (vanilla with maraschino cherries). They also made the Klondike which, not having evidence to the contrary, I boast was a Pittsburgh invention. They licensed other companies to sell it—or did they pay another company to sell their own version? Is my history wrong, slippery, suspect? I can't imagine my grandmother with a shotgun. In any case, if your Klondike had a pink center, you got another one for free. If it had a green center, you actually won a dollar. I think there's an Isaly's in Chabon's *Mysteries of Pittsburgh*. If not there, then in the short stories in *A Model World*. Some of them take place on Forbes and Murray up in Squirrel Hill, two streets I know with a startling intimacy, even after twenty years. To see them transformed in another writer's imagination is both difficult (hey, that's my material!) and fun (wow, you got it right).

My *Mysteries of Pittsburgh*

J

For Josh Gibson, Hall of Famer and maybe the greatest catcher and power hitter of all time. Called signals for Satchel Paige, who could throw a lambchop past a wolf. 800+ career homers. Pittsburgh fielded two of the premier teams in the Negro leagues, the Pittsburgh Crawfords and the Homestead Grays, regularly drawing mixed crowds of up to 35,000. Because of travel expenses, visiting teams were likely to play both the Crawfords and the Grays—a brutal road trip. Lore has it that in the mid-'30s the Pirates and the Grays secretly played a game one morning at Forbes Field, with the Grays winning 5 to 2. (A wishful fabrication? Maybe, maybe not.) While everyone knows Western Pennsylvania as football territory—producing players like Larry Brown, Tony Dorsett, Dan Marino, Jim Kelly, Joe Montana, Johnny Unitas, and Joe Namath—the city itself was historically a baseball town until the '70s, when Forbes Field was torn down and the city built Three Rivers Stadium on the North Side. Even when the We-Are-Family Pirates won the '79 World Series, regular season attendance averaged less than 18,000 in a stadium that holds 50,000. We'll lose the Pirates eventually, and we love them dearly, always have. The mystery here is that most American mystery—the mystery of money.

K

For Kennywood Park, oldest trolley park in America, with at least two world-class stomach-emptying rollercoasters, the Thunderbolt (traditional wooden) and the Steel Phantom (briefly the fastest coaster in the world, with the longest vertical freewheel). The first week the Thunderbolt was open, a boy stood up at the top of the big, curved drop that faces the midway. As the cars rocketed down, he left his feet. The cars hit the curve and sent him flying out sideways at about seventy miles an hour. He flew through the sheet-metal picnic tables of the Potato Patch, a big french-fry concession, his head smashing on the asphalt. Pronounced dead at scene. The next week our annual school picnic was held at Kennywood, and we ran off the bus clutching our orange and blue tickets and dashed for the Thunderbolt, then tried like hell to cut the line. My other Kennywood memory is when the Ghost Ship burned down. It was your basic funhouse; you sat in the padded, clanking car (sort of a wheeled banquette) and screamed when day-glo skeletons jumped out of the dark. Mirrors and strobe lights, a puff of water at the end that didn't even get your hair wet. A makeout place for seventh graders—not enough time or privacy to do anything sustained. It burned in the off-season, but everyone pictured it going up with them inside, the flames dancing in the mirrors as you and your date-for-the-ride jumped out of the car, holding hands, lost in the funhouse.

Also for Michael Keaton the actor, a native Pittsburgher actually named Michael Douglas. Now what are the odds?

L

For the public library, donated to the city by Andrew Carnegie. Carnegie donated libraries all over the Northeast, but this was one of the first and certainly the biggest and, with the library in Braddock, the one used most by the people who slaved to make him the money he would later give away. At the library's 100th anniversary a few years ago, John Edgar Wideman gave an eloquent speech reminding us of a free library's value to the community, especially a community hungry for knowledge, starved of opportunity. It moved me, and reminded me of my own reliance on the children's room, the Bookmobile, the Squirrel Hill branch I haunted all summer. But why did it have to come from Andrew Carnegie? It's a Pittsburgh conundrum. Beautiful Frick Park is named after the man who called out the Pinkertons on the Homestead strikers, Mellon Park after the family who bankrolled the steel barons. As a child, I read a history of the mills that had a page with a calendar charting the number of industrial deaths on the South Side. 1906, I think. The days were filled with little *xs*. These were people happy to have a job. Let's not even get into child labor.

M

For Michel Briere, Penguin rookie star. Obscured now, after the supernova of Mario Lemieux. The Penguins joined the NHL in 1967 and floundered through their first two decades, an embarrassment in a town that calls itself The City of Champions with reason. But for one year Michel Briere appeared to be the Pens' savior. Like Mario, he was young and fast and handsome, at once humble and brilliant—the first star the Pens could sell to the city. After the end of his rookie season, one night in Montreal he crashed his car into a fire hydrant and fell into a coma. At first there was some hope he'd come out of it, but soon it became apparent he never would. The Penguins named their rookie of the year trophy after him, set up a fund for his beautiful fiancée. A decade passed, his monitors beeping. He lived on life support for so long that when the papers announced his death it was a surprise. Then Mario showed up.

N

For *Night of the Living Dead,* the greatest horror and maybe truly low-budget movie ever made, at least ten years ahead of its time, and never seriously challenged. It was shot in Carnegie (yes, that name again) by local auteur George A. Romero and released in 1968. Sets the standard for all films of its genre. Best line: Chilly Billy Cardille is interviewing the local police chief and asks him about the zombies who are attacking. "They're dead," the chief says. "They're all messed up." Our English teacher, Mrs. Epstein, supposedly played the Naked Zombie in Graveyard, baring her breasts for her art. No one has ever verified this with her.

Also for Nick Perry, bowling show host and all-around nice guy who with his friends rigged the Pennsylvania Lottery so it came out 666 and then went to jail.

O

For the Original Hot Dog Stand. Not the Dirty O in Oakland, which still cuts the best, saltiest, greasiest fries in town, but the original Original, gone now, over behind the Nabisco plant in East Liberty. All-beef weenies, with crisp rubbery skins. No tables, you just stood at the steel counter and ate off butcher paper. On the walls above the grill area hung pictures of famous people eating Original Hot Dogs. I don't mean just famous people, I mean *famous* people. Martin Luther King Jr. John Fitzgerald Kennedy. How they heard about the O I don't know, but I'd eat mine and look at them eating theirs, knowing they stood where I was standing, dreaming big.

P

For Bob Prince, The Gunner, radio voice of the Pirates. Famous for saying, "We had 'em all the way," no matter how tight the game was. He spoke out of one side of his mouth, like a stroke victim. Legend is, as a young man he drank a bit, and one night some players dared him to dive out of a fifth-floor hotel room into the pool below. Prince did. He was an ornery man who wore ugly clothes as a joke on other people, and he could make vicious political jokes and in the next breath sincerely wish Mildred Magillicutty a happy 83rd birthday. His last years at the mike, his voice and his strength were both going, and it was hard to listen to him.

Q

For WQED, our public TV station, home of *Mr. Rogers' Neighborhood*. Actually, I grew up in Mr. Rogers' neighborhood. He lived two blocks over from us in a big house at the corner of Beechwood and Hastings. Never once saw the man, despite innumerable paper routes. He's a minister, and back then he was active in St. Peter's (I think) over in Highland Park. My sister-in-law swapped the gospel with him. Unlike the rest of Pittsburgh's institutions, Mr. Rogers is still there, still punching the clock, doing the show.

My *Mysteries of Pittsburgh*

R

For Roberto Walker Clemente, the true Great One (no offense and no apology to Wayne Gretzky). Only Major League MVP on a last-place team. Willie Mays said he was the greatest player he'd ever seen. Clemente carried the burden of being the first great Puerto Rican star with grace and dignity in a city with almost no Puerto Rican community. Like Jackie Robinson, he spoke with his talent and suffered baseless criticism in silence. Exactly 3,000 hits lifetime. He was ferrying supplies to earthquake-stricken Managua when his plane went down in the Caribbean. Or, rumors persisted, was he on his way to see his other family there? Body never found. As boys, we dreamed a desert island life for him, a kind of heaven he deserved. I still see him there, older now but still fit, listening to the games from Miami on a cheap table radio like the one in *Gilligan's Island*, playing dominos in the shade while the green sea washes in.

S

For Soldiers and Sailors Memorial, a huge marble hall near Pitt used for graduations and other formal occasions. Never actually been inside it, except when I watched *The Silence of the Lambs*. The scenes where they're waiting for Hannibal Lecter to come down in the elevator were shot in the lobby. Spooky echoes. When I was young I thought the dead from World War II were actually buried there, the building one gigantic crypt, walls honeycombed with morgue drawers.

T

For Stanley Turrentine, the Pride of Pittsburgh, whose *Ballads* on Blue Note I had to go to Minneapolis to discover. For Ahmad Jamal and his *Pittsburgh*, and for Art Blakey, Roy Eldridge, Erroll Garner, Billy Eckstine, Billy Strayhorn, Earl "Fatha" Hines, and Walt Harper, giants all.

U

For the Underground River beneath the Golden Triangle. This third tributary of the Ohio joins it invisibly beneath the Point, creating—or so the kids in my neighborhood claimed—an undertow which, if you fall off the Point, will suck you ineluctably beneath the tip of the city. It's this mysterious source that feeds the oh-so-photogenic fountain you always see on TV, spewing geyserlike. So far no one has tracked it beneath the streets, canoed through its dripping, rat-filled passages. A place for sodden, bobbing bodies nibbled by blind fish. A place for chase scenes at the end of a long, convoluted novel.

V

For venison and Vietnam, bound together by Michael Cimino in *The Deer Hunter,* set in nearby Clairton. The snow-capped peaks Robert DeNiro and his friends hunt the great stag in belong not to Western PA but Oregon—the Cascades. And the buck itself isn't the right kind, any local hunter knows that. While some critics harped on these flaws, others questioned the accuracy of the Russian roulette scenes, pointing out the fact that no such underworld was even rumored to exist in Vietnam. No matter; the movie was so powerful it inspired a veteran named Jan Scruggs to go home after watching it and sit all night in his kitchen, writing up a proposal for a monument to the nation's war dead. Less than four years later, The Wall was a reality, a reminder far more powerful than the film.

W

For Wilver Dornel Stargell, Pops. In the '70s he owned a number of chicken joints, the first of which was in the Hill District. Every time he hit a homer, a lucky customer would get a free bucket and Bob Prince would cry, "Chicken on the Hill with Will!" He lived down the street from us on Conover Drive, and supposedly he'd pay you ten dollars to wash his van. His son, Son-Son, played ball with us at Mellon Park, and we all wished our father was Willie Stargell.

X

For XYZ, or "examine your zipper." Also offered as "U.S. Steel is down 100%," which, soon after we passed that stage of taunting, turned out to be a devastating, even conservative prophecy. Mr. Carnegie's company dropped its name and became USX. The plants were closed down, overgrown by weeds and rust, then leveled, the poisoned land auctioned off. XYZ!

Y

For "yins" and "youns" (the *ou* pronounced as in "sh*ou*ld"), meaning you-ins, or you all. As in, "Whadda yins guys wanna do—go dahntahn or just screw arahnd up here?" Mystery: why does half the city say "yins" and half "youns"?

Z

For Fritzie Zivic, great Polish featherweight, either a world-title holder or just one round short of it. And for Billy Conn, another Pittsburgh pug who took the ring against the great Joe Louis and fought him almost to a draw. Like Bronco Nagurski, these fighters were some of the only heroes allowed the South Side. Fritzie Zivic and his family later owned a marina on the Allegheny below the Highland Park Bridge where they moored a whole flotilla of decrepit barges that gradually sank year after year, and then, like so much of that earlier Pittsburgh, were suddenly gone.

You can ask any Pittsburgher about these things, and they'll tell you I'm wrong, that my dates are mixed up, my facts off by just that much. I would hope so. John Edgar Wideman is fond of quoting a Yoruba saying: All stories are true. I'd say that in the realm of nonfiction, this is even more important to remember. Every narrator, being human, is unreliable; *only* the story is true. These are tales told over and over, freely embellished on, left tantalizingly open, and all the stronger for it.

Naturally as children we're drawn to the fantastic, the strange and unexplained, the feats of heroes, and my hometown—like everyone's, I guess—seemed full of that stuff. There were other, real mysteries, of course, like why Mary down the street shot herself in the parking lot of the East Liberty Kroger, and how the Vitas who lived next door to her ended up with her car, a rusty blue Nomad, how they could drive it around for years afterward without thinking of what happened in it. And there were the heavy mysteries to come, like love and hate and joy and disappointment, guilt and pride, exile and belonging, but back then these were the deepest mysteries we could comfortably appreciate. Like the Pirates, they were ours.

Stewart O'Nan's first collection of stories, In the Walled City, *won the 1993 Drue Heinz Prize. His first novel,* Snow Angels, *set in Butler, Pa., has won numerous awards and was, strangely, a bestseller in Germany. His newest novel,* A Prayer for the Dying, *was recently nominated for the Bram Stoker Award for best horror novel of 1999.*

We Fish

OMARI C. DANIEL AND

JACK L. DANIEL

I felt a strange confusing pain when I heard that, during a 1993 Kwanza celebration, a sixteen-year-old African-American male said he wanted to give thanks for having lived to see his sixteenth birthday.

I read the January 1 front-page news stories detailing county murder incidents for 1993 and 1994; most of them were African American.

From 1980 to 1993, young African-American males had a 63 percent increase in suicides.

I longed for solutions rather than yet another recitation of statistics associated with young black men killing each other, themselves, and others, day after day. One woman quoted in the article noted, succinctly, I thought, "We don't need any more forecasts of rain. We need to build the ark."

While I was stuck in my slow funk of depression from having had a lot to say about all aspects of African-American life as a black revolutionary college student in the 1960s, but having so little to say about resolving African Americans' problems in the 1990s, my son, Omari, shared with me some poems he had written. As I read them, I experienced a surge of excitement; this young man had escaped the time period and circumstances that had caused others to be jailed, killed, or

45

in other ways destroyed. My son was in college, and had made the dean's list.

The content of the poems reminded me that at least four consecutive generations of "Daniel men" had more than survived, despite the mountains and valleys each had to conquer. His poems shed light on the strengths of the men in his life who had helped him grow. As I read Omari's work I began thinking about the substance necessary for the building of the ark.

The fact that Omari was writing at all, let alone poetry, came as a surprise since I still recalled how he had to be force-fed his handwriting assignments in grade school. By the time he was in third grade, my ultimate threat had become that I would never permit him to watch television again, no matter how well he did in school, until his penmanship improved. His poor penmanship was a reflection of the carelessness that he exhibited with his academic work. As time went on, I found myself having to constantly remind him of the importance of doing well academically and that his school work must come before recreation.

One evening Omari came home with his third-grade report card: An *A* in gym, a *B* in math, and *C*s in spelling, social studies, and handwriting. We still lived in times when African Americans had to be better to be equal; these grades were completely unacceptable. Since he loved playing with his toy soldiers and Matchbox cars as much as he loved watching television, and the television threats had failed, I decided to take his favorite toys away from him.

"Okay, take all of your cars and toy soldiers upstairs, and put them on the bed by my belt. It's going to be a long time before you see them again. Boy, you are too damn hardheaded. I told you to quit playing around in school. You told me that you were putting out 100 percent at school, and then you brought home this trifling *B* in math and this ridiculous *C* in handwriting. Don't play with those cars again until I

We Fish

say so, and if I catch you with them, I'm going to set you on fire with my belt. If you have any free time, then practice your handwriting."

Omari started his usual "But Daddy . . ." Before he could say another word, I cut him off.

"Don't 'but Daddy' me! Just do what I tell you to do. Omari, I am not playing with you. And when you finish your school work, do some of your extra reading. You haven't completed those sentences that I gave you yesterday, and you haven't done any extra reading since I don't know when."

To help him with his handwriting as well as his grammar and syntax, I periodically gave him some sentence fragments to complete. My wife, Jerri, and I always gave him and our daughter, Marijata, books, written primarily by African-American authors, which served not only as their general "extra reading," but also as their learning of African-American literature, which they did not receive in school.

Not wanting to hear more from me regarding his grades, nor have me immediately make good on any of my threats, Omari eased his lips into a childish pout and walked slowly up the steps as if the world was on his back. I was sure that he felt anger toward me, which he knew better than to express, and I was now additionally distressed at the prospect of not being able to play catch with him before dinner the way we usually did. I felt I had no choice but to do what I had to do in order to get Omari to focus on improving his academic performance, however. I was not going to raise one of those "fast runner, slow readers."

I had always emphasized to my children the importance of learning well at least three "alphabets." I told Omari and Marijata that if they could master "A through Z," "0 through 9," and a third "alphabet," then they would not only do well at school, but also at whatever else they wished to do in life. The third "alphabet" could be "sharps and flats," the "primary colors," "dance steps," or any other set of artistic symbols. Ours was a symbol-using society, and if they mastered the two key alphabets, along with an artistic one, then racism and sexism would have a hard time holding them back. Whether Marijata understood and applied this formula consciously, or whether she was simply self-motivated, she excelled consistently in all areas. But with Omari I had to continually hammer home the basic lessons because of what seemed to me to be his desire to avoid working at the highest level of his academic potential. On paper he misspelled words that I knew he could spell correctly; he'd get the right answers to his arithmetic problems, but only do part of what was required in the assignment. At one point during his elementary years, I almost gave up entirely on his acquisition of a third alphabet because it was so difficult to get him to master the two basic ones. Even if he was fully qualified academically, I knew that Omari may well face racial discrimination in college and later, in the work world; I worried about what would happen to him if his grades were less than outstanding.

When Omari was in first grade, Jerri and I moved to a suburban town where she was the director of a daycare center; she loved her job, and the twenty-mile commute from the city, coupled with the difficulty of finding quality child care, had become a hassle. We wanted our children to have the opportunity to interact with other children of color while living in a predominantly white, upper-class community, so we enrolled them in the public school system rather than the local private academy. We certainly did not want them to have the opportunity to develop elitist attitudes.

In third grade, Omari had a black teacher who took a no-nonsense approach with him and insisted that he excel. That year he did extremely well and finished grade school without ever dropping below a *B* average. This still wasn't good enough for my black male child. My father had been rejected by West Point, supposedly because he had failed the admission exam by one point; Jerri's father was denied admission to the University of Alabama Law School, allegedly for academic reasons, although he later was admitted to Yale Law. Accordingly, I viewed Omari's *B* average as a baseline for improvement in junior high school; anything less than an *A* had the potential for being a racially motivated act against him.

As Omari went through his suburban elementary school, Jerri and I watched in dismay as many of the African-American boys were tracked into peewee running backs, fifty-meter sprinters, Little League catchers, and young jump shooters. We watched later as, one by one, many of these same kids experienced difficulties in specific academic areas, failed grades, and got placed on the athletic "fast track." Observing this pattern, and having noted the same thing with many of our own friends when we attended public schools years ago, Jerri and I made academic success a prerequisite for Omari to engage in athletic competition.

Junior and early senior high school English writing classes continued to be traumatic experiences for Omari and his teachers. For the first quarter in ninth grade, Omari received all *B* grades and one *A*. Trying to be supportive of Omari but also to remind him that more was expected of him, and as an alert to his teachers, I wrote on the back of his report card, "We are pleased with Omari's first quarter's performance. Omari has set a goal of improving in everything. We have agreed with his goal. Please let us know, as time passes, if he is improving, and how we can help him improve. Half way through the second quarter, if he is not improving, please call me for a conference. Thanks."

My written message was extremely important to me because of the low academic expectations that many teachers had for African-American males. Additionally, these children all too often had low expectations for themselves, having received no encouragement from any other arena. Educators had documented the significant lag that occurred by third grade for black children as compared to whites. In many public schools, the predominantly white teachers' expectations were so low that a *B* grade was deemed wonderful for an African-American male; I called it the "*B* for a black boy" syndrome. I was not going to have either Omari or his teachers believing that *B* was a satisfactorily high level of academic achievement for him.

By ninth grade Omari was showing great promise in several track events, but I was determined to not let him go down what I considered to be a socially preordained athletic road. High academic achievement had to come first. Maybe he and his teachers thought that his first-quarter ninth-grade report card with all *B*s and one *A* was something wonderful, but I had to let them know that "good" wasn't "good enough" for Omari. I read to him my written comments on his report card to make sure that he knew he needed to convert some of those *B*s into *A*s, particularly in English and math. Jerri, too, gave reinforcement with one of her "bedtime talks." It seemed that he had really understood our messages when one of Omari's coaches tried to convince him that athletics should play a greater role in his life, and that he should run cross country in the fall instead of playing in the marching band, which, at that time, had become his "third alphabet." I was very pleased when Omari refused the suggestion.

At the end of the second quarter that year, however, he dropped to a *C* in science, and a *C+* in handwriting. I wrote in red ink to his teachers: "I am very concerned because I asked that you please call me halfway through the second quarter if Omari was not improving. He went down in three areas, and you never called. I wish to have a conference as soon as possible!"

Jerri and I went to the school and raised hell with both the teachers and the principal. We left only after I threatened to bring my concerns to a school-board meeting, and after having obtained assurances of their strict attention to Omari's performance from his teachers. Several weeks later, one of them responded with a formal "academic deficiency report": "Dear Mr. Daniel: Omari is too interested in entertaining the class to pay attention to me. What would you have me do now?"

Despite what I sensitively took to be a racial jab at me for having raised a "natural-born entertainer," I wrote back: "Thank you for your concern, and its immediate expression to me. You don't have to do anything. His mother and I will handle the matter. I can assure you that his entertaining days are over."

I decided that Omari's conduct required much more drastic action on my part. Too many young black males were going down too many blind paths; even with proper guidance, my son seemingly was veering toward academic detours that led to nowhere. I was not going to have my son travel any of those routes even if, as my father had always said to me, I had to "half kill" him. Because he was in ninth grade and no longer a child receiving spankings, I was prepared to give Omari an old-fashioned, get-down lesson with my belt—until Jerri called a technical foul on me by inquiring gently, "Jack, what about what your first-grade teacher did to you?"

I couldn't believe she stooped so low to get her way; Jerri didn't want me to hit Omari and didn't believe in beating children under any circumstances. She had gotten my first-grade report card out of my high school yearbook and was now waving it in my face. I had always considered this teacher to be a racist who had set me up and then didn't have the heart to go through with her dirty deeds. Since I was able to pass to second grade, there was no way that my academic performance could have been what she had indicated the year before. Jerri's analogy had to be false; I knew that my teacher had had it in for me; Omari's teacher was trying to help him, and Omari wouldn't listen to his teacher, Jerri, or me. I had something around my waist that would make him listen to all of us. To appear reasonable, however, for one more sickening time I looked at the report card.

When I was in first grade, teachers only recorded an S for "satisfactory progress," and an X for "pupil needs to show greater progress in order to reach the standard required." After the first twelve-week period, my teacher gave me an X in everything. After the second twelve-week period, she gave me an X in everything. The fact that I managed to earn an S in everything for the final period and pass to second grade was proof to me that she had been biased for two-thirds of the academic year. After explaining all of this to Jerri, she said in a disturbing voice, "Jack, did it ever occur to you that she passed you because you were black, and she didn't want you in her class for a second year? If so, then neither your brains nor your father's beatings did you as much good as you seem to believe."

I considered this, but I didn't answer her as I proceeded upstairs to get my belt. When I came back down, Jerri barked in staccato, "Don't, hit, Omari, with, that, belt!"

Seeing the fire in my eyes, she backed down a bit, asking, "Why don't you try to talk to him?"

Past reason now, I screamed, "Jerri, I have tried talking, and look at the good it produced! Omari needs to be torn up the way Daddy beat me!"

So I beat Omari, if you can call it that.

As I hit him the first time, my fury was transformed into the sickening feeling of beating myself. When I hit him the second time, my arm movement was slowed by my suddenly rising fear, clearly related to my first-grade report card. My mind raced through the negative effects failing would have had on me. I thought about the possibility that, while repeating first grade, I would have been the class clown just like big ugly Jonathan who had failed first grade and repeated it in my class. My mind flashed over to the teacher's comments on Omari's deficiency report. The anxiety intensified, my fears for Omari intermingling with my fears for my child-self. I realized that I wouldn't have gone on to second grade with my two closest friends, George and Herbie. Our "Three Rocket Boys" space-traveling group would have been split; they might have replaced me with someone like Charles, one of the fastest runners in our grade. My girlfriend Nadine probably would have dropped me for some second-grade big shot. It was bad enough when she started to like that jive-time T.J., the midget-league quarterback...

We Fish

I momentarily turned my thoughts to reflect on the fact that several of Omari's African-American friends had failed a grade. I wondered what it was like for him to make friends with the white students in our primarily white suburban neighborhood. Had Omari's own "Rocket Boys"–type relationships been split up, and his conduct was a way of rebelling and identifying with his friends of color? It was horrible to think that for Omari, passing might have as dire social consequences as my failing first grade would have had for me.

I think I hit Omari for only a third or fourth time, and stopped as I got caught up in these thoughts. As I reflected on Jerri's words, I could not imagine that being whipped about my X grades in first grade had had a positive influence on me. My mind and emotions boiled with guilt for having whipped Omari, anger for the whippings I did receive for school-related reasons, and anger at the teacher—this time for probably passing me when I did not deserve to pass—and the fact that she might have saved my life.

Regardless of the emotional maelstrom it had produced in me, Omari's whipping must have helped some because, during the final quarter, he only earned one grade less than a *B,* and that grade was a *C+,* still in handwriting. Now, though, I was unable to feel satisfied completely with his progress because I had come to focus on the idea that his teacher, too, might have done what was necessary to get rid of her "entertainer of the year."

When he was in junior or senior high school, Omari nearly threw a tantrum when I asked him to write an essay for the local Martin Luther King Jr. "I Have a Dream" contest. I had hardly finished what seemed to me to be a reasonable request before he began with, "Daddy, every year you ask me to do the same old thing. I've written about him and his dream every year. I know, I know. He had this dream. He believed that everybody should love everybody, and judge people by the content of their character, and . . ."

Since he was talking back to me, doing what my mother called "sassin'" me with his "mannish self," I interrupted with, "Omari, be quiet and write the essay!" The way he was talking, rolling his eyes and gesturing wildly, reminded me of just why the "old school" told children, "If you don't listen, you are going to feel; a hard head makes a soft behind." He pushed at me again.

"Daddy, what do you want me to write that I haven't already written?"

"Omari, do what I told you to do before I hurt you! Just write it!"

With that, he left the family room in a huff. As he sat down at the dining-room table he mumbled something just loud enough for me to hear about "this stupid writing." Since he had at least gotten started, I didn't say anything else to him. In his usual "just do enough to satisfy the basic request from Daddy" mode, Omari handed me an essay in about twenty minutes. I refused to read it; as I handed it back, I told him to do a careful review of it and then produce it on the computer.

A short time later, as I came in from work one day Omari rushed up to me excitedly.

"Daddy, Daddy, guess what! I won!"

"You won? What?"

"Daddy, I won the Martin Luther King essay contest! I'm getting a plaque and one hundred dollars for first prize from the Black Child Development Institute!"

I could not believe this young Negro. Omari hadn't won a thing. If I hadn't made him write that essay, this "win" never would have occurred. He failed to remember the fuss he made when I first asked him to write it two weeks ago. He had all but blasphemed King's name. As I viewed it, I was the one who had won by making him write the essay, and to make my point I told Omari he had to give me half of the money.

He protested, screaming, "Daddy, the one hundred dollars are mine!"

We Fish

Quietly and firmly I asked him who had made him write the essay.

He retorted sassily, "Daddy, who is going on television to read their essay?"

I said that I didn't care who was going on which television station to read what essay, I just wanted my half of the money. This scene reminded me of a story my father-in-law liked to tell about a man winning at the track, so I decided to try to illustrate my point by telling it to Omari.

"Omari, listen. A man went to the racetrack with his entire paycheck. He lost five races in a row, and was down to the last twenty-five dollars of his pay. He knew his wife was going to kill him since this would be the second month in a row that they couldn't pay their bills. So the man prayed for God to send him a sign. When the man lifted his head and looked out on the track, he saw one grey horse whose color he took to be a sign from God. The problem was that the horse was going off at 99 to 1 odds. Since he had prayed for a sign from God, the man decided to show his faith in God by putting his last twenty-five dollars on this 99 to 1 shot.

"When the horses came out of the gate, the grey horse was dead last, and so the man prayed earnestly for God to help the horse. 'Lord, this is old Leroy calling on you. I know that the grey horse isn't much, but I know that all power is in your hands. Lord, would you please use a little of your spare power on that horse for me today?' When the horses went around the first turn, the grey horse was still last, and the man started praying heartily about how he was going to attend church every Sunday, quit drinking, quit smoking, and get to work on time every day. Then the man added, 'And Lord, if you let this horse win, I will never return to the racetrack. Please Lord, let him win. Let him win, Lord.' Suddenly, the grey horse started to gain ground. As the grey horse gained on the others, the man started yelling, 'Go ahead, Lord! Go ahead, Lord! Do your thing, Lord! You the man, Lord!' When the horses turned the last corner and headed toward the finish line, the grey horse was in front by five lengths. Suddenly the man cried, 'Okay Lord, okay Lord, I can take it from here myself!'"

He laughed throughout the telling, and when I ended, his devilish grin made me believe that Omari had gotten the point of the story—that he was acting just like the gambler. He was going to collect "his" money, read "his" essay on TV, because "he" had won; he was going to take it from here himself. I just couldn't permit Omari to think that he had really won, could not let him forget how he had had to be made to write the essay, despite his ill-behaved efforts not to do so. More important, I didn't want him to think that he had now achieved the essential level of writing excellence that he needed as a black male in American society. I thought of my mother's adage, "When success goes to a man's head, it leaves him looking in the wrong direction." I decided to turn Omari's head back in the right direction.

"OK, I'll tell you what. Since you now write so well, this weekend I want you to write an essay on Malcolm X."

"Aw, Daddy! Why?"

I answered him with something my father always said to me. "Because it will do you some good."

True to his developing form, Omari asked, "Did the Lord make the gambler bet again to do him some good?"

"Go write," I responded quickly so that Omari wouldn't think that he had gotten the best of me. I was shocked by his question and its implied answer; only after he had left the room wearing a smile did my own face relax into one, too. I had to admire the quickness of his wit.

Throughout the rest of high school, Omari took care of business, earning mostly *A* grades, doing especially well in science courses and in the marching band. He continued to have problems with writing, however. He tried to dodge a twelfth-grade writing assignment by producing a video, "MacRapper," instead of doing the required writ-

We Fish

ten essay on Macbeth. While I had to admit that the video was impressive, and that I was proud of his creativity and his teacher's praise, I also made him write the essay. Although the content was pretty good, it contained spelling errors; he protested when I told him to run it through the computer's spell-checker and print another copy. He just did not seem to "get" my fears about what could happen to him as an African-American male, irrespective of his achievements. He thought I was nagging him, being "the professor," just by asking him to spell-check, to make a substantively good essay better.

The struggle continued into college as he fussed and fumed about his "unfair" composition instructors. He was taking a wide range of subjects, a number of which were in literature. At least once a semester Jerri and I asked him about his plans for an academic major but he consistently responded, "Stop bothering me. I don't know yet." Shock cannot begin to describe my reaction when in the fall of his junior year Omari declared a creative writing major. When I asked him why, he casually replied, "I had to choose something to graduate; most of my courses were in creative writing."

I found out more about his creative writing from one of his professors, who had supervised his writing a collection of poems entitled *We Fish*. I was dumbfounded as she told me about the "fascinating poems" Omari had written, but I thought she was simply being nice because I had helped recruit her as a faculty member. Also, I suspected the often-articulated view that African-American women tended to "raise our girls and spoil our boys," that she was being a little soft with Omari. Perhaps most of all, though, I just couldn't believe Omari's choice of poetry as his area of emphasis.

I had always found it difficult to appreciate poetry and the poetic form, to know when a poem was a poem, or when a poem was just someone's strangely arranged words in structures known and understood only by them. Sometimes I even wondered whether poems were written by people like Omari who I thought were too lazy to write complete sentences, although I must admit to having tried to write poems and I never wrote more than the most elementary rhymes. What further aroused my suspicion was my awareness of how much Omari had gotten into rap music, which he claimed contained "deep" messages beyond what I perceived to be the usual misogynistic sex and violence. In addition, it seemed to me that many young, supposedly politically oriented African Americans were arbitrarily declaring themselves poets with stuff like:

> Blaaacck Man!
> Blaaacck Man!
> This is yo sistah, not yo lovah
> Talking to yah!

As far as Omari's poems about fishing were concerned, I just didn't get it. Omari and I had always fished together; I had never seen our fishing together as anything other than, well, just fishing. I loved fishing so much that I had been nicknamed the Bassman; I was sharing my love of fishing with my son. When I read the collection of poems for the first time, however, I was moved to understand that he had used writing as an effective way of handling some of life's traumas.

> Greek Picnic
>
> Philly
> My people jamming
> with my people
> A rainbow of chocolate
> looming through the streets
> Instinctively being pushed along
> by a soulful bass-filled rhythm
> My people were around me
> My people were with me

then without missing a beat
They were shooting
My people were shooting
at my people
they ran to, from and around me,
and I too ran
ran and hid from my people

There my sister lay
more dark African Blood
spilling into American soil

This time the cause wasn't
Those people
It was my people
I did not stop to help
my sister because
my people were still shooting
at my people
and I was alone

Dealing with That Time

That time when you had me in your basement
where empty pop cans decorated the walls.
That time when I was too young to know better
but old enough to remember.
That was the time you took down my pants,
saying that you had a game for me.
You put your warm lips on my penis.
You said you were making it grow.
I remember you looking up into my face,

your eyes did not lie, so I didn't panic,
didn't fight, didn't enjoy, or at least I don't
think that I did. I just stood silent.

I had it all planned for the next time I saw you.
I began lifting weights, you were seven years
older than me, I needed strength. I practiced
for you. I punched my pillow, I punched the sofa,
I punched the walls, I was going to punch you.
You were going to fall. You would not fight back,
just lay there and know why you were bleeding.

I have seen you several times since then,
and I haven't punched you.
The image of you lying there
mouth bleeding is so sweet to me. I could
not swing. I was arthritic around you,
joints would freeze, muscles rebel, mind unwind.

When your brother got asthma, I went out and laid
in a field of freshly cut grass and watched the day pass.
When your father died, I went fishing with my father,
and we seemed to have caught more small mouth bass
that day than ever before. I made sure to kiss him, that night
you wept for your father, and told mine how much I loved him.
When your step-mother got laid off, I went to work with my mother
and played Duck Duck Goose with the children at the center.
I read to them, chuckled as I envisioned the lady my mother fired
as your step-mother. When you were accused of molesting another
child, I binged on a four course meal. I had golden brown
turkey, prime ribs, corn bread, scalloped potatoes, shrimp,
black eyed peas, and for desert triple layer chocolate cake

We Fish

and deep dish apple pie. When you were acquitted, I purged
myself. I puked up all that I had enjoyed. I tried to throw up all
my memories. I thought of your eyes that
never betrayed you and wanted to vomit in them. I wanted to get
it out, get you out, but I couldn't. Now I am waiting to see you,
I hope I don't freeze, I hope I can end my silent rage.

When I finished reading "Dealing with That Time," my rational faculties gave way to one of the most nauseating feelings I have ever experienced. It stirred in my stomach, anxious to rush up my throat so that I, too, could vomit. I knew the poem's content had to be true because I recognized the actual "basement where empty pop cans decorated the walls," and my mind flashed back to that year when Omari requested weights as a Christmas gift. And the hurt I felt was for more than Omari; it was for the perpetrator, the perpetrator's family, and for the deep dismay I knew Jerri and Marijata would experience upon reading Omari's lines of verse, and for not having known about the incident for so many years.

I became silent in an effort to absorb the pain.

As difficult as it was to learn for the first time of these disturbing experiences, my silence was not simply a function of my dismay. The poem had convinced me that to the extent that one can do so, Omari had managed this darker-side-of-life episode, and therein lay a positive reason for my silence. So much of an African-American male's life could be determined by the way he dealt with violence in its many manifestations. Becoming neither a victim nor perpetrator of violence was a key to African-American male survival, and my mind seized again on the fact that Omari had used writing as an effective coping mechanism.

"Dealing with That Time" moved me in the ways that I had always thought written expression should move people. I always believed that it had to do something for you, had to move you in some fundamental fashion. The source had to conjure up deep emotions, and make the emotions come alive, deep within oneself, had to present vivid accounts of personal, but shared, human experiences. Because this poem affected me in the way I thought a good piece of writing should, it therefore seemed like it had been produced by someone who could write well. Still, I had to consider if this was merely wishful thinking; maybe my emotion came only from the truth behind the words, and not the manipulation of the words themselves.

I didn't know whether to ask him about the reality of the sexual experience, or to congratulate him on his skill in expressing it.

Since I did not seem to be able to be 100 percent sure that he could write this well consistently, and certainly did not want to admit this to Omari, I chose to ask him about the truth of the episode, which he confirmed. Psychologically, I felt the need to keep the content of "Dealing with That Time" to myself, although I was anxious for an evaluation of my son's work by some of my professional writer friends. Mostly, I felt as though I, too, had frozen before ending my silent rage.

I started thinking a lot about how I might have missed the poetic within Omari, and about how I might have missed his ability to resolve complex problems, including those about which I had so many lurking fears. I was reminded of the time as a child I couldn't see what my friends Mabel and Bee Bee claimed to be a "man on the moon." Moving on this memory, I wrote three or four pages of rambling prose from which Omari distilled the essence of the experience.

    couldn't see for lookin

      In grade school,
      I kept hearing
      know it alls

We Fish

like Mabel
and Bee Bee
talk about seeing
some man on the moon
and one night
as I stood with them
staring up at the sky
I couldn't see
and still didn't believe,
but as they pointed and giggled
my eyes drifted
up Mabel's shadow
and I could see
that her legs
looked like two of the world's
most beautiful
dark brown baseball bats
with ankles
just thin enough
for a firm grip,
and legs that got nice and thick
just below her knees
and I could see
that Mabel's butt
looked like two of those curved
salt cured
Virginia hams
that Uncle William brought by
on Sundays.
Later, when we walked,
I watched as
Mabel's hams
pushed each side of her skirt

> up and down,
> allowing me to see
> inch by inch
> of her deep chocolate thighs
> until finally
> I thought I saw
> what my buddy Otis called
> that "wonderful stuff,"
> and it was,
> and I felt wonderful
> until I looked up at the moon,
> and saw him
> looking down on me
> seeing what I saw
> seeing what I felt
> and seeing that now
> I was too ashamed
> to look back
> at that wonderful stuff.

It was a jagged grey face, half there and half not there, but a face nonetheless. The clearer the face became over the next two nights, the more I couldn't understand how I had missed it in the past. I felt so ridiculous that I never did let Mabel and Bee Bee know what I had finally seen. Similarly, I wasn't sure I could let Omari know what I had seen in him. What if it had been there all along, and I had missed it just as I had missed the man on the moon? I just could not admit to the possibility that all of my efforts at chiseling him into a black man could have been more effective if I had worked, in less intrusive ways, with what was always there.

I mused back to another occasion during one of my sophomore psychology classes when the professor showed us the well-known picture of a grey vase; I was one of the last in the room to finally see the reverse image of two identical white faces staring at each other. And now, here I was, a senior academic administrator, still having trouble seeing below the surface of my own son. Maybe I needed to look again, much more carefully, at the person I thought I had seen so clearly. And maybe, I needed to listen more carefully to Jerri when she said, "Jack, leave Omari alone. Don't try to rush him into manhood. He is going to be okay."

> **We Fish**
>
> My grandfather stays with my father
> because he fishes.
> Wading these motherly banks
> of the Juniata evokes memory.
> Each cast, each fish,
> keeps the memory of his father fresh.
> This is how we beat death.
>
> I know if Alzheimer's ever claims my
> father as it did his, all I have to do
> is fish. I will fish the Juniata and
> let the memories of my father flow
> through me. Fishing for channel cats,
> doing the Juniata float, and sneaking
> down the back side of the church
> to fish on Sundays. I will fish
> because we fish, and they fished, and
> I know my father can never leave me,
> if I just fish.

It was not until Omari was in graduate school pursuing a master's of fine arts in writing that some of his poems helped me to realize that

Omari C. Daniel and Jack L. Daniel

our fishing expeditions had provided us with a stage upon which several generations of African-American males had played significant socializing roles. Grandfathers, great-uncles, fathers, sons, brothers, and other old men, not related in any way at all, had leading parts. I began to see how fishing provided me with an antistress medicine more effective than any pill, and how it contributed significantly to the positive bonding between me, my son, and all these other men. Our African ancestors had the healing power that came when they drummed, slaves sang work songs, the Blues emerged, we fished. And Mama crocheted.

After reading Alice Walker's critical essay, "In Search of Our Mothers' Gardens," I asked my eighty-year-old mother why she crocheted so much, though by now I suspected I knew. Mama took a deep sigh, smiled, and said, "You don't know son, but there were times around the house when things weren't so good between your Daddy and me, and I prayed to God, and it seemed like not even God would help me. So when praying didn't help, I would get my needle and thread, sit down, and just do what came to me. Sometimes my hands would get to going so fast that I didn't know what I was doing. Then, about an hour later, I would look at what I had crocheted, and say, 'If that ain't something.' Then, it seemed like everything was going to be okay. You don't know what all Mama been through, son, and crocheting helped a whole lot."

I certainly didn't know what all Mama had been through, but now understood what the vehicle for her own healing and creative forces was. With the help of Omari's writing, and by the time that I was fifty-three years old, I knew that fishing had helped me and some other men in the same ways.

As I finally began to see some of what Omari had seen about the deepening of our father and son relationship while we were fishing, a rush of ideas came to me, and I wanted to express them. Omari would write

We Fish

poems, and I would write related essays. Maybe something real and meaningful could be said about African-American male development outside the confines of sociopolitical texts. Maybe, from our fishing experiences, we could glean some answers to some of the problems facing African-American males in structural poverty. And maybe my time in the struggle had not passed; maybe I did have something to say about "building the ark." At about the same time I was experiencing this excitement of ideas and understanding, came a tremendous Father's Day gift.

Reflections on Father's Day

Daddy, you've written us so many letters like this over the years, I figured it was about time to write you one in return. When I think about many of my friends, and the many young black people in this country, who have never had any reason to celebrate a Father's Day, it really makes me think about how lucky I am. As a Daniel Man you were only doing what was expected, or par for the course, so I can't give you too much credit for that, but I am lucky to have a father who took the time to do so many things with me.

When I beat people in cards, they ask me how I did it, and I tell them I learned to play cards sitting on my father's knee when I was in second and third grade. The same thing happens in ping pong, and just about any other game that I play. It is not so much the actual play of the game, but general strategies that I picked up, and employ in my everyday activities, be it playing to win, finessing, engaging in psychological warfare, or occasionally bending the rules. (I know you are probably sitting there acting like you don't do these things, but you do, and I do, and we both win all the time.)

The things you did with me and for me, as you know, go far beyond games. Basically, as I have expressed in some poems, you made me into a Daniel Man, and you know— all of the things like loving yourself, taking care of your family, etc. that go along with that. It's funny, but a lot of things it seemed like you were *doing to me* at that time, were really being *done for me*. A perfect example of this is when I am editing other people's papers, or my own for that matter, and I have to put in commas. Every time that I add a missing comma, I think back to when you would leave me sentences to do when I came home from school, and I smile or chuckle to myself. Well, I guess I'll move on. I wouldn't want to gas your head up too much. After all, we have your age and blood pressure to worry about (Ha, Ha).

I have been thinking about your book idea. The more I think about it, and the more I see going wrong with black men in this country, the more I think the book might be a necessity. I know you probably want to write most of the prose pieces, and let me concentrate on the poems, but I think I'd like to try my hand on an essay or two as well. We need to discuss the idea more, and lay out the project, because I would hate to miss this opportunity. We at least owe it to ourselves to look into the book idea a little more to see if it is possible.

I think I only have one more topic for this letter, and that is fishing. Over the years, I have never quite had the fever for fishing like you have, and I suppose that is what keeps you on top. But I love going, and wouldn't trade the time I spend fishing with you for anything. When I hear stories of you going with other people, I get a little jealous, but then I am happy that you got to enjoy yourself. When you go by yourself, I wish I were there. I am glad when you catch fish, and love the sound of your voice, and the excitement in it when you tell the stories, and I kind of feel like I was there. I don't really like fishing with other people but so much. It is fun. I spend most of the time playing or talking stuff with the friend I am with, but it isn't really fishing. It is only "fishing" when you are there, because it is "us" together, and I cherish those moments more than you can imagine. Thanks!

Omari,
Bassman, Jr.

It took a day for me to collect my emotions before I could talk about this with Omari. The next evening I called him, thanked him for the letter, and proposed that we begin this book, focusing on his earliest childhood memories of our fishing. He was emphatic in his response. "No, Daddy. You need to begin by figuring out why you have the 'fever' when it comes to fishing."

I was so overjoyed at the prospect of writing with my son that I agreed, even though at that time I didn't know exactly what the "fever" meant. Nor was I anywhere near understanding how my "fever" might have anything to do with helping to build the ark African-American men needed so desperately. I only know that its force propelled me forward.

Thus, the journey began.

Jack L. Daniel is Vice Provost for Academic Affairs and Professor of Communication at the University of Pittsburgh. He conducts research and teaches courses related to African American Rhetoric and African Americans and the Mass Media. His current creative-writing project is a book-length manuscript based on this essay, "We Fish."

Omari Colley Daniel received his BA from the University of Pittsburgh

Omari C. Daniel and Jack L. Daniel

and his MFA (poetry) and his MAT (secondary English education) from the University of Maryland. He is a member of the Cave Canem Literary Community, and is currently teaching English at Springbrook High School in Silver Spring, Md. He is also working on a book of poetry, which will follow the "We Fish" manuscript.

The Conjurer's Profession

LESTER GORAN

The summer's day the war with the Japanese ended in August, I took the bus downtown about three in the afternoon. The Casino Burlesque Theater, where I hustled things in the aisle during intermissions in the stage shows, was closed for the summer. My dream had been—after I graduated from high school in 1946, about a year away—to join the candy butchers, comedians, and strippers in Atlantic City where the nation's burlesque players gathered at the Globe Theater on the boardwalk.

I mumbled about joining the army after high school or going to Harvard or Paris or hitchhiking to see the Grand Canyon, anything at all except facing that I had nothing whatsoever going for me—and, in truth, did not want to do anything at all except attend eight movies a week. Occasionally, sitting and drinking beer with Regis Connors, my closest friend, and a jolly company at the Ancient Order of Hibernians, Division Nine, on the second floor above a bar on Oakland Avenue, I said I was writing a long novel. We talked all night. By the time dawn lit the sky over Pittsburgh I had persuaded myself I really was working at something monumental. It looked like a novel, scraps and dates, names of characters and outlines, but if you approached it from the wrong direction it'd bite you! It was a sorry heap of evasions, unworkable scenes, repulsive events, and no narrative thread at all, but I had convinced myself among the Irish that I was eloquent and well read, virtually irresistible, a novelist in all but the ability coming soon, the power of strong drink more certain than mere talent or persistence or beauty.

Downtown on the day of the Japanese surrender was at first quiet, and then people came out of the buildings. As I walked along familiar streets, in the middle of a hallucinatory spell and remembering these very same streets in recent reprimands of rejection for my poor-boy manners and the dreams of arrival I had had on them, quite simply women threw their arms out, embraced me, and then kissed me. They kissed everybody, sailors, soldiers, marines, merchant seaman. These were not comradely kisses. They were long, passionate, lasting in import and reverberation. Not one woman, not two, many: scores of women were kissing *even me*. I was shadowy in those years, even to myself, my identity a hodge-podge of affectations and doubtful postures. Sometimes jive talk, shy to stammering, sometimes bookish like a berserk children's encyclopedia given gifts of glossolalia, I did not stop talking, dreading the scrutiny I believed came with even momentary silence.

Sexual liaisons were taking place in doorways and on the steps of office buildings. Years of pilgrimage on these streets among people who it seemed would be eternal strangers, and today the women kissed me, again, again, walked holding hands until someone else took their fancy (or I walked off) and the rich promenade of lust and love continued on down the block. I took phone numbers. I gathered addresses on matchbooks.

Tomorrow, dream women in sun-backed dresses and love in your eyes, will you say the war never ended or claim the Japanese won?

Cars were driving through the streets and people were throwing handkerchiefs at the drivers and from the cars scarves fluttering in the air to my feet. The cars might have contained occupying troops riding into a friendly, frantic population. Toward dusk, on a whim, I jumped on the fender of a car cruising downtown, horn blowing, and the rev-

The Conjurer's Profession

eler, a stranger, headed for the South Side, through the Liberty Tubes.

The driver, wild with patriotism and torn between good spirits, perhaps drunkenness and malice, made a game of trying to throw me from the car into the railing of the tunnel. I clung to the hood ornament, and I tried to dig my heels into the fender.

The driver stopped abruptly, putting on his brakes to jerk me loose, speeded up to shake me, careened, twisted abruptly from side to side through the narrow tubes. I made plans for a quick leap, but he gave me no opportunity. He had decided the hell with winning the war, I'm going to break this guy's neck and that's better than surrender eight thousand miles away. There were others in the car with him. He screamed with laughter.

On the South Side I jumped from the car and rolled a few feet. There was a traffic jam at the entrance to the Tubes. People were shouting at each other, some in anger, others in release. Unattached, I felt at bay and defenseless. I ran. I dodged cars. I did not look back to see what happened to the demon driver or his car. It seemed to me that I was the only person on the streets with a healthy destination: everyone else seemed bent on killing themselves or me. And it had all been so lovely a half hour ago when we kissed, held each other, and knew we were in a popular song where the lights would finally go on again all over the world.

In fear of the cars now as I jogged, their horns and cries of friendship as they offered me rides, I walked back through the smoke-filled tunnel. It was a long walk. People threw things out of car windows, not necessarily at me on the narrow walkway, but then again, not necessarily not at me. Beer bottles, milk bottles, oranges and rotten apples and other garbage: I might have been an enemy soldier, afoot while the winners rode.

A soft rain fell in downtown Pittsburgh. As night fell, blue and colored with summer, I saw improbable embraces, reckless and, to put it delicately, unstable and some literally feeble-minded desperadoes from my home wards now making their circuits of the streets. With

73

them, pickpockets and purse snatchers had come from all over the city to assert victory over the Japanese. Whores now respectable until morning, dropouts from the third grade at Miller School kissing women who would have called the police alone on a street with them, con artists sober and working one fraud, then another, and petty thieves and waiting strong-arm men in alcoves and alleys appraising the field.

It had been a day of dreams of love and welcome. No one was barred. It was still a night, for the record, even with the rain coming down harder, of acceptance and no boundaries. We're here downtown and this is the way we are the night the war of sunken submarines and missing aircraft and pictures of babies in firestorms has ended; and the desperadoes have come, too, thinking this is their moment, not knowing they frighten us, and this is the way they are. Watch your purse, lady, some wars never end. Exhausted and moving as if in a play unscripted and with no scenes except infinite greetings and embraces, there were still people on the streets when I took the last bus at two in the morning to Terrace Village, the government housing project where I lived with my mother and father.

A woman tapped on the window for me. I got off the bus and kissed her for a long time. The bus driver waited for me and after the passion and the kisses she and I shook hands.

In the morning, first I wished a world war would end every day and everyone could know what my friends and I felt when we prowled downtown, grandiose possibilities given shape everywhere, the sky the limit, kisses and fantastic embraces between strangers in love and fraternity. And then, remembering the day in all its glories and contradictions, I thought, No, given where even righteous exuberance goes, someone will get killed every night.

The bus to Atlantic City arrived there in the early morning before daybreak, and I walked down to the boardwalk and then the beach. Sitting in the dark and watching the sky, I felt drowsy and laid back on the sand. I had hitchhiked part of the distance from Pittsburgh to Philadelphia and had been awake for twenty hours or more. I woke to find it a gray morning, rain on the winds, but I knew from the solitariness of my situation under that low-hanging sky and the broad and expansive ocean at last I was in a time and place that was going to be my own now and in memory.

It was not enough that there were tall tales and big talk and women promenading on the boardwalk that would have caused the buildings to collapse finally in the Hill District, the slum neighborhood in Pittsburgh where I was born and raised; soldiers returned from every part of the planet to walk the Atlantic City beach; people who paid to come here to sit and walk in the sun where I stood; a job swaggering up the aisle waiting for me (probably the first reference letter ever written for an aisle hustler had been composed for me by Phil Greenfield, the manager of the concession at the Casino); and a promise of an end to staleness. Walk left, turn right: you belong in Atlantic City.

Coming from a government housing project where we paid twelve dollars a month rent, my mother, father, and me, electricity included, I could not be expected to understand that the people strolling the boardwalk were not millionaires. They looked rich to me: everybody, other than my father and mother and other relatives who lived in the projects too, looked rich to me. The conception of a vacation for a weekend or a week, not connected to a settlement house, was as foggy as the mornings of my childhood in Pittsburgh where the sun came out only dimly through the sulfur and smog at two in the afternoon and then was as quickly gone at sunset.

It seemed to me the sun blazed over Atlantic City with a ferocity that in my mind made the occasion of blue sky, bright sun, sand, and surf lit by a kindly nature a time of generosity: brightness at five in the morning, gentle shadows only beginning after nine at night.

At the Casino Burlesque I had been given an apron with pockets and three dollars in change. I sold chocolate bars and boxes of popcorn and soda. Nightly, there was loudly hawked from the microphone on stage reputed drawings of celebrities on a seemingly blank page—to be revealed in pornographic poses when held up to the light in the privacy of one's home. The figures in the poses were nonexistent or vague or indistinct and could have been Marlene Dietrich or W. C. Fields for all the sense they made. But the failure in the magic configuration of life and burlesque fictions making alchemic gold out of a prosaic night at the Globe Theater was never a lasting regret: the promise was all.

From the moment of my first walk up the aisle of the theater shouting, "You want it, I got it . . . ice-cold ginger ale . . ." or "Get it here, get it here . . .," I silently prayed, "Never stop, never stop this one-man procession into crowds, light, noise, confusion, and cash in my hands." Men in rimless glasses turned to my nonsensical declamations, rumpled women daring to visit a *burlesque show,* soldiers and sailors drunk to bellicosity or near sleep, high school boys whooping it up in the presence of dancers in g-strings and blue light about to bare their breasts (all but the nipple—this is 1945 and 1946) and rigid lonely men in the front row, never buying anything, eyes fixed straight ahead.

I made sixty-three dollars my first week at the Casino, twenty-one of it more or less legally.

The rest came from clipping change from the patrons. Not generally considered a moral lapse at the Casino, shorting customers in the rows was an accepted fact of life among the hustlers in the aisle, loosely called candy butchers. So common was the practice and so pervasive, I came to think that the people in the audience *expected* to be hooked. Over the years I've participated in learned discussions among candy butchers that suggest people expect physicians not to diagnose ailments accurately, lawyers to get you sent to jail with bad advice, and ordinary persons on the paying end of things are shocked when they receive full value for their money. Few complained at the Casino: the deed was done quickly, the man in the aisle moved like an apparition, first in lights, then in semi-darkness as the music came up, then in darkness. And who could accurately count their change in the dark? In the blessed night that fell against the music and spotlights on stage, robbing was a way of life.

A dream of ease and wizardry walked with me in the aisle, life forever more punctuated by a drum beat, a cymbal clashing, lyrics to melodies so simple as to seem something at one with blades of grass or starshine on tarpaper roofs of my childhood: the trusting thrusting money at me, faces lit with the belief that racy things were abroad in the theater, dirty things were to be said, fun lay at the end of a dollar ticket to wildness. I knew the need; it was closed to me if too easily achieved. I knew the stagehands shifting scenery too well. But I was happy to pretend the audience and I were in the same dream of restraint gone for an hour or two while chicanery, mischief, and petty thievery accompanied me into the presence of gullible strangers. Enchantment. The time at last of the sweet spot found.

Had I a big bass drum I would have thumped it in Atlantic City. Had I a voice for singing I would have sang. Without either drums or a melodic voice I let the music stay inside me, happy to know at last it was there. I could do here under this sun and thousands more like it what I had done in quest of boldness in Pittsburgh: the terms of my disgrace were my own choice, it had not been a dream to find myself here.

But that summer the wounded from World War II were wandering the boardwalk, becoming aware that the suffering that had already seemed endless was only just beginning: wheelchairs, canes, and stiff back braces as they faced the hot sun coming from the Atlantic in the morning. For them, there could be no past worst than what had brought them here, and now. For me, Howard Johnson hotdogs, fifty-five cents apiece for ordinary people, cost ten cents for me because I knew the men behind the counters at the outdoor stands the company used to have on the boardwalk.

Whatever people paid to live in narrow rooms was no concern of mine; I slept on a plush red velour couch on the second floor of the

Globe Theater, shaved in the men's room, ate hotdogs, and caramel candies all day and drank warm Cliquot Club ginger ale to wash them down.

The universe as far as the eastern horizon was mine: the boardwalk anyhow, shoes on wood, surf calling. And that's how I came to believe that whatever fate had in store for me, a boy with such generally tepid promise, I was for once at the core. No political upheavals in this moment of sunshine and purloined and borrowed suntan lotion where I strode miles finally in the center, no decisions made, nothing monumental occurring (except people openly smoking marijuana on the boardwalk and the police lecturing them, sometimes walking them away from the railing): to be in the crowd sauntering toward the Tarleton, a stop at Howard Johnson's for free orange juice from Lenny or Bucko or Gary and I took a deep breath of ocean air, a fixed entity in the bustle.

My weight dropped to a hundred and forty pounds from its general thirty-five pounds more and all of it chicanery and joy, not an ounce of foreboding slowing me down. My hair became bleached blond by the sun. I quit combing it. I cut it myself. Who cared? My ability to walk twenty miles a day on the sand was an easy accommodation to my various raptures. I lost a lingering shyness and sadness and remoteness, occasioned by my apprehension that strangers were able to see my seedy past on my forehead as surely as my welfare penitentiary shoes and pants had once marked me in grade school as a recipient of public charity.

I talked to people I did not know on any subject whatsoever (whatever their point was, mine was "Look at us. We're here. The sound you hear is the Atlantic Ocean and it will never stop").

Except for weekend matinees at the Globe, I worked only at night, and then I was through before eleven. I sat on blankets with women most of the day, went into the water with them, shared salt and water and screams at the waves. I walked the boardwalk all night. I sat on benches at three in the morning and listened and talked and listened:

I'm not sure people understand what it is like to talk to someone who is listening desperately. Sun, ocean, moonlight, shouting inanities in the aisles for a living and standing with the show's comedians and unofficial comics, the candy butchers, on the boardwalk under pastel clouds at twilight: if I wake up in Heaven one fine morning it will be Atlantic City, 1946, and I will cut my hair again with a blunt scissors and no mirror to guide me.

I lodged with various people once the season was underway. Having come early, I did my occupancy of the second floor of the theater while an occasional cold wind still blew down the beach and boardwalk. The theater had a guard, more an oldtimer who made a nightly brief survey, and he was no problem—except lonely he told me nightly of when he used to drive a truck in South Philly. I fell asleep listening to the rhythms of how he had scammed hams and bottles of wine from people too stupid to count. And, in the interests of truth, none of the people I roomed with in that fine time of youth and dreams was one of those girls from the distilled fantasies on the posters in front of the Globe Theater. With my other limitations, my general invisibility came with the job: I think the loss of status for a showgirl, certainly a stripper, even one of the girls attending a concession stand, would have been catastrophic to have been identified with one of us—particularly the younger, more wild-eyed and raggedy ones. Mostly the eighteen-year-old beauties were the province of eighty-year-old comedians (names on request); and I consoled myself that it was the promise of a career in show business that made their engines turn and it was nothing personal, the invisibility. But who knows? Maybe the old-time comedians made the young girls laugh.

In the raucous exhilaration of my first taste of ocean-bred freedom—do what you want by way of song, the Atlantic makes no judgment—there intruded those pale young men in wheelchairs and braces. Some became sunburned, and their shoulders large with the efforts at their wheels. Among themselves they sometimes laughed; to the nurses pushing their chairs they smiled when they turned to talk to them. I loved those nurses: they were in it with the wounded men in a way that I never could be. Each of the men had a secret, the moment of his wound, the terror and the confusion. They were bound to each other and the nurses. There was no entering the world of their forfeitures.

Dancing down the boardwalk, I was, when I saw them, a reminder of triviality to myself. They were in a sobriety overshadowed only by grim death as a final statement of treachery and precariousness, probably embodying the truth of all things finally. The former soldiers could not dance; and my merry-footed pilgrimages up and down the boardwalk became a reproach to myself if I dwelt on it. I did not want to walk well when I saw them. Was I to be someone who could not let go of awful scenes, dwelling too long on the terrible?

But if I worked it right, I did not have to observe suffering at all except at the peripheries of vision. Fitzgerald and Joyce in their customary sidewalk cafés: where did they learn to look, not to see what passed them on their streets? James and his walking stick, listening to the voices he passed, running his cane jauntily along an iron railing, how did he lose himself in the rhythms of his mind and not be distracted to tears by the wounded of his streets? I could not shake the feeling the young men had caught the shell fragment intended for me.

The men in wheelchairs could understand what I had sensed of loss as night fell on the chimneys across the street and my mother waited at the third-floor window for my father who often would not come home that night or that week: would the malign indifference that had tracked her leave poor, old Jake, my father, dead in a doorway? And the former servicemen understood the truth of the terrors in darkened staircases and who finally it was tarrying, breath indrawn for silence, in monstrous alcoves on familiar landings. It has no name, but, looking back, we know whatever it's called it's coming—maybe not for everyone—but us, yes!

A writer's recriminations with himself for dishonoring someone else's torment by indifference in the pace of his own living, I understand this now, will ultimately fade before the reality of the brace, wheelchair, scar, and the call and promise inherent in his next book. The writer may note your condition of affliction, but for now there is a cashier with arms brown from the sun and her eyes are grey and she is counting the minutes down at the end of the boardwalk at the Blue Diamond Restaurant. She has hair that glints with the late sunlight in it. You are a marvel to her with your nonstop monologue on what you will write, how you will write it, what you saw that day that troubled you and pleased you and how, for the moment, you have nowhere to place it in your life because things do not fit.

And I will hand her my two-dollar dinner tab with a quarter as if I have had only a coffee and she squares it with the cash register. Later, when we are both done at work, I will meet her again. You men recovering your stability at the Thomas M. England Hospital will see us passing and you will think your thoughts about us, dark if that is your disposition and even angry—you have earned your right to rage, you above all—or you will be reminded of better times, if that is your nature, and we are a friendly sight to you and no hard feelings. So, for now, I am late, good-bye, good luck: a writer too close for comfort to your meaning and who trembles with his understanding of what he sees must never, not ever, look too closely at things or he will see what is there and that can be fatal to any well-trimmed narrative.

To move about freely, chained as I had been in youth to my house or street, gangs, unreasonable fears, a frail constitution, Atlantic City was the prospect of a new mobility. With the ability to be places, unknown and unmarked, came a sense of the largeness and perversity of streets and people on them. Surely, people strolled more then, bent on errands, saw more on streets, heard more.

I knew Sid Noble as one of the profound walkers in Atlantic City: and not just displaying his rare, physical presence on the boardwalk where anyone after all could with summer furs and silk suits choose to flaunt their best suntanned advantage, but he walked resplendently with ease and importance in the streets off the main thoroughfares. They knew him on Georgia and South Carolina Avenues as well as the majestic boardwalk.

He stayed at the Washington Hotel the time I too briefly was young and there; and nightly in the early evening and after work at midnight Sid and I would walk. His name was not Noble, but he called himself that in Philadelphia and it fit him in a strangely sympathetic way.

On our strolls he was as handsome and proportionate as the fine night itself, stars in order above the ocean's shore, the air as bright as it can be in Atlantic City when you are me out of a cage at last—when one has just turned 18 and threatens the community of self and outsiders with the phantoms of novels to be written, a trace of Chekhov and Graham Greene for sardonic sobriety, and then, look no hands, the United States Army ahead to be conquered—on those nights I knew the ocean was true and I was in the company of a presence. Right and appropriate for the thousands of light bulbs of the Steel Pier. Resonant as a saxophone from the open door of a bar we passed.

Women loved him. Never before or since have I seen such adulation (perhaps that is not desirable in love—too grasping, too unequal in footing—but women adored Sid and that was the truth of his situation as comprehension of his status settled in on me like the warm night around us). No irony here of the dwarf-like men with no ears women paradoxically love or extraordinarily fat men with liver spots or the colorless or old or feeble—all necessary fantasies of our masculine failure to make metaphor of the urge to reproduce—this was love for an Adonis out of the purity of night in rowdy Atlantic City. Dressed in a white shirt and tie, each night like a colonial raja allowing his subjects proximity, he walked and talked to me, a fine prop, a listener, a handy foil to explain the point of a joke or the meaning of a complex relationship.

For me the act of walking itself in public places was movement in the cause of possibility: one sees those grim streets of my youth, the home of dreams of pursuit and capture, and remembers that free passage on a boardwalk, a side street in Atlantic City, or a barefooted slow shuffle down to the ocean is not a matter of no moment. No, walking was not just dangerous; it was always a statement of mother, father, and strange son.

Walking a block from where we lived one day on our home streets—not a frequent occurrence—my father and I, when I was perhaps nine, a boy a little older than me rushed out of a yard and stabbed me with a fork several times in the back. Mostly the fork hit the leather jacket I wore, but one of his blows caught me in the neck and I bled. The boy turned and rushed back into the yard where he had been hiding. My father started after him, then changed his mind. The bent fork lay on the cracked brick of the street.

"Let's go," he said urgently pushing me ahead of him in the direction of our house.

Thinking he saw some peril I had missed, I moved along, terrified of what was to come. "What is it?" I asked.

"Come, come."

"What is it?" I asked, aware now there was no menace I could see. "What is it?"

"We don't want any trouble," he said, reminding me as my neck burned where the fork had gouged away three inches of skin that our backs, our bodies, maybe our souls, were to be treated on the streets for what we were, provocations to the strong, swift, and cunning to mutilate us.

The open skies of the seashore and the broad endless boardwalk (one had only to walk its length and then simply to return where one had been, walking thus forever where no enemy waited in a doorway) and Sid, confident that he could work miracles: it was long, cotton-candy-scented moments of a time of liberation. The dreams of dismal hallways, skulking figures half-seen, three boys coming at me and separating so that I could not elude them; they linger in dreams, but after A.C. I knew there was something else.

In my daily forays in celebration of not getting stabbed, meditative as Sid summed up the world, nodded to men and women, I was where candy butchers go when all goes right. He was from Philadelphia, a candy butcher too, but barbered and tailored, visiting his subjects, on vacation in Atlantic City. No side-of-the-mouth gymnastics here, he was, by an odd chemistry of being, a person who made people want to do things for him—from buying gewgaws in the theater to, in the case of certain women on nights like no other in the history of the world, the summer of 1946, connect to him with silken cords of sexual attraction, a hunger for general excitement and meaning.

As we walked he stopped often to talk to his constituency. He surely knew hundreds of women, from New York, Philly, Atlantic City; and with each there was a discreet talk, a secret agreement on the terms of a barter. And to directly confront the matter, the exchange was frequently about money.

To say he took money from women was to deprecate the hold he and the women had on each other. He helped them: out of a marriage—or as trusted go-between, into a marriage—advice on a father, mother, runaway sister, a job for them or not for them, clothes, how shoes looked with a certain dress. And, if one read between the lines of murmured comment between them, he did not sleep with many of the women he enchanted. They gave him money for his new apartment, *his* clothes, alimony payments to be sent a long-gone wife and invisible kids, gambling losses, a trip to Boston. He would quietly, if vaguely, explain the money he received (there was often the opening of a purse, the thrust into his hand of rolled bills) and sometimes he gave the women money. For her new apartment, for her kid's shoes.

Each night we passed like shades in a netherworld perhaps a dozen women who had traffic with Sid. I do not know when he had time for private moments with them. He and I walked sometimes until dawn was in the sky over the Atlantic and we'd go to an all-night restaurant and eat eggs and toast—he always picked up the check—and there a waitress would flirt with him.

The Conjurer's Profession

"Where you been, Tyrone Power?"

"Around, you know."

As the sun came out, certain illusions swept away before me in the morning wind off the ocean: Sid was simply a presence. He had little except his cleft chin, solid nose, reassuring deep voice and manner, a sense of kindness about him that drew people to him. He had no favors like a politician to offer, no gifts of stimulating intellect to ensnare the inquirer thirsting after insight or knowledge, no particularly interesting turns of language. He had himself: the damndest thing, I had walked too early for my own good nightly with every man's dream of being a magnet for the love of others, young and old, and discovered, unhappily—at too early an age—that few are really fated to live the life of unearned affection. So, we move on to some sorry substitute—name your field of compromise—for Sid Noble's long, dark eyelashes and unfaltering stride.

I was among people who counted me in. I swam among them, as accepted as a fish out in schools of his kind in the deep, opaque Atlantic Ocean. The outsider boy was gone where even I knew no one could see him, except in my own dreams. I was more interested in people then than I have been since. They were new: every day with the job came an accounting to me of mysteries sweeter than the stolen coin. However wrong my interpretations, I was no longer observing things from a hole in a tree trunk.

Flossy Cunningham possessed a body born to wearing expensive and well-tailored clothes, compact and slender, and he moved in gestures calculated to demonstrate folds and drapes, hangs and quality of wool and cotton blend. He was known as the best-dressed candy butcher in Union City, N.J.

His name was derived from a burlesque sketch: one of a number of names so originated in comic deprecation. There was an "Our Gang" and a "Foo" at the Globe.

Flossy had a beautiful girlfriend named Minx, a showgirl from

Union City. He had a long, thick nose, and she was fourteen inches taller than him. They had been together a long time, and she beat him. He'd have scratches on his nose and bruises on his faces and be morose, but there never seemed serious talk of their separating. Perhaps loving rich, colorful ties as he did, forty-dollar shoes, top-dollar leathers, cufflinks, she was an acquisition to him, valuable as they strolled the boardwalk as something in a short, homely man's collection. Still, a rare wristwatch doesn't break a man's nose, a goblet doesn't throw his back out of joint as he seeks to elude its blows.

That summer they had a particularly violent fight; he had purple bruises on his neck. She had plainly tried to choke him to death.

Flossy, in his early fifties then and a longtime bachelor after a disastrous early marriage, was afraid of Minx's uncontrolled rage. She had hit him once with a bowling pin, a prop in a sketch, in a theater in Union City and sent him to the hospital. People wondered why he stayed; she was remarkable in complexion and body generally, but what good would it all do him under a tombstone when she discovered the right prop in her hand for his demise?

She had disappeared after the latest assault, and he asked me to take residence in his two rooms at the Washington and when she returned there to explain to her he wanted no more trouble. To simply say: "Flossy says he loves you but wants no more fighting." Unless she held her vicious temper, he told me to tell her, he would break up with her, forever. She may well have thought she killed him after their last brawl. He limped, he wheezed; he had two deep scratches down his forehead, across his monumental nose, and over his jutting chin.

"What if she lays into me?" I asked.

"This has nothing to do with you," he said. "I'm asking you because you're a stranger to her. She knows the other guys."

The point was: What did it matter if she hit me with a brick?

The first night I gave up my nightly boardwalk pilgrimage to wait for Minx. The Washington was noisy; I slept badly.

The next day I checked *The Wasteland* out of the Atlantic City library and all night long I was bewildered by its permutations. I fell asleep finally into dreams of the voices in the poem and Eliot and Flossy insinuating themselves into the depths of my consciousness. Rising early, I paced around the hotel, morning cluttered with figures from the infernos in the discreet mind of a genteel Englishman by way of St. Louis. The stately Minx—called on stage "The Queen of the Night" in one skit, "Evil's Loveliest Daughter" in another—arrived only in the fantastic voices of T. S. Eliot on the morning breeze, the shadows on the sidewalk. I waited two more nights; she did not come; neither Minx or Eliot yielded their mysteries easily.

On the fifth day, I told Flossy I planned to move back downstairs to my room. We stood on the railing to the beach in front of the Globe Theater, and the sun struck fully the explosive nose, the chin of a man twice his size, a mask of anguish in sun and depths of shadow. He said, "You don't give a damn if we never get back together, do you? Do you? As far as you're concerned I'm a mutt off the street, a whipped animal that nobody cares about. Punk, I put more time in rooms in crummy hotels than you have hair on your head. I've been an orphan since I was seven; and all I know is burlesque and rooms on the road from when I was a kid, but things changed with her. She built her whole life around me and I ain't going to let her down. It's not easy: and you ain't coming between us."

He gave me fifty dollars and hardly ever spoke to me again. She came back a few days later and I saw the two of them walking on the boardwalk at midnight, he in polished brown and white shoes, Minx in the peak with the best cosmetics and good health. Her hair was dyed blonde to white, and she was tall and busty and wore loose off-white pants and a bright yellow silk blouse. She held his arm as they formally strolled the night.

I put the five tens Flossy had given me into my shoe. Love flowered in Flossy, I have seen in my imagination its odd designs: between patterns in the faded wallpaper of the orphan boy's lonely rooms in Union City, Wichita, Denver, and Boston, in the heat of the hot plate where he cooked Campbell's baked beans, the sound of a tiny radio playing foxtrots at four in the morning, the unwashed windows and the threadbare carpets. Love for Minx in Flossy grows indomitable, blossoms, he will forgive her anything. Flossy, I think, would have loved a sharp-clawed polar bear if the bear held the promise of alleviating the tedium of those shabby one-room days and nights.

Across the street from the Washington Hotel there was a small restaurant called Sonny's Luncheonette. Sonny had returned from the war burning to make his fortune, tall and avid, his eyes blue and piercing. He was Italian and working with him in the restaurant were his wife, his mother and father, his two brothers-in-law, and his brother.

For no discernible reason, every member of the family grandly waived the check when I came in for breakfast or lunch. I ate a mountain of tuna-fish salad sandwiches; but when Angelo, Sonny's brother, was cooking or when Sonny himself saw me they fixed me waffles with coffee ice cream, huge almost angry scoops of ice cream thrown on ridiculously piled–high layers of waffle. Breakfast took me three-quarters of an hour to get through the bounty. I do not know why they chose me for this fate. I came in the first day they opened, I was accorded this treatment, and it continued for weeks and months.

Had there been a sister there, I would have understood I was her best prospect for marriage. Such kindness, unrelieved and insistent, was uncomfortable. "You brought us luck," Sonny occasionally said. Sometimes, I stayed away for a few days, anxious not to take advantage of the family's generosity, but when I returned I could see I annoyed them by not making a daily appearance. At rare times they accepted my payments on the check: but the next time the waffles would be piled higher, the coffee ice cream would cascade over the sides of the waffles.

It was a moment in which Sonny, shrapnel in his leg, had lived out in veterans' hospitals, dreamed about in France and Germany, and before that in high school in South Philly. A national moment too:

optimism as thick as syrup on a waffle, largess bottomless at the end of the too-long war. Our summer, 1946, was the consummation of all the troubled nightmares of men never returning and whatever had been good before gone forever in the senseless imperatives of history. Good times at Sonny's Luncheonette and the length of America: this was Sonny's own place, from here in ever-increasing strides onto the Bellevue-Stratford, and beyond. There was no limit. An old movie; suddenly the mother and father throw down their canes and begin jitterbugging, Angelo turns out to be the world's greatest banjo player and Sonny and his wife dance on the formica counter of the luncheonette, shaking their shoulders and swiveling their hips, and the cop on the sidewalk dances with another cop in a mock waltz.

That was how America felt to me as I prepared to leave Atlantic City. I had a date in mind I was going to enlist. If anyone questioned me, I had a story with the best of them. I could, interrogated, answer in consecutive sentences. When other boys on the street said, "What do you mean you don't eat supper in your house?" I had been tongue-tied. I was satisfied now I could say: "I guess I'll put in a couple of years in the army and then go to college. Maybe writing, you know, books, not journalism."

The people at the Globe Theater shook hands with me as solemnly as if there was a shred of truth to my unhappy evasion of going to the army and then going to college to become a writer. They gave me addresses. I had told the story so many nights at the Irish Club, waiting for the inspiration to rise out of the beer bubbles for a great book, I had come to believe it. I went down to the courthouse downtown in Pittsburgh and enlisted in September. My pose was ludicrous to me. I thought it possible I'd be too embarrassed to apply to college. I had failed three courses in high school and never made them up, but worrying about that was a long way in the future. I felt myself after Atlantic City a young man with prospects: if I didn't get to college, so what? If I didn't become a great writer, what did it matter? *This moment with me in this place.* Say *Atlantic City, 1946,* and then savor the sound. I was there; no, more immediate, *I am here forever when things go well.*

An edge on two billion people on the planet who might eventually find their place in the sun, blundering into great discoveries in medicine, composing symphonies, or simply putting in the nine-to-five at mostly someone else's bidding, I knew what I wanted, to work and shout in the aisles of burlesque theaters for the rest of my life.

Lester Goran currently teaches in the English Department of the University of Miami, where he started the Creative Writing Program and, later, the MFA in Creative Writing. He attended Pittsburgh public schools and the University of Pittsburgh. He has published (1994) a memoir, The Bright Streets of Surfside: A Memoir of a Friendship with Isaac Bashevis Singer. *His latest novel,* Bing Crosby's Last Song, *was published in 1998, and his third collection of short stories,* Outlaws of the Purple Cow and Other Stories, *was published in the fall of 1999.*

In the Woods

LESLIE RUBINKOWSKI

1

The day my grandfather saw the naked woman began at dawn. He and his brother Louie had parked the Chevy pickup at the edge of the woods and stepped down between the trees, carrying their rifles. When they lost sight of the road they parted, Louie disappearing deep. My grandfather found a stump, sat down, and waited.

Hours passed with no sign of deer or any other living thing. The middle of the day came but among the trees it was dark and still.

Then my grandfather heard a sound, a shuffling in the leaves. He looked up.

"Louie," he said, "is that you?"

It was not. It was a woman and she was standing before him, naked. She was young and very pretty and shivering in the cold. My grandfather stared at the woman. She hugged herself, made some small joke. She offered no excuse for her nakedness and it did not occur to my grandfather that she needed one. She smiled at him and the woods fell silent again.

After a long time my grandfather stood, still cradling the rifle in his arms. Then he turned and leaned the gun against the stump. He slid off his jacket and held it up for the woman to see.

"Here," he said. "I got long johns."

"I'll bring it back to you, I promise," she said.
"No," he said. "It's okay."

My grandfather turns to look at me. It is not deer season anymore but a night in July, maybe August. We sit on his back porch. I am fourteen. I know my grandfather wants to see what I am thinking so I lower my eyes and stare at my bare feet. While he talked the sun slumped below the trees just behind the beagle pens at the back of the yard. The sky is purple turning over to blue. In the kitchen behind us my grandmother says, "Oh, God." Neither of us moves. I scuff my toes on the fake grass carpet. I study my feet. They are huge for a kid my size.

He knows he has me.

I know he is lying.

I hate my grandfather's lies but I love a good story even more. I know this fact will either be my salvation or the reason that I will never get a date. But I also know I must hear what happened next. I need to know so much that I might as well be naked. I am too young to understand that I already am. And that this truth is both my future and my everlasting doom.

I look up.

"Then what," I say.

That is where it all starts, doesn't it? *Then what:* That lovely painful pull of the thing you need to know, whether you need to know it or not. One thing follows another and you tell yourself you know all the answers but suspect in the end you are still stupid because you lack the strength to say: enough. Because you also know that your stupidity can teach you something.

This is a true story about lies. I spent my childhood listening to my grandfather lie. That is not what made me a writer, but it is what made me the kind of writer I am, the kind of person I am. The kind of person who asks too many questions.

Like: Then what?

Like: Did you ever get that jacket back?

Like: Have you ever wanted to know the truth about something so much you made it up?

2

Some facts about my grandfather:

He was born September 10, 1910, in Phillips, Pennsylvania, to Hungarian immigrants, the second child of six. He dropped out of school in the sixth grade and went to work in the coal mines after his father died. He began smoking around the same time—unfiltered Chesterfields. He met my grandmother at a dance. The first time he saw her she sat at the edge of a dance floor on a wooden folding chair, wearing a white lace dress.

They married on July 31, 1931. They had three children—my mother, who was the middle child, and two sons. My grandfather was a mechanic in the mines and he settled his family into a company house in a neighborhood of other miners and their families in what people called a coal patch. Sometimes he drank. Sometimes he drank too much. On one of those nights my grandmother threw a bottle of ketchup at him and when my mother and her brothers saw the spatters on the wall they thought she had finally killed him. In 1941 a mine ceiling collapsed on him; a sheet of slate shaved off his face and the crush of rock nearly killed him. They rebuilt his face but he was different. After the accident he got softer, stopped drinking. Started telling stories.

He loved professional wrestling. He used to sit in front of the television in his favorite recliner—the armrests sticky from where my grandmother had taped the cracks in the vinyl—and shadow-box while the wrestlers dropped on each other like meat falling out of a grinder. When he swung his recliner lurched and by the end of the show his knees nearly touched the screen.

He had his teeth pulled around 1945 but hated the way his false set felt so he went around toothless. He used to open a box of chocolates and squeeze each piece to determine which were the creams. Anyone in the house hungry for candy had to decide whether they wanted it badly enough to eat my grandfather's dented rejects.

He wore his teeth only for special occasions, like weddings and deaths. At those times he disappeared into his room and emerged wearing a blue suit, white shirt, black shoes. He lingered outside his door, studying the plastic runner in the hall, and when his eyes darted up his smile shone like a burst of flashbulb, an unexpected slice of moon, and from the living room everyone already dressed and waiting would smile back and say how nice he looked, and he would open his mouth a little more and his eyes would get shiny behind his glasses and he would study the runner again, and though I am not a child anymore I still ask myself: What wrong could ever live inside a man bashful about having teeth?

Almost nothing, except that he lied to me every time I saw him— once a week, minimum. Most Saturday nights my parents would drop off my younger brother and me at my grandparents' house and go off dancing; we would sleep over and they would pick us up in the morning after my grandmother had served us a breakfast of pancakes and hot dogs smothered in homemade syrup that tasted suspiciously like whiskey. I remember those Saturday nights as an improbable cocktail of Lawrence Welk hours and marathon story sessions. Sometimes my grandmother would corner me and explain the recipe for this soup she made that had an omelet floating on top or confide her dream of becoming an accountant, killed when her mother made her quit school in the eighth grade to clean houses. My grandmother never lost the sense that she was destined for better, and she was always trying something artistic. Her garden took up two-thirds of her backyard. While supper cooked one afternoon, she spray-painted every surface in the living room gold. We all had to agree it looked pretty amazing.

But most nights when I tried to slink across the side yard into the house, my grandfather would catch me. "Hey, farmer," he would holler. "Come here. I gotta tell you somethin.'" Sometimes I would be paddling across the living room with a plate full of nut rolls and a head full of adolescent disco misery and he would say something like, "Boy, I'll bet Mazeroski was cold," which was my signal to sit down and start listening.

Some stories were set in the mines where he worked, tales of horrible accidents involving heavy machinery and rats as big as lunch pails. A few took place in his childhood, like the one about George Washington, a kid in second grade who was so stupid my grandfather sold him his own shoes.

But most of my grandfather's stories unfolded in the woods. Infinite possibilities, no witnesses: wilderness. Most people went into the woods and got lost. My grandfather found things. Once he saw a laughing monkey in a tree. Once he stumbled upon a truckload of shih-tzus. Once, when he was a boy, he found something in the woods and he didn't know what the hell it was. It bristled with quills just like a porcupine but the quills were more like fur. It had a bill like a duck and beady black eyes.

Like a platypus? I asked when he told me this. I was probably twelve.

He looked at me as if to say: Shut up. "We put it in a bucket and filled it full of water," he said. "We called the game warden. He came over and looked at the thing. 'I don't know what the hell that is,' he said. He took the bucket and left, and that's the last we heard of him."

As I am writing this, I realize that I am lying to you. I am telling stories that I know to be untrue. And I am filling them with memory, the clumsiest editor of all. I don't remember my grandfather's exact words. I do remember the color of the summer night sky, though maybe time has simply convinced me this is true. But in one thing I am honest: I accept that in some ways I am no better than my grandfather. Writers lie all the time, even when they deal in fact. We try to sell ourselves as natural-born architects of polished sentences and balanced arguments when bias and doubt force and influence every word. My first draft of this story looked nothing like what you are reading now. In an earlier version I began with a story from another hunting season. My grandfather was sitting on a stump, holding a rifle in one hand and a walkie-talkie in the other.

The walkie-talkie crackled.

"Louie," he said, "is that you?"

"No, John, it's me," a woman's voice said. "You want some pie?"

"What kind?" my grandfather said.

"All kind," the woman said. "I just made 'em. My house is just through the trees."

My grandfather walked for a while. He saw the woman's house. He saw the pies, steaming on a kitchen windowsill. He saw the woman. Good God, she was ugly. My grandfather was not an educated man but he knew he wanted no part of any ugly woman's pie. He slipped back through the trees.

A year later, he was sitting on the same stump. The walkie-talkie crackled.

"Louie," he said, "is that you?"

"It's me, John," the pie woman said. "Where you been?"

When I was a kid, this story would not let me sleep. On nights when I stayed at my grandparents I would lie awake listening to the beagles moan in their pens out back and try to make sense of what I'd heard. How did this woman find my grandfather's frequency? How did she know when he'd return? How in the hell did she know his name? *What kind of pie?*

I was a pretty sad kid.

It was probably inevitable that I grew up to be a reporter.

3

Three A.M. on a Thursday. I lie in bed in my own home obsessing over a stranger who told me she used to be a star on *Hee Haw*. To be exact, a Hee Haw Honey, one of those women in hillbilly bikinis who pop out of a cornfield and tell awful jokes. My past warns me she is lying; I can feel it. Nothing feels like the feeling I get when I sense I am being lied to, that hot whine behind the eyes, that cold pressure beneath the bridge of the nose. I love that feeling: Not surprise or shock but a wash of comfort and relief. People lie. You can count on it.

If she is telling a lie it is a small one, and in the scheme of things—in the book I am writing—it means next to nothing. Rationally, I know this. Truthfully, I don't care. Size is exactly the point. The smaller a lie is, the harder I scramble to expose it. Because one tiny lie slides past and then bigger ones follow and then rot sets in and then everything flies apart and because it is 3 A.M. I believe that if this happens I will die. This is how pathetic my life is: This is the tension, the engine that drives my days and wrecks my life. I am never more miserable or more alive than when I lie sleepless, trapped in my past and happy in my pathology.

Her last name sounds like a first name. I tried once, in a bright-orange booth at a Waffle House in Erlanger, Kentucky, to see if it was her real name when she pulled out her wallet to pay for her eggs. Instead my eyes went *thwock* on her driver's license photo: Postapocalyptic corona of platinum hair. Pillow lips. Eye makeup straight off a cathedral ceiling.

"When I leave this world," she informed me at an Elvis impersonators' contest in Memphis, Tennessee, "first person I want to see is my Lord. Second person is Elvis. I want to touch him. I want to say, 'Thank you.'"

We huddled in the back of a nightclub while up front some guy in a jumpsuit popped his hips to a drum roll. She told me about her history and *Hee Haw,* offered vague insinuations about Elvis. I asked if Elvis gave her the TCB necklace around her neck, the kind he gave people, the one she claimed she never removes. She started to weep. She proclaimed she didn't love him as a lover but as a man. She said she has a tapestry of Elvis on her ceiling. "It looks like he is going up to heaven," she said.

In bed, I stare at my ceiling. A car grinds past. My head began to hurt the moment she began to cry. It was all so beautiful I knew it couldn't be true.

I trust nothing but I am prepared to believe anything. This seems to me like common sense. Reporting relies mainly on common sense. This may explain why so many people are so bad at it. So I consult reference books. The dates the woman says she appeared on *Hee Haw* don't jibe with her account of the year she met Elvis. I feel wronged. I feel wonderful.

The show is no longer in production, but at the time it ran in syndication on the Nashville Network. I ask the TV listings editor at the newspaper where I work if she has a phone number for the network. She hands me a fat binder full of numbers. I fish one out. I make a call.

A receptionist ships me to a public relations woman's voice-mail. I identify myself, explain my dilemma. She calls back. I explain my dilemma in more detail. It occurs to me I sound like a nut. I don't care. Reporting also relies on the willing suspension of self-loathing. She tells me the name of a woman in the *Hee Haw* office who knows everyone who's ever been on the show. She will call her and get back to me.

A day later, she calls back and leaves a message: No person by the name I gave her ever appeared on *Hee Haw*.

I call the self-proclaimed Hee Haw Honey. She has moved, so I get her new number from a couple who takes turns checking me out on the phone. The alleged Honey is happy to hear from me. I was so nice to her, she says. She's married now, and happy. I'm glad, I say. Discrepancies, I add. Could she clarify?

Of course. She worked on *Hee Haw* in Bakersfield, California, at a ranch owned by one of the stars. Ah, I say. Again we verify dates, times, years. And again I ask her to spell her name. I have it on tape, but still. One *n* in the last name, right?

No, she says. Two.

I call back the woman from the Nashville Network. Discrepancies, I say. She sounds frightened. Take the *Hee Haw* number, she says. I call

Nashville. I love the *Hee Haw* historian as soon as I hear her voice. She finds my drama funny but is happy I'd rather not lie. She will check records, files, and the memory of the show's former star and get back to me. A day later, she does. The show never filmed in Bakersfield, she says. The woman is lying. I ask her, "Why would anyone say they were on *Hee Haw* when it is so easy to find out they weren't?"

A few times a year, she says, she gets calls asking about people claiming they used to come out of a cornfield on *Hee Haw*. After all these years she still has no idea why.

We hang up. I put a picture of the woman wearing a black and gold evening gown and a ring on every finger into an envelope with a letter. Could the historian kindly look at the picture to, without a doubt, verify that this woman definitely never appeared on the show? A few days later, she returns the picture. "I must say I've never seen her before," she writes, "and she most definitely was not a member of the HEE HAW Show Cast—ever—under any circumstances. You are to be commended for checking the information which is represented as fact."

I change the passage in what I am writing but still I cannot sleep. At first I decide it's because I'm happy. It takes me a few dream-state days to realize I am miserable. Deep down, I wanted that woman to be a Hee Haw Honey.

I used to think I was trying to expose the same lies that annoyed me when I was young, but as I've gotten older I realize I was lying to myself. There are lies that attempt to hide, and then there are those that reveal. These are the ones that haunt me because of what they say about loss and hope. I could count on my grandfather lying to me the same way I could count on him loving me. He lied to me because he loved me, I think. And because he didn't think he was lying. In his mind he was the guy who rescued naked women in the woods, resourceful and dashing even without teeth, a coal-patch Cary Grant. *This is who I am*, he seemed to be saying. *Never mind that it isn't true.*

In his lies he offered up his best self, and he taught me the possibility of strange and powerful things. Naked women may not roam the woods, but coal miners with sixth-grade educations can burn with stories and the desire to tell them.

So maybe what I'm looking for aren't lies at all. Maybe what I'm looking for—hoping for—is a happier truth.

Maybe what I'm looking for is the way I felt another summer night, the summer of the year I turned seventeen.

4

I am standing at the edge of my woods listening to my grandfather meow like a cat. Seventeen years old and I have nothing better to do on a Saturday night than scowl into a stand of trees beyond the garden so my grandfather can prove something.

He seldom repeats stories but for a couple of weeks he has refused to let one of them go. "Hey, Joanne," he says, as always calling me by my mother's name, "I was up in the woods and I hear this sound, and you know what I seen? This Siamese cat. Just like yours. Cried like a baby. When I tried to come up on it, it ran from me."

"Really," I said.

"Honest to God!" he cried.

So I stand next to him while he makes a sound that suggests his foot has been pinned in a trap. The beagles out back believe him; they yelp and throw their shoulder blades against the chicken-wire doors. "Get in there!" he yells at them, then resumes mewing.

I cannot see the moon. My grandfather caterwauls, dressed in his usual plaid shirt and dog-running pants, patches on top of patches. Legacy in action. I regard my unfortunate feet and wonder how it came to be that I am damned. I am a strange child, given to memorizing soliloquies from *Hamlet* and the lyrics of Barry White songs. I wake at 5 A.M. to write poems, all of them containing the word "darkness." Nothing I see this night gives me any hope.

Then I see something coming out of the woods and I don't know what the hell it is. Except that I know exactly what it is. It strolls, shoulders rolling, wet and yowling and with its blue eyes wide. I half expect a naked woman to stroll out of the woods behind it, carrying a pie.

    I cannot lie. I do not remember the speed of the wind or the velocity of my shock and bewilderment, though I can still feel it, how everything in the world seemed to lift and spin, and how it seemed perfectly normal that everything was weird, and how in some way I'd always expected it, and how my grandfather leaned forward and shot me one of his bottomless smiles. And I do remember that its fur looked like wet feathers, and when it cleared the woods it walked right past my grandfather and headed straight toward me.

Leslie Rubinkowski teaches writing at West Virginia University and at Goucher College. She is the author of the book **Impersonating Elvis.**

That Sweet Anarchy We Call Youth

CHUCK KINDER

*T*he story swept through the mining camps like wildfire across West Virginia that Sid Hatfield and Ed Chambers had been shot down like dogs in front of their wives on the courthouse steps at Welch, and the killers were free on bond, paid by the coal barons who ruled southern West Virginia with the old proverbial iron fist. And while the lowdown murderers went free, hundreds of Mingo County miners, the miners Sid had stood up for his whole short life, remained thrown under the jailhouse. Newspapers hollered the news in headlines all over the country, and the United Mine Workers of America closed its district office in Charleston, West Virginia, posting a placard upon the door which read thusly: "Closed in memory of Sid Hatfield and Ed Chambers, murdered by Baldwin-Felts Gunthugs while submitting themselves dutifully to a court of law." In Charleston miners held a mass meeting on the lawn of the capitol, whereupon they passed a resolution of outrage and perpetual grief. Soon thereafter, miners along Little Coal River, halfway across the wild mountains between Charleston and Matewan, began arming themselves and multitudes of men with guns began to come down out of the dark hills calling out for their rights and for sweet vengeance in Sid Hatfield's name. These drastic actions touched off a series of tragic events which culminated in the Battle of Blair Mountain in August 1921, a basically unplanned, leaderless rebellion in which 10,000 miners battled coal-company gunthugs and lackey state police for three bloody days before lackey federal troops finally intervened, in what was the largest insurrection in the United States since the Civil War.[1]

For many of the combatants on both sides, who were World War I veterans, the Battle of Blair Mountain was as fierce as any they had fought in France. Although no accurate count was ever made, there were many casualties on both sides, including, according to family legend, my Great-Uncle Alfonso, who was my paternal grandfather's older brother, and who had been a rather reluctant draftee during the First World War, and then later had returned home suffering from a chronic shivery condition due to shellshock. So it had been unfathomable to family members when Uncle Alfonso, a mild-mannered bookkeeper by nature and trade, and nearly spastic with that nervousness, and who had been considered peculiar anyway because he was rumored to read books he didn't have to and even pen poems, had for some reason donned his old uniform, including his "tin derby" trench helmet, and loaded his rifle for the first time since he had returned from the Big One, and he had marched off with several of his coal-miner uncles and cousins to join Sid Hatfield's avenging army.

Somehow Uncle Alfonso had become lost on Blair Mountain during the battle and had wandered about for a whole night essentially in solitude, while men on both sides who couldn't see one another sought pleasure shooting into the darkness all night purely to see the flames spit out from their gunbarrels. The next morning Uncle Alfonso had emerged onto Crooked Creek Pass, where he stumbled into a miners' campsite, certain that he was the ghost of a doughboy who had been killed by a single bullet in a French forest far from anybody who had ever loved him. He was wrong about that, both the ghost business and the love part, for while Uncle Alfonso had been put

---

1. I am utterly indebted for all the historical material to a wonderful book by Lon Savage called *Thunder in the Mountains: The West Virginia Mine War, 1920–21* (Pittsburgh: University of Pittsburgh Press, 1990).

away for his own good for the rest of his natural life, he had remained beloved and unforgotten. My own middle name is *Alfonso,* a name which occasioned more than a few fistfights for a secretly poetical boy trying to grow up tough in southern West Virginia.

Another story about poor old Uncle Alfonso has come down in the family, which perhaps helps explain why that gentle, fragile soul armed himself to the teeth and marched off to avenge Sid Hatfield. Apparently Uncle Alfonso was once traveling by train at night from his current coal-company bookkeeping job in Williamson to his home with his folks in Charleston, and he had gone back to the smoker car for a cigarette. Uncle Alfonso had been all alone for a spell, until a slim, rather handsome, well-dressed young man walked in and took the seat opposite him. They nodded and presently took to talking. At some point, it finally dawned upon Uncle Alfonso that he was conversing with the notorious Sid Hatfield. After a time, Sid pulled a flask from his pocket and suggested they have a little drink. Whereupon my Uncle Alfonso, who was not as a rule a drinking man, had said no thank you anyway, sir. Sid Hatfield had nonchalantly reached back under his coat, and this time he pulled out a long revolver, which he laid on the seat beside him. Then Sid had offered Uncle Alfonso the flask again, and this time he smiled that famous smile of his, and quietly commented: "There's nothing lonelier than a feller drinking all by hisself on a train late at night." In telling of this experience later, my Uncle Alfonso was reputed to have always wound up the story with the remark: "I never had so much fun or got so drunk in my life."

There came a point in my life a while back, when I took the notion to get to the bottom of my curious lengthening existence by writing a book about my regional, redneck roots in the southern West Virginia hills and hollows, and I began to drive from my home in Pittsburgh down into the dark, pyramidal mountains of my haunted home state often, moved back down there for a spell in fact, as I vainly sought the ghost of my lost, handsome, youthful self. But I was seeking something more than that essential silliness. As I drifted alone, for days sometimes, around those twisty, country roads traversing that sacrificial landscape, little town to town, what I was really seeking was linkage to the vital—albeit violent—stories of another time, attempting, I suppose, to invoke the fervor of that other time, a dangerous, bloody, adolescent era, when folks imagined they harbored hopes worth living and dying for, and in the midst of disastrous events had a few laughs to boot. The bloody saga of Sid Hatfield had caught my attention early.

I had heard stories about Sid Hatfield since childhood, but I first became truly interested in him when I watched John Sayles' critically acclaimed 1987 movie *Matewan*, which basically deals with the people and events that led up to and included the bloody gunfight where ten men died. In the movie, the character of Sid Hatfield (played by a young actor named David Strathairn) emerges rather slowly, appearing suddenly at key points in the narrative and then fading back into the shadows of the story like the *Lone Enigma*. Early on, Sid is an armed and clearly dangerous presence on the edges of the action, but mostly an onlooker, until the final bloody showdown with the Baldwin-Felts gunthugs in the streets of Matewan, in which Sid was a principal participating shootist.

In true life Sid Hatfield had gone into the mines at thirteen, and had grown into a tough, hardnosed but rather good-looking young man, slight but wiry with muscle, maybe 150 pounds soaking wet and five-feet-six, with light brown hair, high cheekbones, jug ears, a dimple in his chin, and an engaging grin that sported gold in his teeth (picture the actor Matt Dillon with a real sunburst of a smile). At night Sid raised hell in Matewan, a town as wild and dangerous and corrupt as any in the old Wild West. Sid played pool, poker, and slot machines, chewed, smoked, drank at the Blue Goose Saloon, and chased the gals. He fought often, putting at least one fellow in the hospital. He shot guns with buddies along the riverbank, and they still say down in Mingo County that Sid could toss a potato in the air, draw his pistol, and split it open in the blink of an eye. These qualities won respect in Matewan, and they caught the eye of C. C. Testerman, the mayor, who appointed Sid as the town's first chief of police.[2]

Sid had become fast friends with Mayor Testerman, a thirty-seven-year-old, pudgy, balding man who dressed nattily in a suit and bowtie and who tended to favor the miners. Mayor Testerman also had a lovely twenty-six-year-old wife named Jessie. Sid wore his badge and guns but no uniform and he pleased the miners by enforcing the law fairly. When miners brawled, Sid pulled them apart; when they got drunk, he took them safely home; when they became wild and woolly, he cooled them off or joined in the fun. Rarely did a miner occupy Sid's little town jail. To the amusement of Matewan's miners, Sid even got into brushes with the law himself in the winter of 1919–20, once for possessing illegal whiskey and once for fighting. Both times Mayor Testerman posted bond and kept Sid in his job. The campaign to unionize the miners was under way, and Sid was supportive. Night after night that spring miners filled Matewan's little Baptist church to learn about the union, while Sid stood by to assure that the meetings went undisturbed. Three hundred miners signed up in a single night. Among them was boyish Ed Chambers, newly married and Sid's best friend. As the union drive heated up, Sid's popularity was such that he announced as a candidate for the Democratic nomination for constable of the Matewan district.[3]

Then Al Felts, field manager of the Baldwin-Felts Detective Agency, bragged that he would break the union-organizing effort "if it puts one hundred men in jail and costs a million dollars." He came to Sid and Mayor Testerman and offered them five hundred dollars for permission to place machine-guns in Matewan, in case they might have to mow some striking Commie miners down. Sid told Felts to kiss his ass and get the hell out of town. By May 15, Sid's twenty-seventh birthday, three thousand miners along the Tug belonged to the United Mine Workers. And hundreds of them, who had been fired and

2. Ibid., 12–13.
3. Ibid., 15.

evicted from their company homes the moment they joined the union, lived in tent colonies, where women and children circulated hungrily around the swampy cities of patched canvas on boards for sidewalks, and raggy clothes flapped like hundreds of sad flags on lines along the dark Tug Fork. The miners were angry and seething for atonement, for mountain revenge, for frontier justice. Guns bristled everywhere.[4]

What we cannot forget is that those were fierce, feudal times, bloody, barbaric Dark Ages down in the mountains of West Virginia. A deep feel of the frontier had lived on in West Virginia's interior far after its values had eroded in the rest of the country, even in the faraway vanished Wild West. In many important ways, you can imagine West Virginia as one of the final frontiers, where even today there is a great nostalgia for the habits and customs and old ways of life in the mountains, which, like life on the frontier, were often crude and violent, with a great predilection evidently for drinking and dancing to excess, and fighting and feuding and fornicating wildly until dawn, and risking all for love or revenge, and discharging guns into the air simply to express despair or confusion or joy or for just the general old-timey frontier fuck of it.

This frontier spirit was due in part to West Virginia's isolation deep in the Appalachian Mountains, which for a long time kept the forces of modernization and her sister moderation out. Also, there were economic aspects of mountaineers' lives which help explain the lingering survival of frontier conditions. Subsistence farming and the grazing of hogs in the forests remained for years the principal forms of agriculture. If a mountain farmer produced any market commodity, it was probably whiskey (and, more recently, the best marijuana money can buy), a vastly more efficient and fun way of storing and selling corn than handling bushels of those slippery little items. Another traditional frontier avocation was pot-hunting, which was

4. Ibid., 16.

nothing more than the ancestral practice of a man shouldering his gun, hollering up his dogs, and going out into the woods to kill some forest critters to feed his family. Hence, long after the frontier spirit that had driven the Wild West, such as it was, had passed except as a ghostrider before the storm in songs and in Western movies that come back to haunt us yet, that same free, wild, rough-and-tumble, fun-loving, sexual spirit survived deep in the dark hills of West Virginia, where, as I have commented, it lingers to this day, particularly in pockets peopled by my own rowdy relatives. I, for instance, would forsake my university professorship in a heartbeat if I thought I could make a decent living grazing hogs in the woods. And I drink whiskey.

Because of the Wild West pulp fiction popular early in the century, and later the shoot-'em-up cowboy movies, the particular mythos of the old Wild West found its way back even into the mountains of West Virginia. It was as though the Wild West sense of frontier had folded back on itself there, layered itself like a seam of coal running through the West Virginia hills. And that Wild West movie mythos had found itself resurrected there in that ongoing frontier called Appalachia. "Mountaineers Are Always Free" is the state motto of West Virginia. In their imaginations, mountaineers moved freely within a fiction of the old Wild West, where dead-tired at kitchen tables after farming rocky hillsides or working deep in the coal mines or cutting timber until after dark, they could be cowboys or lawdogs or outlaws in their daydreams as they ate their cold suppers late and alone. They could become frontiersmen, holy outsiders, magical West Virginia warriors, who would join up with the union no matter what the risks, and fight tooth and nail for their rights as men and miners and shoot down fucken scabs and Baldwin-Felt gunthugs and strike for as long as it took, passing that Mason jar of moonshine around the blazing campfire night after night, until hell froze over if it came to that.

Basically the Wild West showdown-in-the-street was made up by Hollywood; the shootout was mostly pure cinema. But in that remake of the Wild West movie state-of-mind called the Great Coal Field Wars, bloody showdown shootouts blossomed into a sort of art form, into a sort of poetic cinema verité of pure, spastic, orgiastic violence. In terms of the numbers of guns blazing deadly fire and fallen men and the entanglements and intrigues of moral issues, the famous *Gunfight at the O.K. Corral* was child's play compared to the *Battle of Matewan*.

It was on May 19, in 1920, a gray, drizzly Wednesday, when near the railroad tracks in the center of Matewan Chief of Police Sid Hatfield and Mayor Cable Testerman confronted a force of thirteen heavily armed Baldwin-Felts gunthugs, led by Al and Lee Felts, who had come to town to evict unionized miners from company homes. Mingo County folks still argue about who fired the first shot. Sid said Al Felts shot Mayor Testerman and then he, Sid, pulled a gun and shot Felts. Others say miners in the hardware store shot first, killing Mayor Testerman by accident. The Felts family always claimed Sid shot first. One witness testified that Sid came up behind Al Felts, jerked a pistol hidden under his coat, and fired directly at the back of Felts' head, who crumpled onto the sidewalk. Others claimed they were certain a bullet from Sid's gun was the one that killed Mayor Testerman, making a widow of the woman Sid was known to admire. But whoever fired first, on the rainy streets of Matewan that day the scene suddenly erupted into an orgasmic explosion of gunblasts and splurting blood and blasted men tumbling into all of death, and in a heartbeat Albert Felts and Mayor Testerman lay on the ground dying, and before it was all over seven Baldwin-Felts gunthugs, two miners, and Mayor Testerman were hillbilly history.

At Sid Hatfield's trial for murdering Albert Felts the following year in Williamson, the scumbag company spy Charles E. Lively, who had infiltrated the union and befriended Sid, testified against Sid. One of the things Lively claimed was that Sid had told him that he would like to get Mayor Testerman out of the way. All of Sid's supporters had figured that that was simply scumbag bullshit, of course. But after reviewing all the evidence, it had occurred to me that maybe that was true. What if late one night while Lively and Sid were up drinking whiskey together and talking nooky (as pre–politically correct men were wont to do), Sid did say what Lively said he said about being in love with another man's beautiful, brown-haired wife and being willing to go through hell to have her? It is, after all, only the supposedly scumbag company spy's word against that of the hero of the minefield's sacred hills and hollows. What if Sid, the miners' two-gunned mythic hero did, in fact, plug poor old Mayor Testerman, his best friend and benefactor, when the opportunity presented itself in the chaotic midst of general firing and thick gunsmoke in order to have Testerman's dark-eyed, creamy-skinned wife with wondrous breasts? Was Sid Hatfield capable of such a monstrous deception and betrayal purely for the sake of nooky, if not love? Not unlike that complex precision in the relationship between predators and their prey, the nature of the relationship between the betrayed and their betrayers is a unique, almost ceremonial linkage, as they give one another what they each suspect they deserve or want or need or fear the most and dream about nightly, as though they are merely channels for the insidious, arbitrary jocularity of the universe.

Somehow I can imagine Mayor Testerman burying his sad, fat face in his hands and weeping while he tells his lovely young wife Jessie that if anything happens to him she should go ahead and marry Sid Hatfield if that's what she has her heart set on. Sid would take care of her and be kind and good to her and get up in the dead of night to hold her when she wakes up screaming as though she is being murdered in those crazy nightmares she has and make her cocoa. I can imagine Mayor Testerman sitting there sobbing and hoping with all of his heart his wife would say no, no, honeybear, baby, that's not what I want to do ever. But Jessie doesn't say anything of the kind. Jessie simply sits there quietly at the kitchen table looking so heartbreakingly lovely in the soft lamplight. The same kitchen table where not twenty minutes earlier perhaps Sid had sat, his chiseled features rugged and handsome and dramatically shadowy in the same lamplight as he talked about the danger he would face when the Baldwin-Felts came back to town. How dangerous and daring Sid had seemed, how tough, yet somehow tender, and even innocent, boyish and brave at once, and vital and intense and sincere and so in love with Jessie he couldn't keep his dark, hungry eyes off her.

I can even imagine Mayor Testerman burying his sad, fat face in his hands and blubbering his heart out in front of both Sid and Jessie while he asks Sid to please treat Jessie good. While he asks Sid to love his little Jessie-lamb with all his heart and treat her good like he, Mayor Testerman, had always tried to do himself. Perhaps it was the night before the big battle when Jessie and Sid confirmed the mayor's worst suspicions and those rumors rampant around town that Sid and Jessie had been seen walking hand in hand down by the Tug Fork. Perhaps Sid didn't have to plug the mayor at all to win his Jessie-lamb. What if the mayor, a fat, ugly, smart, philosophical man who was just thankful to have had it all even for a little while, to have held heaven in his fat arms a few times, he was just thankful for that, what if that philosopher had gone down into harm's way the next day unarmed and gentle and soft-hearted and unendurably sad and sacrificial. I can imagine such a romantic, sentimental, fat, hopeless, heroic husband offering himself up for the sake of his beautiful, beloved wife's future happiness, and maybe even stepping in front of that beneficent bullet meant for his best friend, Sid, who had gone and betrayed him like that.

Sid Hatfield became an instant hero to the unionized miners in the coal fields. After ten days of intense mourning, Jessie, the lovely young widow of Mayor Cable Testerman, eloped to Huntington, West Virginia, to marry Sid. Sid and twenty-two other defendants were acquitted of charges arising from the shootout after that lengthy trial in Williamson. Only a little over a year after the famous battle, Sid and his friend Ed Chambers, along with their wives, Jessie and Sallie, after being promised protection by the local sheriff but against the better advice of their friends, rode the train south from Matewan to Welch, the McDowell County seat and a coal barons' stronghold, to stand trial on some trumped-up charges stemming from still yet another shootout between miners and company gunthugs.

The streets on August 1, 1921, in Welch were packed. Folks flooded up from the depot toward the courthouse on the hill, everybody in town for the forthcoming trial, many as witnesses or codefendants. Sid's name was on everybody's lips. The massive stone, ivy-covered Victorian McDowell County Courthouse, with its high clock tower, loomed like a fortress on the hillside. An eight-foot-high, heavy stone wall bordered the sidewalk, and above the wall the lawn sloped upward toward the courthouse. A double set of stone steps, running parallel to the street, intersected at a common landing at the top of the wall. A single wider set of steps then turned perpendicular to the street and led up the hill to the front entrance of the building. Standing athwart the sidewalk and along the grass at the top of the steps were the scumbag spy Charles Lively and a half-dozen other heavily armed Baldwin-Felts detectives. The gunthugs watched steely-eyed as the Matewan group strolled along on the far side of the narrow street and then crossed at the corner.

Sid, Jessie, Ed Chambers and his wife, Sallie, started up the steps amid the slow-moving throngs of people. The sunny, bright day was dazzling. Sallie carried a parasol. Ed, blond and boyish in appearance despite his reputation for explosive violence, led the party, one hand on the stone balustrade, the other holding his wife's arm. They reached the first landing and started up the next flight toward the courthouse. Behind them Sid put an arm around his lovely young wife, Jessie, as they mounted to the first landing. Sid looked up the stone steps to where his old friend and mortal enemy, Charles Lively, stood waiting and their eyes met and seemed to lock for a moment, and some say they both grinned. Just then a group of Sid's friends reached the landing from the opposite direction, and Sid Hatfield took his arm from around Jessie to raise his hand in friendly greeting.

That Sweet Anarchy We Call Youth

He smiled his famous, golden, sunburst smile and spoke the last words he would utter upon this Earth, "Hello, boys."[5]

Every time I dipped down to Welch, I'd park in front of the old courthouse on the hill, and for a few reflective moments settle my butt on that third stone step from the bottom of the landing, the one where the head of Sid Hatfield had come to rest nearly seventy-five years earlier. Then I would walk around that tired, gritty-brick town with its frequent empty storefronts and almost deserted streets for a time. Right around the corner from the courthouse on McDowell Street, I had found the entrance to the building which once housed the old Carlton Hotel, where Sid and Jessie and their party had rested up before walking over to the courthouse for Sid and Ed's trial that fateful summer day. Big gold letters above the Romanesque corner entrance, which still retained a certain old-hotel elegance with large carriage lanterns attached to its white stone pillars, announced that the three-story brick building was now named TYSON TOWERS. Now the spacious old lobby was home to Taylor Optical, which advertised quality eyeglass service. Right down the street under a small, green-striped awning, I found another entrance, which had the old Carlton Hotel crest above the door. This entrance now opened into the Pizza Plus dining room. There was a sign in the window that advertised that the Robert Tyson Realty had a furnished apartment for rent, and for no good reason I wrote down the number, 436-4358. You could never tell. Anything was possible at that point in my own do-not-go-gently, grouchy, grumpy coming-of-old-age story.

As best I could figure, the old railroad depot down over the hill toward the river where Sid and his party had disembarked that day was now a nearly empty concrete parking garage building. But across the street from the old Carlton Hotel corner entrance was Ray's Barbershop. I recalled that Sid had gone out alone to get a haircut that morning before the trial. When I had peeked through the window of

---

5. Ibid., 69–70.

the shop one day, the barber, Ray himself as it turned out, who was sitting in his barber's chair reading a newspaper all alone in the place, waved for me to come on in as though I were a long-lost son. So I had ducked into that barbershop, whose high walls were lined with shelves filled with what could have been literally thousands of beer cans, which was what had caught my attention in the first place.

The friendly barber looked like still yet another hillbilly version of a local aging Elvis, with black shoe-polished, piled pompadour hair and thick porkchop sideburns down to his sagging jawline, and he began babbling as soon as I walked in the door that his name was Ray *the Third*, and that this here personal beer-can collection was the biggest in the world, and how he had personally emptied every dead-soldier sonofabitch on those shelves over the past six years, two months, and five days. So what appeared to be a regular old everyday barbershop I had stumbled innocently into was in reality a world-class beer-can museum, and I had never felt so quickly at home. Suddenly I felt something akin to that old tingly, expectant, hopeful feeling I recall as a sense of arrival. I love beer-can museums. To be a barber named Ray *the Third* disguised as Elvis in a cozy corner barbershop that smelled like hair tonics from a bygone time and housed a world-class beer-can collection struck me as a wonderful way of life. What was each of those empty beer cans anyway but a good-time trophy.

But then the friendly barber found it necessary to inform me that every one of those empty sonofabitches up on those shelves was like a tombstone over some good time wasted loving a bad woman. The barber's voice turned sad and theatrical and holy at that point, religious with loss and pure Elvis, as he launched into a clearly old lament about the woman who had done him dirt six years, two months, and five days ago. I, for one, didn't need any of that boo-hoo business. I interrupted that whiny barber. I asked that barber a historical question. I asked him if this could have been the barbershop where Sid Hatfield got his last haircut that day he was shot down like a dog nearly seventy-five years earlier. Yes, buddy, it was, the barber said, his voice still resonant and churchy. It was my own old granddad, old Ray *the First*, what gave Sid Hatfield his last haircut in this world as a matter of fact. And a shave, too. And my granddad always told how Sid Hatfield was the friendliest fellow you'd ever want to meet. Sid Hatfield sat in this here very chair and popped jokes and wisecracks while he got his last shave and a haircut, and not one hour later that fellow was laying dead as a doornail on the courthouse steps.

I asked the whiny albeit friendly barber if I could sit in that chair, and, eyeballing my aging-hippy ponytail, he said yes, indeedy. I stepped up and settled down slowly into that barber's chair, whereupon I tried to put myself in Sid's shoes. I tried to imagine being Sid Hatfield as he sat in that very barberchair nearly seventy-five years ago not an hour before he would meet Mister Death. I imagined the barber, old Elvis *the First*, turning Sid in the chair to face the mirror. The old barber, old early Elvis, who was famous in those bygone days for the stories he told and his jokes and his generosity of spirit, put a hand on either side of Sid Hatfield's head. The old barber positioned Sid a last time, and then he brought his own head down next to Sid's. They gazed into the mirror together, the old barber's hands still framing Sid's head. Sid was looking hard at himself, and the old barber was looking hard at Sid, too. Maybe Sid cracked that famous grin of his, or tried out some dangerous expressions in the mirror for a laugh, but maybe not. Maybe Sid and the old barber simply looked into Sid's eyes together, as though some hidden inkling of the future might be reflected there. But if the old barber saw something, he didn't offer comment. The old barber ran his fingers through Sid's thick hair. He did it slowly, as if thinking about something else. The old barber ran his fingers through Sid's thick hair tenderly, as Jessie might have done it, like a lover.

As I have previously commented, what we cannot forget is that those were fierce, feudal times, bloody, barbaric Dark Ages down in the West Virginia hills, a period of pure rebellion, which is romantic and adolescent in nature anyway, in other words, a perfect time and place in which to clutch that sweet anarchy we call youth, and Sid had a big decision to make. Sid had spent a year trying on his new life with Jessie over the store back in Matewan for size, and he had to make up his mind about how much this new life meant to him in terms of what to risk. It was so different from his old, wild, free, shootist life, this new married life settled over a store, feeling hapless and stuck in time to grow old just like everybody else through the long years. What if Sid went back to the hotel and fetched Jessie, and they simply left town on the next train. Sid Hatfield could do that. Nobody would blame him. Folks would think Sid was smart, not afraid. Surely that thought must have passed through Sid's mind. To go back down to Mingo County and dare the Baldwin-Felts to come and try to get him there if they thought they could. Or he could just go around to the courthouse in less than an hour and face the music like the legendary two-gun shootist he had always imagined himself to be.

Everything that day seemed so dreamlike to Sid, from the moment he first awakened in his old friend Mayor Cable Testerman's big brass bed and for a full minute could not remember where he was, much less why, and who the beautiful, young, sweet-smelling woman asleep beside him was. All day long Sid felt strangely unstuck in time, like he did sometimes when he was drunk, as though everything had already happened five minutes ago. All day long Sid felt a sort of weird elation, a sort of weightlessness. Maybe Sid gazed at his reflection in the barbershop mirror, and his eyes looked unbearably old to him, and maybe even a little bit frightened, as did my own eyes that day I tried on that barberchair for size, but not necessarily of old Mister Death. Maybe Sid was thinking that in less than an hour he really might say hello to old Mister Death. That the Baldwin-Felts would surely try to shoot him down. He sure would if he was them. Maybe during that time he looked at his reflection in the barber's mirror, Sid tried to apportion what could turn out to be his last moments on Earth in terms of what to remember and reflect upon. So many moments from his life to reimagine. To see anew in the light cast by these his last moments. And, Lordy, so many lives left to live, even now. A whole hour of lives left, an endless stretch of time, no need to imagine the last moment.

A part of Sid couldn't imagine growing old, couldn't even bear it. So what if he was dying today, truly, twenty-eight years old, healthy as a horse, strong as an ox, and this hour ahead of him was his old age. And maybe another part of Sid thought, Oh how I want to live some more, how precious life can be in the arms of that sweet-smelling woman! Was it really possible that in less than an hour he might no longer be around? That he wouldn't breathe this sweet old mountain air again, he wouldn't see old Mister Sun rise higher in the old sky, casting its sweet light on this old world? Could it be that he would never lick up the front of Jessie's smooth, white legs again? Dimple her soft, creamy skin with his tongue? Turn her over and taste that favorite old fishing hole, too? All this could still be his, this old world, and Jessie, Jessie, the taste of her mouth in the morning, her warm, sweet breath on his face and neck and agoing on down warm on his body real slow, if only he didn't have to be who he had always figured he was and maybe have to quit his life now for it.

So long, old-timer, Sid had said to the old barber named Ray *the First*, and flashed that famous grin as he strolled out the door toward death. Lately Sid had felt as though he was somehow sailing backwards into his life, as though somehow the future was a distant, receding shoreline. Sid strolled out of that barbershop young and strong and handsome and in love and famous with a fresh shave and a haircut and smelling of that ruby-colored hair tonic and talcum powder toward all of death. Sid had practiced for death all his life. Everybody knew the future was all smoke and mirrors anyhow. Freedom was knowing that a choice made today, in the right here and now, throws itself backwards through our lives and changes the nature of everything we have ever done, making us all live finally backwards to be free. Old Sid was a philosopher in his final moments. It's pretty to think that Sid had made up his mind about what he was going to do and why he was going to do it while sitting in the old barber's chair. Sid's choice had had something to do with that sense of calm he had felt when he closed his eyes and let Ray *the First*'s tender old barber fingers move through his hair, the sweetness of those fingers, his hair already starting to grow again.

In her testimony before a select committee formed to investigate the shootings on the Welch courthouse steps, Ed Chambers's widow, Sallie, who was a lovely, auburn-haired, young woman of twenty-four, described the murders in minute detail thusly:

> Well, as we went up the first flight of steps, just as we landed on the first landing, the other defendants and their witnesses were coming up the other flight of steps on the other side of the landing, and Sid kind of hesitated just a little bit when the boys were speaking to him and kind of waved his hand at them, and at that time the first shot was fired about three steps up the second flight of steps that led into the courthouse. I don't know how many of them were there shooting. It looked like there might have been a hundred or two hundred of them there shooting that day. But I reckon there was about six or eight of them right there on the steps firing down. Mr. Charles Lively put his arm across in front of me and shot my husband Ed in his neck. Right there was the first shot. I don't mean that that was the first shot that was fired, but that was the first time my husband was shot. Sid was shot first. Sid Hatfield. My husband was shot about eleven or twelve times. Some say Sid was shot nine times, and some say eleven, so I am unable to say how many. My husband, he rolled back down the steps and I looked down and I seen him rolling down and blood gushing from a hole in his neck, and I just went back down the steps after him, you see, and they kept on shooting him, and when he kind of fell on his side leaving his back up, you know, toward the

steps and they were shooting him in the back all the time after he fell. And then Charles Lively shot my husband Ed right behind the ear. My husband was lying down kind of on his side at the time that Charles Lively shot him the last time. Mr. Lively just reached down and put his gun just about a inch from my husband Ed's ear, but before he did that, though, I seen him coming down the steps toward us, and I said, "Oh, please Mr. Lively, don't you shoot at him any more, you have killed him now." But I didn't know if Ed's life was gone then, but you know I just said that because I knew in my heart Ed would die, so Charles Lively just run down and stuck the gun behind my husband's ear and fired it. And then I struck Mr. Lively with my umbrella, and he turned around to me and said, "Oh, don't you hit me with that umbrella again, you dirty devil, or I will shoot you too," and he stuck his gun out, but he didn't shoot me, and then he went back up the steps. I went down on my knees beside my husband and had hold of his hands, and I just begged for someone to come to me and no one did come, but there was some men started to run up to me, you know, and those detectives told them "Go back, stay back, we will take care of this," so those men had to stop, you see. I was rubbing my husband's face and had hold of his hand, and Mr. Salter, the man that had been shooting at Sid, and Buster Prince, of course I didn't know the men's names at that time, but I recognized their faces, and I said to Mr. Salter, I said, "Oh, Mr. Salter, oh, what did you all do this for? We did not come up here for this." And then he said to me, "Well, that is all right, we didn't come down to Matewan last year for that either." Then they took me by the arms and pulled me away from my husband and I told them, "Oh, no, I am going to stay with my husband." But they pulled me up the steps toward the courthouse and as

> we got up at the top Charles Lively was standing there and he looked at me like he was so glad he had done what he had done that I could not resist the temptation and I just had to hit him again with my umbrella.

Two thousand people walked in the procession that carried Sid Hatfield and Ed Chambers to their final rest in a Kentucky hillside graveyard across the Tug Fork. The rain poured down in buckets and Jessie and Sallie were near collapse. At one point Sallie had to be helped to a chair when she grew faint, while Jessie sobbed nearby. As her husband's casket was lowered into its grave, Jessie Hatfield cried out, "I'll never forget you, sweetheart, ever."

The Baldwin-Felts gunthugs were tried in the same courthouse where they had gunned Sid and Ed down and were promptly acquitted by reason of self-defense. Charles Lively worked in the coal mines around Mount Hope, West Virginia, for several years afterward, and later as a railroad detective and hotel operator in Roanoke, Virginia. He died in Huntington, West Virginia, in 1962 at the age of seventy-five.

Sallie Chambers married Harold Houston, the UMW attorney who had defended Sid and Ed in the Matewan Battle trial, and eventually retired to Lake Worth, Florida. Jessie Hatfield married a state policeman and moved to Huntington. She later divorced her third husband and married a fourth. Jessie lived with the son she had by Mayor Cable Testerman in the last months of her life in Huntington, and she died in 1976 at age eighty-two.[6]

Whenever I park my butt on that third step from the bottom on the courthouse steps down in Welch, where Sid Hatfield's head had come to final rest that day over seventy-five years earlier, one thing I reflect upon is what went through Sid's mind the moment he heard those first apocalyptic explosions. In that sudden, omniscient burst of

---

6. Ibid., 167.

final clarity, perhaps Sid realized that in the end all that is left of self is story. And that to have been lured down into that clear deathtrap unarmed was simply a real enigmatic failure to imagine the future and his place in it, and that now all he had left to do in his lifetime, as he felt the impact of the first of his own beneficent bullets, was to die purely impenitent.

Chuck Kinder is the author of the novels Snakehunter, The Silver Ghost, *and* Honeymooners, *forthcoming from Farrar, Straus & Giroux. "That Sweet Anarchy We Call Youth" is a chapter from a "fictionalized" memoir called* The Last Mountain Dancer.

Passing Through Pittsburgh

HILARY MASTERS

The Greater Pittsburgh phone directory lists 191 numbers under the family name of Coyne, and there must be other households of that name that are not listed or who may not have a telephone. Not exactly in the same league with the Joneses, but yet a sizable Irish colony, which may explain why my grandfather showed up here around 1875 at the age of fifteen, his first stop on a trek toward a citizenship that always seemed to elude him.

Tom Coyne, his three brothers, and one sister all immigrated together, having walked from their village of Leenane west of Galway City to Queenstown, or Cork, where they took the boat for America. Whispers in family archives gossip a melodramatic flight from British authorities due to the body of a priest found pitchforked on the family sheep farm. This was the time of "the tithe" and the Coynes' father, Black Phillipe, was supposed to have had enough of the ecclesiastical ripoff, whether by the Roman Church or the Church of England. So, the story goes, they were on the lam and someone may have said, "You have cousins in Pittsburgh, Pennsylvania. They'll take you in." But they all split up once coming ashore in the New World, further suggesting they were running from something, and, in fact, when my grandfather made his only return to Ireland at the age of ninety he tried to get a passport under an assumed name. He might still be wanted, he feared. Whatever, he was the only one of that family to come to Pittsburgh, and he was vague about his time here in 1875. It seems he was only passing through.

Carnegie, McCandless & Company had been founded by 1873 and the Edgar Thomson Steel Works in Braddock had already installed the first Bessemer. Frick's coke empire was under way; glassmaking was a close second to steel as an industry in this boomtown where one could feel "the actual physical presence of power," to use the words of a contemporary *Wall Street Journal* article.

Tom Coyne must have breathed the power of the place, felt the heat and rhythm of its industry. The great number of steamboats and barges on the rivers probably impressed him for they served the largest inland harbor of that time. He was fond of such assessments; the largest *this*, the greatest *that*, the most powerful *other*, maybe because he was a small man himself, wiry and resilient but with a Celtic fury in his eyes to compensate for his stature. After his Army career, his life would be fitted to heavy machinery, locomotives, the great locks of the Panama Canal—engines to cross and move the earth, divert oceans. Along with the river vessels, the six railroads that focused on Pittsburgh must have firmly centered this fascination.

And in all probability, he arrived in Pittsburgh by train, coming from Kings Point, Brooklyn, where he landed—this some twenty years before Ellis Island—to Philadelphia and then Pittsburgh. Just two years before, in 1873, the train trip from Philadelphia to Pittsburgh had been cut down from twenty-five hours to only twelve—what better proof to this young immigrant of the powerful society he thought he had joined. The place fired his sentience for human invention to a white-hot fervor that was never to cool.

Why didn't he stay? "The mill work was too much for me. I wasn't strong enough for it." But he was strong enough to break and handle cavalry horses only a couple of years later. Strong enough to construct railroads all through Mexico and Central America. In Ecuador he built and ran the railroad from Quito to Guayaquil—an arduous construction that crossed the Andes. In his seventies he was strong enough to disarm two muggers in Kansas City, send them fleeing, and capture one when the man fell over a fireplug. When the police showed up, they found Tom Coyne kicking the thief's behind. He had to be restrained. So it wasn't that he was weak or fragile, but for some other reason he got back on another train after a year or two in Pittsburgh and headed West. He was a Connemara lad and perhaps there were aspects to Pittsburgh, with all its industrial wonder, that were too much for him. Or not enough.

Some years later, I am going by train in the opposite direction, and I am eight years old. My mother and I take a Missouri-Central from Kansas City to Chicago, where we change to a Pullman sleeper on the Pennsylvania Railroad. The next morning my father will meet us at the Pennsylvania Station in New York and we will taxi across town to Grand Central, where we will get on a train of the New York Central's Harlem Division that will take us, on a roadbed laid down in 1852, to a small town near a rented farmhouse in New York's Columbia County. The whole trip will take the better part of two days and a night. It is a summer pilgrimage I would make many times to fulfill my parents' peculiar concept of a family, for my grandparents kept me nine months of the year. But that's another digression.

This particular trip East occasioned my first look at Pittsburgh, and it was a sleepy look from beneath the blind of my Pullman berth's window, but it was a sight that burned into my remembrance. Midnight or early morning, the train's scheduled arrival in Pittsburgh is unknown to me, but it is pitch dark. Some change in the train's rhythm has awakened me. I snuggle down in the cozy cave of my upper berth —no bed linen will ever match the crisp luxury of Pullman sheets; they had the cool freshness of a fine memory.

Nor, if I may switch onto a little sidetrack, has the special effect of train travel been matched by any other form—something's been lost. Train travel permits a passenger to encounter others in a different space, poses a relativity between object and viewer which Einstein fully appreciated. These days we mostly travel cut off from the world we traverse, only our destination and arrival time are defined. But to pass by train through a countryside, to take up temporary residence in another place, and to intersect, however briefly, with other lives waiting patiently at a road crossing, that particular human experience has been all but lost, and I think the human imagination, without this free association, has been impoverished.

But, here I am, entering Pittsburgh at eight years of age, on a Pennsylvania Pullman to New York City, coming up the Ohio River, McKees Rocks on the right, then into that cut through West Park and across the Allegheny at 11th Street into Daniel Burnham's gorgeous terminal, erected to replace the old depot that was burned down during the 1877 railroad riots. The riots would have occurred a couple of years after Tom Coyne came to town.

I raise the window blind and, still drugged with sleep, look out on a scene that Turner could have painted. Violent explosions of color, of whiteness. Billowing clouds of fire blossom from the dark to metastasize into orange and scarlet plumes. The sun is coming apart. I am terrified and fascinated all at once, as it is always awesome to look into the center of power. My mind's camera was permanently marked with this image of the mills turning common ore into iron and steel, making something new out of the ordinary: an immense, catastrophic breakdown and integration.

Tom Coyne must have had a similar view. The air was clogged by the particled residue of coal fires, not just from the mills but from the city's fireplace grates. Perhaps my grandfather warmed himself on cold winter mornings at one of these narrow grates; let's say, staying with a Coyne cousin. He never said. So I am free to wonder. Maybe he didn't hit it off with the relatives—personal relationships were not his forté—so he might have rented a bed in one of the many rooming houses that boarded single men, mill hands, and perhaps in one of the rowhouses of my neighborhood on the North Side in which the floor planks of yellow pine still show the old nail holes that marked off those cramped corners that transformed a normal-sized living room into a crowded dormitory.

Surely, he might have thought, this was a paltry citizenship he had exchanged for the fresh air of Connemara, the dew of Galway still upon him. For these grimy alleys he had left the clear streams where trout fought for a place on the hook. For this gritty domain, he had turned away from the long vista of Killary Bay where salmon entered to spawn and Viking ships had once ghosted on a westerly breeze. It may have been this mystical perspective that pulled him away from Pittsburgh, and not the hard work, for his whole life was one of hard work, and it would be too clever a hindsight to suggest that he objected to being separated from the product made by his hard work, and with borrowed tools, or that he felt himself made expendable, dross to be burned out to make more efficient fuel. Those ideas were around then, of course, but he never thought that way. No, I think those mythical images he carried from Ireland pulled him away. He tried to duplicate them on the coulees of Montana, in the jungles of Central America, and the heights of the Andes. Then, there were those riots of 1877.

The management of the Pennsylvania Railroad, the same company that had brought him and me through Pittsburgh at different times, had decided to do a little downsizing in 1877. Trainmen's salaries were to be cut 10 percent; moreover, freight-train lengths were to be doubled, thereby reducing the number of jobs. The city rebelled. Burghers blocked the tracks. Mayor William C. McCarthy refused to call in the police, and the members of the local state militia would not raise arms against their neighbors. Under pressure from the railroad company, Gov. John Frederick Hartranft called up the militia quartered in Philadelphia, and after arriving by train, these men assembled, confronted the citizenry, and, on July 21, fired into a crowd, killing twenty people. All hell broke loose. The mob drove the troops out of Pittsburgh. Over a thousand freight cars were demolished and nearly a hundred and fifty locomotives were destroyed. Dozens of downtown buildings, including the depot, were burned to the ground. The city was brought to a halt, to the edge of total anarchy, and it was the most violent uprising in America since the Civil War, not to be equaled—if then—until the riots of the 1960s. I can understand how it discouraged my grandfather. How was this oppression of a citizenry any different from the history he had just left? Exchange the Pennsylvania Railroad's board of directors with Queen Victoria's cabinet, and it looked like the same sort of tyranny he had learned to hate at his father's knee. It had been waiting for him here, in Pittsburgh, and the air was bad, too.

Something else to conjure. Almost exactly a year before, on July 4, 1876, George Armstrong Custer had led the Seventh Cavalry to its destruction on the banks of the Little Big Horn River. The battle had made all the papers. The stupidity of Custer's foray was glossed by the glory of his death, for his opponents this time around were not the old men, women, and children slaughtered at Washita and Sand Creek but, as my grandfather was to say later, "the greatest light horse cavalry ever to go into battle." So it was something like a fair fight, and in the clean, open air as well. He even might have been cheered by the Sioux victory; the underdog had won this time, and though he was to spend five years in the U.S. Cavalry, his sympathies were always with the Indians. The irony was not lost on him that to gain his own citizenship he had to suppress and diminish the status of others. The awful paradox would sometimes make him weep.

So he left Pittsburgh. "I worked on the railroad," he would say when asked how he got to California, and that was all he would say. The Irish laid a lot of track, going east to west, as the Chinese did from west to east. Unskilled labor, such as a mill worker, was about all that was available to him in a society that discretely placed signs in its windows: *No Irish Need Apply.* "Sometimes I was called a white niggra," he told me once, and the confusion still welled up in his pale-blue eyes. Yes, the comparison offended him, but also he was outraged that men, African or Celt, should be put into such an equation at all. In San

Francisco he enlisted in the U.S. Cavalry at the Presidium: five years' service would give him citizenship, at least on paper, and these were to be "the happiest days of my life." He was assigned to the Yellowstone, whose trout-packed streams and the clean air reminded him of Connemara, and where he witnessed the American Indian's harmony with nature. Their way of life would become a lifelong paradigm.

But what looks smooth to me this morning on Monterey Street was actually a disjointed record. We make such narratives to iron out the discontinuity of our lives, give tumbled events a cause and effect—even a reason they may not have possessed, and the endeavor comforts us as it helps us believe that we were, in some way, in charge of the past when it was happening; a condescension as much as folly. This behavior, though, might explain the myopic affection we have for the past, worked into sweet nostalgia like a piece of leather until it is soft and supple to our self-appraisals. Worked on until past events come out right. We prefer unity in these revisions, everything under one roof, so to speak, and the piecemeal configurations of the original smoothed over. Card players illustrated by Norman Rockwell pleasure this nostalgia; the same game pictured by Cezanne scares the hell out of us.

So I admit to a certain lack of control of this material, and merely to put the different parts of my life and my grandfather's life, and Pittsburgh, into a pretty cohesion will only be my arbitrary arrangement of the bits and pieces. The particles themselves will remain unaltered and unexplained and the inquiry unoccasioned: an idle amusement and nothing more.

However, two years after my first passage through Pittsburgh, I came through once again but this time by plane. My grandfather gave me a round-trip ticket to join my parents via a Trans World Airlines DC-3 which stopped to refuel in Chicago and Pittsburgh. The flight took over six hours, about the same time it took Tom Coyne to go from

Philadelphia to Pittsburgh, and I mention this commonplace only to recall his exultation when I became part of this proof of modernity, this demonstration of human invention. My grandmother was more of a traditionalist and apprehensive of all gadgets, especially those that lifted a person several thousand feet into the air. "I can see his little legs dangling through the clouds," she said worriedly.

 I enjoyed the trip, pampered by the stewardess with extra helpings of chocolate cake and chewing gum, but the time spent on the ground in Pittsburgh draws a blank. Unlike that other early morning passage, I can call up from memory no views of the steel mills, no clouds of fire and smoke, nor even a trace of the rivers' fork. Moreover, we landed far outside of town at the old airport. The plane's altitude and flight path separated me from these citymarks so my memory is left holding an empty contour, but I was distanced from more than a place.

 Back on the ground of this Pittsburgh where I live, a similar separation from place, from a past meant to nourish the present, has been happening here and in all American cities the last half of this century. It goes by such names as Urban Renewal and Cultural Renaissance, and it is a process born of the suburban mentality that has always lived outside a city's limits and is uncomfortable within the rough edges of its neighborhoods. So bulldozers are called in to smooth the awkward edifices of the past, selected artifacts installed in museums to be viewed safely on weekends.

 My own neighborhood had been a part of Allegheny City, an independent urban entity across the Allegheny River from downtown Pittsburgh. Fifty years ago, the five hundred buildings of this commercial center were torn down and replaced by a mall—that vulgar pastoral of suburban zeal. Today this mall is all but empty, a derelict of corrupt planning because the local populace had been isolated by its very construction, separated from their natural thoroughfares and haunts. Most of these places have been obliterated and major streets truncated.

To build the Civic Arena, home of the Pittsburgh Penguins, fifteen hundred black families were made refugees in their own city and neighborhood. Perhaps there is a connection between this displacement and a finding that puts this city at the top of the list for having the greatest number of impoverished African-American families. Cut off the circulation in a hand, and it becomes numb, useless, and it is the same with a neighborhood. Cut off the flow of its inborn traffic, and its citizenry are diminished. The place rots. Perhaps city people should beware of suburbanites seeking, if not bearing, culture.

Lately, a so-called Cultural District has been marked off in the center of the city and designed for attractions that will lure culture hounds from the glens of Fox Chapel and Sewickley. But how can culture be segregated, and is it wise to do so? Culture is diminished when set apart from the community that is supposed to inspire it, indeed, from which its own inspiration is drawn. This current undertaking is merely another mall that will market the national chains of entertainment enterprises: fuzzy reproductions of Broadway boilerplate and the weary appearances of celebrity *artistes*. It is more than a passing irony that the "renewed" area previously hosted the city's prostitutes and porno dens, agents of another kind of veneration that was also set apart from the community. But vice has always been segregated—now, in Pittsburgh, it seems to be culture's turn. At the same time, I would guess that in the neighborhood bars of Bloomfield, Homewood, and the South Side, more genuine, spontaneous culture (neighborhood myths and local heroes remembered) is celebrated on any night of the week than in a whole season of imported attractions in the glittering halls downtown.

Tom Coyne, in his quest for citizenship, wanted to join the power of Pittsburgh. He wanted to contribute his energy and invention to that power, but he had to move on because he found the power was exclusive, misdirected, and made harmful to the very people it was supposed to enhance, to amplify. My search for identity is neither as desperate nor as direct; after all, I am second generation, and I can afford to loaf a little on the banks of these three rivers. But I am no less mindful of the struggle for identity, for a place on river delta; so, in the temporal coincidence some call history, Tom Coyne and I are merely passing through.

Hilary Masters's recent novel is Home Is the Exile. *His essays have been published by many journals and newspapers and two of these appear in Anchor/Doubleday* Best Essays of 1998, *edited by Philip Lopate, and* Best American Essays of 1999, *selected by Edward Hoagland. In Montaigne's Tower, a collection of these essays, was published by the University of Missouri Press in January 2000.*

Lessons in Persuasion

KATHLEEN VESLANY

There was the cat to think of. And the motorcycle. On Saturdays we walked through neighborhoods collecting addendums: windows, bus lines, safety. How much we could afford. Enough room to work without distraction. David wrote down addresses; I called them with questions, called back when we'd been stood up. Finally the apartment we wanted opened up. We notified the post office, signed the lease, made arrangements for a phone, gas, heat.

David and I are not planning to get married but have come to both living together and ballroom dance at a time when wedding invitations arrive for us like flowers: a bunch at a time. In between budgeting for a security deposit and returning RSVPs, I remembered David and I having kicked around the idea of taking dance lessons. I called for a course catalogue: "Begin the beguine—won't it be romantic? Under the guidance of popular ballroom dancer Bernard Fiske, students will reach across time and culture to essay lessons in the style and nuance of the fox trot, waltz, jitterbug, tango, cha cha, and other forms of social dance behavior!"

David and I signed on for seven weeks. We gave the lessons as an anniversary present to ourselves while everyone around us planned weddings. We expected receptions to be good practice.

Tonight, three weeks after we've moved in together, we arrive for our first lesson. A small man in glasses, wearing khaki pants and a bland shirt with a shiny tie, moves to the center of the studio floor. Grinning wildly, he welcomes us to Big Band Social Dancing, rubbing his hands together while he talks as though preparing for a big meal. Bernard introduces himself as a man who wears many hats, and for a quick minute I'm amazed by the joke, mistaking his figure of speech for a reference to his own badly shaped toupee, a wavy gray patch that makes his age, at best, a fuzzy guess. In addition to teaching ballroom dance for the past thirty years, he is a hydrologist and cartographer. Without asking us who we are or how many hats we wear, Bernard gets down to business by staggering the group of us into two lines from where we learn our first dance.

Although the course description didn't mention it and there's nothing Big Band about it, I'm too optimistic to complain when Bernard shows us the electric slide. It is arguably social in a hokey-pokey sense—a dance you'd only do with a large group after a few drinks. We all seem sober, but Bernard wants us to have fun and to never have to leave a dance floor because we don't know how to stay. The electric slide is a dance Bernard believes in.

We learn the three steps to the right, to the left, the forward step, the backward step, the way to change directions. Once the claps are integrated, we deserve music, and Bernard makes his way over to the stereo in the corner and begins the song that too zealously reminds us that "It's electric!" In ten minutes we've all caught on, even the large man in the hiked-up shorts who moves in a strange palsy. We could do this in our sleep. Dancing is easy.

I've seen this dance done before and it reminds me of the wedding receptions I went to with my parents when I was young. After a long Mass, guests were anxious to stretch their legs. Large halls were full of round tables, an open bar, a long buffet, the bride's bouquet finally falling toward a woman then destined to be the next one married. I never caught it but always tried, even as a girl who knew nothing of marriage but enough to dream of its white dress. Enough to know I wanted it. Old men I didn't remember asked me to dance because there were no cousins my own age. My mother and her sisters tried to teach me the alley cat. This dance also started in lines with a repetition of steps, ad infinitum, that got more difficult as the music's pace escalated, and the old and amateur knew enough to accept defeat. My mother could keep up with the song until it ended.

My family believes in marriage the way Bernard believes in the electric slide. Both feel that it should be taught early on and is a lesson that bears repeating. My childhood was a succession of weddings and receptions. Catholic sacraments include seats for the children, so I learned young the way things were done. I've sat through bridal showers, learned all of the superstitions. I know that the vein in the ring finger leads to the heart, whose family sits on which side of the church, that song I had in my ear: love, marriage, house, baby.

I haven't been to a Catholic wedding since I've known David and haven't seen the alley cat since it's been ripped off and thrown out by the electric slide. After we've memorized its steps, Bernard announces the fox trot. He tells us that this is the dance we'll do the most in our lives, and then he parts the men and the women like the Red Sea. David and I watch from our respective lines. Bernard is lean, short, and smooth on his feet as he moves through the dance with his assistant. Bernard tells us that she works at a downtown department store as though she was not standing right there beside him.

Bernard explains the men's footwork first, that their first step is always forward on the left foot. Then his assistant moves through Bernard's commands as they are given; a woman's first step is always backwards on the right. His assistant never elaborates or hesitates on Bernard's instruction for women. Instead, she is a demure and neatly dressed demonstration model with legs and high-heeled shoes of the same fleshy-tan color that carry her fluidly through the steps. Beneath her tidy blonde haircut she looks blankly at Bernard and then at those of us studying the path of her feet. Occasionally, she is joined by Bernard so that the men and women can see what the collaboration of their respective steps will look like. None of us can take our eyes off of them.

When Bernard's assistant is not demonstrating, she watches us until Bernard sends her to dance with a man whose lead is weak. She tries to teach him how to persuade her. The word "persuade" belongs to Bernard and I'm laying all bets that it's his favorite verb. He calls the man's right hand, when it rests in the small of a woman's back, "the persuader." After we have learned the forward travel, the side step, the open travel, and the magic step, Bernard goes on at great length about the powers of persuasion.

The fox trot has no pattern, only a series of steps that are used in a dynamic sequence depending on the space a dancing couple has to move through. In ballroom dance, it is the man's responsibility to gauge that space and to pick each step the moment before he takes his partner into it. The woman waits for news of the lead's choice through the hand on her back. If the heel of the hand presses into her back, she is meant to move right. If the fingertips curl in, she should go left.

Bernard gets animated when he explains persuasion. In exaggerated form he shows the men how their hands will shift for different directions. He dances across the room with an imaginary woman and uses the words "push" and "pull" to clarify how persuasion can work, making guttural noises while he moves as though a woman's spine was something other than bone beneath skin. Between grunts, he reminds the men not to make such noises out loud when they are leading. Bernard's a real card.

Finally Bernard plucks a woman from the line in what he likes to call her "debut." He demonstrates the result of a strong lead, and with him she dances perfectly. I try to figure out which man across the studio is her partner, look for a face of shock or envy of pride, but find none. I'm convinced by the woman's graceful ascension in Bernard's arms, and when he drops her off in our line and encourages us to applaud her, we're happy to do it.

"He does all the work," she says. She is glowing. "With him, it's so easy!" The tidy-haired assistant gives the transformed student a knowing smile, and I wonder if David will be as persuasive as Bernard.

There is a question from the men's line: How do you persuade the woman to move backwards? Bernard stands in front of his assistant, he leans his chest towards her, looks straight ahead, and begins moving forward. She retreats with each step that he gains. In this case, persuasion comes through the eyes.

It's an option to take Big Band Social Dance without a partner. To come alone costs more than the couple's fee split in half, but people still come. In our class, only women do this, and they take their turns with Bernard while the couples-proper circle past them. If a man comes to class when his partner cannot, he dances with one of these women. One woman who comes alone stands beside me in line. She is very friendly and plain, and I root for her to get the spare man, when one's available. Another woman has long blonde hair and a lot of gold jewelry. She is dressed to the nines in a black linen dress, cut high on the thigh. She is very tan. Bernard picks her out for a debut early on in our first lesson.

Otherwise, it's a world of pairs. There's a young couple from West Virginia, who drive an hour into Pennsylvania every weekend for their lesson. There's an older couple who, as far as I can tell, are the best dancers in the class. There is an ease between them that the rest of us lack. There is the man who moves strangely, with his long-haired, athletically built wife. They don't talk to anyone other than Bernard and laugh at all of his jokes, seem competitive on the dance floor. There is a squat, Italian-looking older man who asks questions constantly and cuts Bernard off mid-answer. I find his manner both abrasive and satisfying, depending on how I feel about Bernard at the time. This man's wife is tiny and much younger than he is, and she never says a word.

Most people seem to be in our class for weddings—to dance in their own, to brush up for their kid's, to become the smooth-moving couple in a bridal party. Bernard even tells us that he has been invited this weekend to give a quick lesson at a reception. The newlyweds are not only former students, but one is also the child of former students. They must have loved their lessons, embraced Bernard as a tradition.

Finally, Bernard sends us to find our partners and begins a record. We're excited to merge our new steps into a seamless path around the studio. David will lead and I will follow. When his left foot moves forward, my right will glide back. We have met each other's families, integrated our furniture, claimed our sides of the bed—so it's hard to believe how graceless we are when we begin ballroom dancing together. We bump into couples. We step on each other. We stop. We begin again.

I am stunned as the couples careen around us, both at their bliss and our stagnant huddle. I hate moving backwards, seeing where I am only after I have arrived. David hates that I am slow to follow his lead, that I seem to be taking a different path than the one his hand prescribes on my back. After one song, Bernard begins another and we search for the way that we will make the fox trot work.

I ask David to call out the steps before we take them, wanting to know by name how I am expected to move rather than being pulled and pushed at whim. Soon this fails us. We are pausing after each step as David decides which steps he wants to take next and then mentally flips through the catalogue of names before finding a match.

I suggest that we agree on a pattern, our own predictable fox trot. We agree to a sequence of four steps that we commit to repeat over and over, an incantation to ourselves that will deliver us from anger. But we soon learn the dynamics of a ballroom. The space around you changes without logic. Territory is temporary. We wind up on the outskirts of the counterclockwise circle. We dance ourselves into corners.

I blame David, David blames me. Our anger turns acidic. I cannot lead or suggest the way I want to follow. As a partner, I'm wholly uncooperative. I take issue with David's lead. His hand lacks persuasion; it's a wet rag. For the rest of the record and the one after that, we feign effort only when we think Bernard is watching. Otherwise, we mangle our steps around the studio floor in an uninspired circle, as though we are trains on a track—inanimate and responsible for nothing. I stop meeting David's eyes, disconnect myself from the hand on my back. When we move past the mirrors, I refuse our reflection.

These lessons are a gift, a present in honor of time spent together. Bernard is all smiles and jokes, an enthusiastic monument to the timeless joys of the ballroom, generation after generation. Bernard thinks this is fun and I look for the reasons it is not. I am not used to being led, to conceding the powers of persuasion, to being forbidden to anticipate. The women who make a poor debut with Bernard are easily corrected. They either ignore Bernard's lead or imagine how Bernard will lead them before his persuasion begins. I hate that what Bernard calls the forward travel means I must move in reverse, that I never know where I'm going, that Ginger Rogers had to do everything backwards and in high heels. Even though this is only dancing, I bristle at the lack of equity in the fox trot. But in Bernard's class there are no protests or questions about it. The women are persuaded. I must learn to like being led, to admit in breathy relief that "He does all the work!"

Finally, Bernard separates the men from the women. It is time for disco dancing. I remember my parents taking dance lessons when I was young. Again, those wedding receptions return to me—my parents moving toward and away from each other, my father spinning my mother, my father turning himself as my mother's hands slid over his back before falling again into his sure grip. The steps Bernard shows are identical to those I remember—the forward-back-back-forward footwork with his assistant. Bernard likens the hand-holding to an accordion. We will press our hands together and then widen them apart. In and out. In and out. Together and apart.

Bernard has selective methods on interpretation. The electric slide, now disco. I'm beginning to wonder who the liar was who wrote the course description. And even though there was a sexual revolution in full swing during the days of disco, not to mention two hundred years between the hustle and the fox trot, Bernard is unconcerned. Persuasion is not open to reinterpretation. It is the sun to his dancing orbit.

There are only a few minutes left tonight and Bernard teaches too quickly, so that when "Ring My Bell" begins and we are sent back to our partners David and I are no worse than everyone else. The floor is a swarm of broken travel, couples stepping out of sync, hands losing their grip. During the spins, either David is not lifting his arm high enough or I am holding on too tightly because I keep whacking myself in the head with my forearm. Learning a dance we will never use, David and I are less invested in this one, and our mistakes are what makes "YMCA" bearable as the evening's last song.

Two forkfuls into my curry shrimp, David tells me that tonight, for the first time, he saw our relationship spiral away from him. I look at the blue eyes and long chin across from me and keep chewing. I'm not surprised at what he says. In one dance lesson, a mere two hours, we've become a bickering old couple, oil and water, cat to bird.

To live together does not dull the lessons of my girlhood, that song in my ear, the volume of the weddings David and I attend. But I'm suspicious of tradition, that which relies on repetition, history, blind faith. I want something of my own invention with David, even though I know every couple is bound to tradition if only as a means of measurement—how closely they adhere, to what degree they diverge. I've watched the men offer and the women accept, the men eating what the women cook, the wives riding beside their husbands who drive. Dancing places me face to face with these gendered prescriptions, that being a woman beside a man brings a host of expectations from which there is too little departure. It is either lead or be led.

I want to ask the women whether they mind the arrangement, tell Bernard that we have alternatives, offer David my lead. I'm unsure about how much to make of this, but am afraid of not making enough. Should I give voice to my silent protest or remind myself that this is only ballroom dance? There is no winning.

Collapsing the borders of two lives within one home has become a litmus test. As much as we've agreed that moving in is absolutely not a trial run or impending promise of marriage, I have watched the way we've moved around each other in these past weeks. There is significance, when you look, in whose name is put on which bill and what groceries get bought and when the laundry gets done and whom a room is cleaned by. I am not looking to split hairs or halve the chores in all their minutia, but I am looking for a collaboration that soothes my fear of domestic and societal predictability—that he will this and I will that, etc., etc., ad infinitum.

I am watching and listening to the both of us to see how we lay claim to a single space collectively. We've been dancing for nearly a month without knowing what to call it: the distance necessary for privacy, how to rise without waking the body that remains in bed, the pleasure of absence and return, the power of habit, the alarm triggered by a tone of voice, the subtle and changing demands of time and space, the affect of one body in a room on another. This is a new song about instinct and habit and movement. Everything is a lesson in persuasion.

My irritation with Bernard and impatience with David come less from the dancing and more from my fear of gendered tradition. I'm afraid of losing myself in the role of wife that I have not embraced but cannot ignore—the person I may be preparing to become. I'm afraid of turning into someone I don't recognize until I find myself tracing her footsteps. I'm afraid of repetition, history, blind faith. I'm afraid of knowing too well the song in my ear—love, marriage, house, baby—and forgetting what else there is. I'm afraid of euphemism, that word "persuasion."

I taste David's soup and decide I'll order it next week if we come here again for dinner. There is much to be said for sitting across from each other, having a meal cooked for us, plates brought to our table, our dishes washed by anyone other than ourselves. David continues talking about how awful we were, says that during our fox trot he was grinding his teeth so hard that he was afraid he might damage some fillings. I am not offended. Away from Bernard, we laugh at our miserable debut, pick off each other's plates, vow to practice as soon as we get home.

And we do. We move without music through the living room, in and out of the bedroom, settle in the study. We do a lot of forward travel, David's favorite step, and open travel, which is mine. In fifteen minutes, we perfect the magic step, a direction change Bernard has taught us to use when we're backed against the bandstand or close to colliding with another couple. In our apartment, we use it to move away from his desk, to avoid backing into my bookshelves. We practice all week.

There are books about ballroom dancing. Old ones. Some suggest that dancing most likely predates language. A mode of self-expression before words. There is also the idea that dance is first and foremost instinctual. The most primitive art seen even in the behavior of apes, ostriches, penguins, insects. Dancing as release, as recreation, as courtship, as initiation, as territory. I think of these animals separated from us by language, but contributing to it: henpeck, hound, pussyfoot, weasel, bully, fox trot.

Tonight after most of us have arrived, a small man in glasses, wearing khaki pants and a bland shirt with a shiny tie, moves to the center of the studio floor. There is a strange sense of *déjà vu* during our second lesson. We begin again with the electric slide. Bernard is a creature of habit. He is slowing the pace of our class down, devoting tonight to a review of what we learned last week before we move into the waltz.

When David and I begin the fox trot tonight, I suck in my breath before I remember: anticipation is forbidden. I do not know what will happen; I must trust David. The practice rounds through our apartment pay off. Like Bernard, we are all smiles. We compliment each other through the first song. David has learned a firm hand and I've learned to accept his persuasion. Halfway through the second record, Bernard stops us.

"You've got the footwork down nicely," says Bernard. David and I pretend it's natural. "But you're not listening to the count."

Bernard takes me out of David's lead and into his own, speaking the count out loud, "Slow, slow, quickquick. Slow, slow, quickquick." Bernard says that some people have to listen harder to the count than others. He returns me to David, but I have no idea what he's talking about.

When we return to our respective lines, Bernard reviews again the steps to the fox trot. He calls out to the students to make sure they're paying attention: Which foot, Steve? The magic step, right, Ruth? Is Bob persuasive enough, Vicki? Bernard is a whiz with names. After the quiz, Bernard walks toward me with his arm extended, says, "And now, Kathleen will make her debut." I am drawn along by Bernard through a dozen steps. With a lead like this, dancing becomes swimming—fluid legs, strong arms, no hesitation. Every week more of us are transformed before our partners' eyes.

David grins from his line, confirming the theory he has that Bernard gives the lessons to get to dance with all of the women. Soon Bernard drops me off, his assistant gives me a nod, and the other students applaud. I've been initiated.

Bernard doesn't acknowledge the body politic of ballroom dance. You take your lessons, you practice, you use the magic step to get yourself out of a tight corner. In Bernard's class, dancing requires tradition, the negotiation of space, the way two people move in synchronicity, the repetition through which grace may, hopefully, be learned.

David and I continue to fox trot, this dance we will do the most in our lives. We come within the counterclockwise parameter and say the count softly between us, trying for our version of perfection. The other couples are peripheral forms we navigate beyond, too intent on our own path to look anywhere else for more than a few seconds.

David's hand is firm on my back, and I can't see the space we're about to step into.

I imagine Bernard making maps, marking precise boundaries and ageless waters with his persuader. I remember Bernard's instruction and lean back slightly to receive David's lead. I don't allow myself to anticipate.

Kathleen Veslany's work has appeared in Sycamore Review *and* you are here, *among other journals. In 1999 she won second prize in the Annie Dillard Essay Awards. She currently lives in Tucson with her husband, David, and works at the Udall Center for Studies in Public Policy as an editor.*

Who Am I to Speak?

NATALIE L. M. PETESCH

A fiction writer may, within the limits of her imagination or from among the murmuring echoes of her interior dialogues, take on any role—saint or sinner, hangman or hanged, traitor or patriot, perpetrator or victim, faithful lover or devastated betrayed: Saint Joan or the Marquis de Sade. The narrator may be any sentient being, even a woodworm burrowing through the labyrinths of history, as Julian Barnes has shown us. We fiction writers have a very long leash: because any invention is acceptable, we do not have to prove that anything is true. We may, of course, end up hanging ourselves by this very leash, but this is considered a tolerable risk, the worst punishment for which is to have the yawning reader shut the book in our face.

Thus, for a fiction writer whose essential art is to create That-Which-Has-Not-Existed, to create a work in which nothing is to be invented and all must be held up to the test of Truth is a formidable challenge. And no sooner had I accepted such a mission than I was at once faced with the soul-shaking question: Who am I to speak? What do I know for certain about *any*thing? At first it seemed to me that the only topic about which I could be certain that it was something I had *not* made up was My Own Life—so I was at first convinced that I absolutely must write an autobiographical memoir. But then a faint cricketing voice within demurred: What, after all (it cricketed), would

Who Am I to Speak?

such an autobiography be but a record of my relations with others? I hadn't been a tree falling in the forest where no one heard; I hadn't sprung into the world *de novo*. I'd had to await contact with others before I became myself. And, moreover, the small voice added admonishingly, there was this immobilizing paradox: even if I were to write a memoir in which naturally I would bind myself to tell the absolute Truth, there would still remain all those people who, knowingly or not, had made me myself, and who were now wandering nearly forgotten (never understood) in the dark corners of a Past now quite unillumined by any enlightening flashes of memory. Who was I to speak for *them*? And this question once having been raised—one that seemed to me to threaten the very foundations of my creative Reality—still another immediately followed. Even if (the no longer faint but now strident voice of my relentless Interrogator pursued) I were to convince myself that I could write an honest memoir, one that would be unwaveringly truthful about myself and faultlessly fair to others, wouldn't I nevertheless (considering the great strides of science) be obliged to begin, not with David Copperfield's disingenuous "I record that I was born (as I have been informed and believe)" but with my actual, not-invented grandparents, or with, as we now refer to it, my gene pool? But alas, to my eternal loss, every one of those relatives had perished before my orphaned and impoverished parents ever set foot on Ellis Island. Thus this, too, as a requirement for a truly honest memoir was impossible for me to fulfill.

And so, finally, in spite of my every effort to cling to some external source of authenticity, the only absolute Truth that remained to me—firm, authentic, and forever unchangeable—was: that I am the daughter of immigrants.

Nevertheless, to compensate for this extremely limited authenticity, I felt there was one other piece of information that I could offer, one for whose absolute Truth I could not vouch, but whose historical reliability I might offer with reasonable certainty. This historical Truth—one, at least, which was held to be true by the millions of immigrants who thronged through Ellis Island and other ports of entry—was that these turn-of-the-century immigrants would be *welcome* in America. Indeed, many of the hundreds of passengers who had left their native villages to endure the triage of steerage had been persuaded by the colorful brochures and glowing stories of professional recruiters, who assured them that America needed tens of thousands of workers—for its steel mills and textile mills and meatpacking houses and canning factories and assembly lines and coal mines and iron mines; that America needed, also (as far west as Minnesota and Montana), thousands of farmers to feed a miraculously multiplying population. And during those utopian decades before World War I these 20 million immigrants—strong in mind and body: the lame and the halt or those who might become a "public charge" were ruthlessly deported—became within a generation or two the most energetic, most ambitious, and in many ways the most grateful new arrivals to land in the New World since the seventeenth-century settlers seeking religious freedom. Most of these steerage passengers brought with them little or no money, but only a passionate desire to be free from persecution and poverty (yes, *poverty:* no longer considered a valid reason for coming to the New World). Inspired by their longing for education (many, like my own parents, could neither read nor write), and for land of their own, they were willing to work at dangerous jobs under conditions almost inconceivable to us today. Tens of thousands of them died at workplaces that offered little or no protection from collapsing construction, chemical poisons, incinerating metals, mine disasters, exploding granaries—at all those deadly workplaces, in short, that have moved out of America to countries where industry will not be troubled by OSHA or unions or environmental regulation. But the rewards for the survivors of this industrial gauntlet were enormous—free public schools for their children and education for working adults, but, above all, freedom from the terrors of persecution and arbitrary laws. We all know the astounding success

Who Am I to Speak?

stories of these millions of immigrants and their descendants—scientists, architects, physicians, artists, entrepreneurs, and millionaire philanthropists—a record of achievement unparalleled in the history of Western civilization.

But this is not the turn of the century, and America no longer recruits impoverished, barely literate laborers for its industrial revolution.

So let us put aside for a moment my earlier observation that the only absolute Truth I could lay claim to was my identity as the daughter of immigrants. Let us assume, instead, that I am an actual present-day immediate and very-much-alive emigrant trying to get to America. In my native country—Guatemala or Nicaragua or Mexico or the Dominican Republic—there are thousands like me. Let us assume, further, that I am a young man—perhaps sixteen or seventeen years old. At home I have five siblings, all younger than I am. My mother works in a *maquillador* just across from the U.S. border where she earns about three dollars a day stitching jeans.

And let us assume, further, that I have made it finally across the U.S. border: that I did not drown in a drainage tunnel during a flash flood, that I did not wander through the Southwestern desert half-mad with thirst, my skin ripped by cactus and underbrush, that I did not suffocate in a trunk or in a sealed van, that thieves have not stolen my fifty pesos folded in an aspirin tin—or worse, that my plastic shopping bag with its bottle of water, more valuable to me than any pesos, has not been swept away during my river-crossing along with my sandals, my one clean T-shirt, and the photographs of me with my sisters which might help identify me if I don't make it across the desert. Let us assume that I have outmaneuvered the helicopters with their nightscopes and slashing lights searching for me all last night, that I have not fallen sick with fever or snakebite, or fallen into a ravine in whose rocky depths filled with sagebrush or snakes I may never be found, nor even that I have not, with foolish and fatal timing,

Natalie L. M. Petesch

"fallen" in love: God help me, what would I do with a wife or sweetheart on this now-endless ride in this closed van that has at least kept its promise to pick me up and may at last transport me to America?

Let us assume that I have survived all that and that I am now heading for Chicago. It's true that I could perhaps have gone elsewhere—in my case, to Minnesota, where I have a cousin who is an American citizen. But he says that under the new law he cannot afford to sponsor me, that now he has to prove he has an income of 150 percent above poverty level, and since he only works in a canning factory at minimum wage he can't possibly afford, he says, to guarantee, as the law requires, that he'll take care of me even if I become sick and disabled.

Perhaps I should have tried to get to California. That might have been simpler—and warmer. But California scares me, what with its new Proposition 187 which I don't understand except that it obviously hates me and the thousands like me who are costing them, they say, a billion dollars a year, and they won't let me attend school (God knows I should have gone to school instead of shining shoes ever since I was big enough to carry a box and a rag). California, I'm told, won't educate me, they don't want kids like me in their schools, and they won't let my kids, if I ever have any, be educated in their schools. And I've been hearing lately that American-born *mejicanos,* descendants of those who came earlier, that they, too, are angry with us, complaining that we're not like the immigrants used to be, that in El Paso and Douglas and Nogales we "new ones" steal the clothes off their lines and urinate in the bushes and sleep on the ground. Ay, people like me, once we leave a country, we are homeless, stateless, loveless.

But all those decisions and possibilities are now in the past. The happy moment has arrived. *I* have arrived. At the sight of the lake and of the Sears Tower I burst into unmanly tears. Suddenly I understand all those stories about the Statue of Liberty and the huddled masses kissing the ground at Ellis Island. But my tears quickly dry (or freeze): I have arrived here on a day when it is 10 below zero. I have never seen

Who Am I to Speak?

snow. I am dressed more or less as when I trekked through the desert. My sandals and T-shirt are in shreds. Any other possessions I might have had are now pure nostalgia, lost God-knows-where. My driver is anxious to get away. It is early dawn, but already the streets are beginning to fill up with pedestrians. I want to protest to my *coyote* that only an insane man or an alien would walk the streets in a T-shirt and sandals when the temperature is 10 below, not counting the wind that blows off the lake like the end of the world. But my driver is already revving the engine; he must get away.

I know no English, yet I must find a place to sleep. I must find work. I do not know what jobs there may be for me. I have been warned that there are no longer any jobs for people like me in America, that America, after all, is approaching the twenty-first century, not the twentieth, that there are no longer jobs in factories, in coal mines, in textile mills (they've been moved to countries just like mine). The gates of America are shutting down, they warned me, Americans no longer have any patience with our so-called excuse, "the lure of jobs."

Well, I dare not think about that now. I will think about that tomorrow. Maybe my *patrón*, if I find one, or someone who sees the hunger in my eyes, will let me wash dishes in his hotel or clean his storefront windows or mop the floors of his restaurant or let me lay flagstones in his patio, or let me—even—shovel snow. (But how would one do that? It seems to me an alien and hostile substance into which I might sink and never be found.)

The van has disappeared around a corner. Tentatively I place my foot onto the ice glazing the sidewalk. I am shivering with cold. The wind hits me like a cannon blast. But within I am laughing, drunk with joy, with ecstasy, because I have made it alive to America.

Well, that is Miguel, and I cannot speak for him, since I am not a young man of seventeen and I am not Mexican. Miguel is, anyway, a special case perhaps, for he lives close to us, just across the Rio Grande.

Natalie L. M. Petesch

Let us assume instead that I am Liu, from mainland China. After a tearful departure from my wife and daughter, I have boarded a freighter headed for the United States. One of the reasons I feel I must leave China is that my wife has recently been subjected to an abortion: we would like, eventually, to have another child or even two, but we dare not challenge the one-child law. The freighter I am on is crowded with several hundred refugees like myself. Some of them are fleeing the interrogation and imprisonment of suspects ever since the Tiananmen Square massacre. Some are Christians facing punishment, or who have wearied of practicing their faith in secret, of hiding in the catacombs. Some of them, I admit, have heard that Americans are blessed with the highest living standard in the world and they, too, would like to enjoy some of those blessings.

Like myself, many of the passengers have sacrificed their life savings: some of us have paid the entrepreneurs of this voyage as much as thirty thousand dollars. We are as crowded as steerage immigrants of the nineteenth century. All of us share a single toilet. Nevertheless, we are happy. We are optimistic that we will make it, finally, to America. We have taken a circumnavigating route—a seemingly endless voyage—but by traveling this route we at least have avoided the dangers of disembarking at Alaska, where, we have been told, the immigration authorities deal out immediate and irreversible deportations with an iron hand. We have also avoided any port of entry in that erstwhile bastion of liberalism, northern California, where we hear that there has lately been a lot of anti-Asian feeling.

And so we are now heading for America at last—not far, they tell us triumphantly, from the Statue of Liberty and Ellis Island. But we are unlucky. Within two hundred yards of our longed-for Paradise, the boat strikes a sandbar and we are trapped. Some of us jump overboard. Ten of my friends drown. A few, I later learn, do miraculously reach land and vanish into the anonymity of New York or Chinatown. Others even manage to escape farther west, to the sheltering byways of a big city. But I am one of the unlucky ones. I am manacled and car-

Who Am I to Speak?

ried away to a prison in Pennsylvania. Who knows me here? No one. Who knows my language? An interpreter, perhaps, but even she has a problem with my dialect. The laws here seem to me so harsh that I feel I am back in my own country.

For reasons that are complex beyond my understanding, I am held prisoner here for three years. Not only me—no personal punishment is being meted out to me. All forty-five of us have been equally held prisoner. All of us have sat in despair day after day, month after month, and—incredibly now—year after year, waiting for our fate to be decided: will they deport us? Will they keep us here till our children have grown and have forgotten us?

Thus three years pass while we wait in despair. But not all the prisoners sit idle. Some of them God has blessed with "extraordinary ability." Some of them are artists who have dreamed their way through their thousand days, transmuting their grief into art—creating something of and for themselves that transcends our prison garb, our (to others) incomprehensible language, our failed effort to gain our human rights by this desperate but illegal attempt. Some of these prisoners (not I—I have no such gift) have made exquisite paper sculptures—of pagodas and dragons, of dream ships to Utopias, of birdcages, and of that symbol of the forever uncaged: eagles. All these my fellow-prisoners created from our prisoner supplies—threads from towels, toilet paper dyed with grape juice and tea, or with the simple toys of children—pencils and magic markers and colored cutouts from magazines.

During these three years some prisoners have perfected their art, and several of them have, miraculously, drawn the attention of influential and kind-hearted people, so that now one of my dearest friends here is finally to be released as "an alien of extraordinary ability." My friend, for whom I feel great love and also great envy, will soon be free to go out into the vastness of America, free to get a green card that will permit him to apply for residency, and thus he will be allowed to work while he learns the language of his new country: he has lost three years of his life, but he has found America after all. But what about those of us who remain behind? Are we not extraordinary too? What about me?

Well, I cannot speak for Liu any more than I could speak for Miguel. Perhaps I fail because they are men? Perhaps for a woman I might speak? Someone like myself?

Let us assume, therefore, that I am a woman from San Salvador. I work in a big house, five or six bedrooms (one is a "study"), for a lady who, I think, is not a tyrant. The house is far from the city, many miles away from roaring traffic, from air pollution, from urban crime. It is also very isolated and lonely, far from all that might be familiar to me—nothing like my country. There is no public transportation, not even to the village eight miles away, where there are a few shops, churches, and restaurants.

When I first arrived at the house "my lady" (as we domestic workers call our employers) greeted me in Spanish—*Buenos días, bienvenido,* a few words like that, nothing complicated, maybe to put me at my ease, which it did, it made me feel accepted. Her four children were told that I would be like an older sister to them, that I would be one of the family. But this is not true: I have not been one of the family. When her friends come I am made to understand—sometimes in small ways I have to interpret, sometimes in some sudden and wounding remark—that I am expected to disappear into the kitchen or remain upstairs with the children until the children are finally ready to go to bed. Often this means that I am working until after ten or sometimes eleven (though I had been told on my first day that I would work from seven to seven). The children must all have their baths, and the bathrooms afterwards must be left as clean as if during those prolonged bedtime rituals they had not tossed their clothes, their toys, their towels, and even their pretty little animal-shaped bars of soap onto the floors. Then they must be put into their pajamas. I must be certain that Heidi and Ariadne and Ronald and Robin have all brushed their teeth and that they really go to sleep, that they don't turn on the TV when I leave their rooms, or make phone calls to crazy people. (Now they have computers and that is fearful for me, for I understand nothing of these machines: who are they writing and "talking" to?)

Some weekends, it's true, I'm called downstairs to help in the dining room with a special party. I dress up in my black uniform with my white apron (the bow is always tied like a perfect figure eight in the back. You can tell a good maid, my lady observes with a smile, by how she ties her bow: it should rest like a white flower on her behind). At these parties I do at least get a chance to see the elegantly dressed and highly educated people who will by midnight be leaving their canapé saucers and olive pits and their empty glasses nearly anywhere—in the flowerpots, on the stones of the patio, under lawnchairs, even propped among the bookshelves. Sometimes she will introduce me to one of her guests, a special friend of hers maybe, singing out my name "Yo*land*-a" as if it meant something other than itself, some exotic musical instrument maybe. These weekend parties will easily round out my work week to eighty hours. But I'm up again for everybody's breakfast—after which there's cleaning, there's laundry, there's ironing (always), there's furniture to be dusted and polished, and cooking (always). But at least I don't do the shopping. Ever since I spoke Spanish to my Guatemalan friend, Inés, who works as a cashier at one of the village groceries, I have felt my lady doesn't trust me. I think she thinks that by some collusion my friend will add to the bill and there'll be a kickback.

My lady buys a lot of food, and there's a lot of cooking, as I say, but I don't mind cooking, cooking can be pleasant. But when how much you eat is noticed and counted, when she asks you why do you eat so many olives, "olives are expensive," or she notices that I drink a lot of coffee and tells me "imported coffee is ten dollars a pound, and besides too much coffee is not good for you," well, you can't even enjoy your food if someone is watching you.

Natalie L. M. Petesch

I work six and a half days a week. My pay is supposed to be two dollars an hour. I have Sunday mornings off so that I can go to Mass; I take Communion every week; then I stay a little while afterwards so that I can talk to the others, the *encerrados,* as we are called, which means, literally, the locked-up ones.

The long hours expected of me and her remarks about coffee and olives—that I can stand. It's, after all, my job. And also I work in a nice house with hot water all the time and bathrooms in every room. It is far better than in my country where there is nothing for a woman if she does not marry, and even if she does—what is there? My real problem is this: that my lady has not paid me the money which is owed to me. At two dollars an hour from seven to seven she owes me about two thousand dollars by now. She does give me a few dollars now and then, but she has always insisted that she is saving the rest of my money for me (she keeps it in a small safe in her room). But repeatedly she has explained to me that she must charge me what I owe her—for some careless thing she claims I have done, that I have broken a piece of valuable china or that I have ruined a dress she bought for a trip to the Virgin Islands. Even such petty meanness I could endure (in my country it is a shameful thing to be called a miser) because in the long run it would be as nothing to me. So I have pretended not to notice. But now the trouble is very serious for me. She has accused me of theft—yes, theft, the worst thing you can say about a maid. But I swear that it's not true. I have not taken a penny from the money I have seen always lying around—the lunch money and bus money for the children, the open wallets in the master bedroom, loose bills in my lady's purse, or money sometimes folded away in her husband's pants or jackets. Now she says she will not pay me until I return her pocketbook which is missing and which had in it two hundred dollars. I am hurt and confused by this accusation. This is the worst thing that has happened to me in my new country. If she dismisses me and says to everyone she knows that I am a thief, no one will hire me. I will not have a good reference and I will not receive my back pay either. I think,

Who Am I to Speak?

sometimes, that I should maybe finally "steal" something—my own savings perhaps. But if she were to have me arrested, and if I were convicted of a felony, I would be "barred from naturalization" and they could deport me, or maybe something worse—God knows what power they may have over a "felon." I have been told by the other *encerrados* that the immigration officials have become very harsh and unpredictable, that since the new laws their decisions can no longer be appealed as they used to be. Perhaps I should complain about all this to the people at my Church, but would they have the power to protect me? Who will speak for me?

Alas, not I. I cannot speak for Yolanda, nor can I speak for Tannina who fled her native country to escape genital mutilation and who, upon arriving in the United States, was at once imprisoned for false documentation; nor for Amélie who failed to reach America from Haiti after all, but drowned off the coast of Florida; nor for Antonio, who managed to float his leaky *yola* from the Dominican Republic to the coast of Puerto Rico (that almost-to-New-York stop) because he says, "at home we are hungry"; nor for Käthe, who must leave her young son behind and is forced to return to Germany where she has not lived for many years, and who may be denied reentry to the United States for as long as ten years because she overstayed her student visa by "more than a year"; nor for Ahmadou, fleeing unspeakable tortures in West Africa, but who arrived "without valid documents," and so he may be returned to his torturers unless he can prove within forty-eight hours that he faces "a credible fear of persecution," who, if he is "convicted"—not by an officially appointed or elected judge but by a randomly encountered immigration officer allocated him through the tectonic shifts of good or bad Luck—has no constitutional right of redress (he does not have the right to be represented by an attorney): he must be deported.

Alas, I cannot speak for Ahmadou or for Miguel or Liu or Yolanda or Tannina or Amélie or Antonio or Käthe. For whom, then, can I

Natalie L. M. Petesch

speak? Or must I remain resolutely silent—remain silent "with dignity" as they say one should be allowed to face death? But while I ponder this moral problem of whether I have the right to speak, thousands huddle at the closing gates, dozens die in the desert, hundreds die by sea, thousands more languish in prisons. What is my moral responsibility? Who, if I dared to speak, would listen? Or as Rilke asked, *Who, if I cried, would hear me among the angelic orders?*

Natalie L. M. Petesch has published five novels and five collections of short stories. Among her awards and honors are the Iowa School of Letters Award for Short Fiction, the New Letters Summer Prize Book Award, the Pittsburgh Cultural Trust's Award for Creative Achievement by an Outstanding Established Artist, the Swallow's Tale Press Short Fiction Award, the Kansas Quarterly Fiction Award, the Louisville Review *Fiction Competition Award, and inclusion in* Best American Short Stories. *Her most recent books are* Wild with All Regret, Flowering Mimosa, Justina of Andalusia and Other Stories, *and* The Immigrant Train and Other Stories.

A Way to Make Some Money

LEA SIMONDS

Charles H. ("Teenie") Harris (1908–98) was a self-taught Pittsburgh photographer who devoted his forty-year career to documenting the life of his beloved childhood home, the Hill District (*Wylie Avenue*). The Hill, as it is still called, though an ethnically and racially mixed population at the time, was predominantly African American and the heart of black social, spiritual, and cultural life in Pittsburgh. The Hill was home to the most widely circulated black newspaper in the country, the independently owned *Pittsburgh Courier*, which hired freelancer Teenie Harris in 1936 as its principal photographer. The *Courier* was a critical voice during the 1930s, '40s, and '50s when, as a weekly paper, it published a local, a national, fourteen regional, and four international editions. During these years the urban African-American experience in neighborhoods like the Hill District was a complex narrative, interweaving pride and prosperity with the pain and frustration of racial discrimination. The irony of segregation as a factor in shaping an economically and socially self-sustaining community of strong values and fellowship is evident in Teenie Harris's comprehensive photographic history. According to the late Rollo Turner, a sociologist and historian of black history, Teenie's estimated 70,000 photographs constitute "one of the most complete chronologies of a black community in the United States."

Lea Simonds

Working for the *Courier* and out of his own studio (*Teenie Harris in Studio Doorway*) Teenie Harris photographed everything from disasters to demonstrations, political events, weddings, funerals, fashion shows, birthday parties (*Child's Birthday*), family portraits, and street scenes (*Two Men in Front of Kathleen's Beauty Salon*). Teenie's images of work and educational environments and inspirational and recreational activities (*Hunters with Trophies*) made apparent the vitality and richness of a lively, socially complex, and sophisticated community. Discrimination required that the Hill not only have its own clubs, restaurants, and other venues for recreation and entertainment but encouraged the formation of organizations like the Hill District's all-black police unit (*Portrait of a Policeman*), which kept the neighborhood one of the safest in the city. The Hill had its own thriving businesses, professional schools, and even a baseball team, the Pittsburgh Crawfords. Edna McKenzie, a reporter for the *Courier* who went with Harris on many of his assignments, remarked on the "dynamic and beautiful social life in the black community, a community which was not behind, but doing the same thing everyone else was doing."

The foundation of social life in the Hill District was the church, the most influential and formative institution in most people's lives. Not only did people seek spiritual support at Sunday services, prayer meetings, and Bible classes, but they could count on financial assistance when needed and expected to find their closest friends and future spouses among the congregants. A great variety of dynamic clubs, guilds, and associations in the Hill District were also venues for social interaction. There were some fifty organizations for women alone, and as many fraternal, professional, and special-interest groups for men. Elite clubs like the Luendi and the Frogs had national membership and held weekly dinners and week-long celebrations every year.

However, the most glamorous and lively social scene in the Hill District was to be found at the numerous theaters (*Roosevelt Theatre*), nightclubs (*Patrons in a Night Club*) and private clubs that operated around the clock and earned the Hill the nickname "Little Harlem."

A Way to Make Some Money

Pittsburgh was a convenient stop on the railroad between New York and Chicago and a destination for the great musicians of the day. Big names like Duke Ellington and Cab Calloway were frequent visitors as were Ahmad Jamal, Lena Horne, George Benson (*George Benson at the Piano*), and Billy Eckstine, who all called Pittsburgh home at some time. When the downtown gigs were over the performers would head to places like the Hurricane, Stanley's Tavern, and the Crawford Grill, where elegantly dressed patrons—both black and white—would have turned out for a long, full evening of good food, music, and dancing. There was so much activity in the Hill that even Goode's Drugstore and Soda Fountain stayed open twenty-four hours a day.

Sports, a major source of pride and entertainment all over America, were central to black culture. Pittsburgh was home to many fine athletes and a venue for frequent sporting events. The Crawfords—started by Teenie Harris and bought by entrepreneur Gus Greenlee—played in the Hill at Greenlee Field. The Crawfords and the Homestead Grays (*Homestead Grays Teammate*), which claimed the legendary Josh Gibson as a player, were two of the finest baseball teams in the Negro League. Segregated leagues kept black teams from going head to head against white teams with any frequency, but when they did teams like the Crawfords and the Grays usually prevailed. Boxing was another favorite sport in town, and when Pittsburgh's own Billy Conn got into the ring with frequent visitor Joe Louis, Conn's near-victory over the famous boxer became such a part of Pittsburgh folklore that "it was better than winnin'!"

The Hill District owed much of its prosperity to the resourcefulness and success of enterprising citizens like Teenie Harris's brother Woogie and his friend Gus Greenlee. Frank Bolden, their friend and editor at the *Courier*, would have referred to them as the kind of people who could make "stepping stones out of stumbling blocks." Although antidiscrimination laws had been passed in 1935 they were mostly ignored in practice, leaving the African-American population without access to lucrative employment, public assistance, or loans from downtown banks. Woogie and Gus masterminded the introduction of numbers writing (*Numbers Writers Counting Money*) to the Hill District and, through this illegal but profitable lottery, effectively served as bankers to the community. A one-cent bet could earn a seven-cent return for the bettor, but it was Woogie and Gus's take that helped to provide—through loans or outright gifts—the much-needed capital for tuitions, rents, repairs, and the startup costs of businesses like Teenie's own photography studio. Woogie and Gus became so revered in the community for their trustworthiness, generosity, and class that they were referred to by the dignifying moniker "the Digitarians."

In his personal and professional demeanor, Teenie Harris was disciplined, determined, and principled. He always worked in a suit and tie and earned the nickname "One Shot Harris" for his efficiency. "They called me 'One Shot' because that's all I ever took." Mayor David L. Lawrence gave him the nickname because "whenever I'd go into him [his office], there'd be four, five, six photographers there and they'd be shootin', shootin', shootin'. I'd wait for them to get through. Then I'd walk up and—bam! One shot. And he liked that." Not only did Teenie save money on flashbulbs and film, which the *Courier* did not provide for him, but he became uncannily good at knowing which shot he needed to tell the story.

While Teenie did not consider himself an artist and referred to his career simply as a "way to make some money," Frank Bolden remarked that "Teenie was never a picture snapper. His photographs always said something, if it wasn't anything but good-bye." Notwithstanding his modesty Teenie clearly understood that his images had the power to please and inform but also to influence and inspire. Teenie satisfied his studio clients with thoughtful portraits that he would handcolor at their request, and his photographs of birthdays and weddings became family treasures. But Teenie also used his talent as a political tool to draw attention both to the contributions made (*Women Selling War Bonds*) and the inequities suffered by Pittsburgh's minority population. When no blacks were hired for a construction job, Teenie would photograph the all-white crew or the picket line (*Labor Demonstration*) and publish the image in the *Courier*. He took pictures of poor housing facilities and dirt roads and sidewalks that in any other community would have been paved. The photographs, either published or sometimes hand-delivered by Teenie himself, would often compel the embarrassed officials into making immediate changes. During World War II Teenie covered the activities of the Double Victory Campaign—a civil rights campaign to win the war abroad and the war for opportunity and equality at home. Teenie was once offered a job by the white-owned *Pittsburgh Post-Gazette*, but refused it and the salary increase because, he said, "They would've had me taking shots they were interested in, and that surely wouldn't have included blacks."

While segregation had been a factor in shaping the extraordinary character of the Hill District in its glory years, it was, ironically, the processes of desegregation and urban renewal which contributed to the decline of the neighborhood. When living restrictions eased, more and more of the African-American and other minority residents left the Hill District and moved to other areas of the city. In 1968 Teenie's camera was turned on the scenes of anger and frustration that characterized the riots in the Hill following Martin Luther King's death, scenes that stood in stark contrast to earlier images of a thriving and self-confident community. Today the Hill District, for a long time blighted by derelict buildings and drug traffic, is home to a new generation of citizens who are committed to and investing in its future. New businesses and attractive housing are being built, Crawford Grill II is offering good food and jazz, and the *New Pittsburgh Courier*, though no longer published in the Hill, is still telling the story of Pittsburgh's dynamic African-American community.

Lea Simonds is a member of the Editorial Advisory Board of **Creative Nonfiction.**

Wylie Avenue

(Reproduced with permission from the Estate of Charles "Teenie" Harris.)

Teenie Harris in Studio Doorway
(Reproduced with permission from the Estate of Charles "Teenie" Harris.)

Child's Birthday
(Reproduced with permission from the Estate of Charles "Teenie" Harris.)

Two Men in Front of Kathleen's Beauty Salon
(From the collection of the Carnegie Museum of Art.)

Hunters with Trophies
(From a private collection.)

Portrait of a Policeman
(Reproduced with permission from the Estate of Charles "Teenie" Harris.)

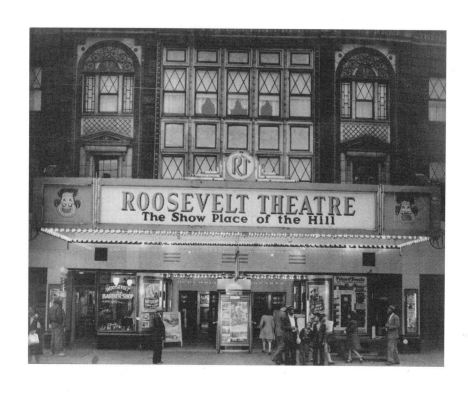

Roosevelt Theatre
(Reproduced with permission from the Estate of Charles "Teenie" Harris.)

Patrons in a Night Club
(Reproduced with permission from the Estate of Charles "Teenie" Harris.)

George Benson at the Piano
(Reproduced with permission from the Estate of Charles "Teenie" Harris.)

Homestead Grays Teammate
(Reproduced with permission from the Estate of Charles "Teenie" Harris.)

Numbers Writers Counting Money
(From a private collection.)

Women Selling War Bonds
(From the collection of the Carnegie Museum of Art.)

Labor Demonstration
(Reproduced with permission from the Estate of Charles "Teenie" Harris.)

Language at Play

DIANE ACKERMAN

*A*ll language is poetry. Each word is a small story, a thicket of meaning. We ignore the picturesque origins of words when we utter them; conversation would grind to a halt if we visualized flamingos whenever someone referred to a *flight* of stairs. We clarify life's confusing blur with words. We cage flooding emotions with words. We coax elusive memories with words. We educate with words. We don't really know what we think, how we feel, what we want, or even who we are until we struggle "to find the right words." What do those words consist of? Submerged metaphors, images, actions, personalities, jokes. Seeing themselves reflected in one another's eyes, the Romans coined the word *pupil*, which meant "little doll." Orchids take their name from the Greek word for testicles. *Pansy* derives from the French word *pensee,* or "thought," because the flower seemed to have such a pensive face. *Bless* originally meant "to redden with blood," as in sacrifice. Hence, "God bless you" literally means "God bathe you in blood."

We inhabit a deeply imagined world that exists alongside the real physical world. Even the crudest utterance, or the simplest, contains the fundamental poetry by which we live. This mind fabric, woven of images and illusions, shields us. In a sense, or, rather, in all senses, it's a shock absorber. As harsh as life seems to us now, it would feel even worse—hopelessly, irredeemably harsh—if we didn't veil it, order it, relate familiar things, create mental cushions. One of the most surprising facts about human beings is that we seem to require a poetic version of life. It's not just that some of us enjoy reading or writing poetically, or that many people wax poetic in emotional situations, but that all human beings of all ages in all cultures all over the world automatically tell their story in a poetic way, using the elemental poetry concealed in everyday language to solve problems, communicate desires and needs, even talk to themselves. When people invent new words, they do so playfully, metaphorically—computers have *viruses*, one can *surf* the Internet, a naive person is *clueless*. In time, people forget the etymology or choose to disregard it. We dine at chic restaurants from *porcelain* dinner plates without realizing that when the smooth, glistening *porcelain* was invented in France long ago, someone with a sense of humor thought it looked as smooth as the vulva of a pig, which is indeed what *porcelain* means. When we stand by our scruples, we don't think of our feet, but the word comes from the Latin *scrupulus*, a tiny stone that was the smallest unit of weight. Thus a scrupulous person is so sensitive he's irritated by the smallest stone in his shoe. For the most part, we are all unwitting poets.

When we create with words, in the literary arts, we raise the stakes. Then we stare straight at our inherently poetic version of life, make it even more vigorous and resourceful. Poetry, for example, speaks to everyone, but it cries out to people in the throes of vertiginous passions, or people grappling with knotty emotions, or people trying to construe the mysteries of existence. At a stage of life remarkable for its idealism, sensitivity, and emotional turbulence, students tend to respond for all three reasons.

Sometimes when I pass a basketball court I'm transported, thanks to the flying carpet of memory, back to my first real teaching job in the early eighties. At the University of Pittsburgh I taught various undergraduate writing and literature courses, but I remember most dearly the graduate poets I taught. Not much older than most of them, younger than a few, I found their blue-collar enthusiasms a tonic. All the elements of their lives breathed with equal intensity. They played as hard as they worked as hard as they loved as hard as they wrote. It was typical of them to discuss Proust in the stands before a hockey game. They bought poetry, read poetry, wrote poetry in the seams between work and family, met at a bar after class to drink Iron City beer and continue talking about poetry.

After class one evening we all went to a nearby basketball court so that one of the students could teach us "fade-away jump shots," an image he had used beautifully in a poem. Sometimes I went with them to the Pitt Tavern after class, where we would continue talking late into the night. With an unself-conscious fervor that amazed me then, and in retrospect still does, they demanded to be well taught. They knew instinctively that words could change their lives. My job was to keep pace with their needs. I had no choice but to teach them everything I knew, learn with fresh energy, then teach them even more if I could.

At the end of one semester, in the closing hour of the final seminar, I asked if there was anything we hadn't talked about that needed to be addressed. One of the best writers raised his hand. "How to make love stay," he said simply. For the remaining hour, that is what we discussed. I can still see his soulful face. Smart, romantic, unpredictable—he was all poet. Even now, a dozen years later, I worry about him, hope he survived the intensity he craved but could not live with. I hope he continued writing. I see the faces of the others, too, and wonder how they've fared. Although I could not tell them so at the time, I knew where some of their emotional travels might lead them. They were intense young poets. In vital ways, we were similar. We shared a common currency—we understood the value of poetry.

When I was a freshman at Boston University, in the late sixties, I used to stroll beside the Charles River with a copy of Dylan Thomas's poems in one pocket and Wallace Stevens's in another. I was drawn to the sensuous rigor of Thomas and the voluptuous mind of Stevens. Together they opened the door for me and many others into a realm of ideas, song, word play, idea play, discovery, and passion. What I loved about Thomas (and still do) is the ways his poems provide a fluid mosaic, in which anything can lose its identity in the identities of other things (because, after all, the world is mainly, as he put it, a "rumpus of shapes"). By mixing language and category with a free hand, he seems to know the intricate feel of life as it might come to a drunk, or a deer, or a devout astronomer freezing to death at his telescope. His poems throb with an acute physical reality. No poet gives a greater sense of the *feel of life*.

Then he goes even further, to recreate the *process* of life through a whole register of intricate and almost touchable images and events. Working himself into a state of neighborly reverence, he invents metaphors that don't so much combine *A* and *B* as trail *A* and *B* through a slush of other phenomena. He ardently weds himself to life's sexy, sweaty, chaotic, weepy, prayerful, nostalgic, belligerent, crushing, confused vitality in as many of its forms as he can find, in a frenzy that becomes a homage to Creation. In this way, he seems to create a personal physics to match his ideas, so that the language of his best poems echoes the subject matter, and both suggest the behavior deep in our brains, hearts, and cells. He really does nibble the oat in the bread he breaks, intuit the monkey in the newborn baby, see the shroudmaker in the surgeon sewing up after an operation. Sometimes he's cryptic, as when he writes, "Foster the light nor veil the manshaped moon." Sometimes a clear-eyed observer, as when he refers to "the mousing cat stepping shy, / The puffed birds hopping and hunting." Sometimes he's lyrically emphatic: "The hand that signed the paper felled a city." Sometimes he's a maker of schoolboy jokes, sometimes a celebrant seer. But, above all, he can transform the Saturday afternoon reputation of the planet—a couple of imposing-sounding topics, its being called a "star," the pyramids, Jesus, Adam, illness, birth, death, sex— into something sacramental. Not neat. Not well behaved. Not explicit. Not always argued or even structured. But bold, wild, and tenderly voluptuous. How could I resist all that?

Other poets took my fancy, too. I loved the way poets illuminated life like a holy text, drawing my attention to how dreams were made, and to the beauty at the heart of the most commonplace dramas and things. Poetry had a way of lifting a feeling or idea out of its routine so that it could be appreciated with fresh eyes. In "the foul rag and bone shop of the heart," as Yeats called it, I knew words, and especially the charged reality of poetry, had everything to teach me about life.

Poetry was all I knew to write at eighteen. Much has happened in my writerly life since then. Although I still write poetry, I've learned to write prose, too, and that has brought its own frustrations and freedoms. In both genres, writing is my form of celebration and prayer, but it's also the way in which I inquire about the world, sometimes writing about nature, sometimes about human nature. I always try to give myself to whatever I'm writing about, with as much affectionate curiosity as I can muster, in order to understand a little better what a human being is, and what it was like to have once been alive on the planet, how it felt in one's senses, passions, and contemplations. In that sense, I use words as an instrument to unearth shards of truth.

These days, I do that more often in prose. But the real source of my creativity continues to be poetry. I've just published a new collection of poems. I read poetry regularly. My prose often contains what are essentially prose-poems. Why does poetry, with its highly charged words, play such an important role in my life? For centuries, poetry was vital to the life of nearly everyone. In the nineteenth century, poets such as Byron and Tennyson were superstars of Hollywood status. Movies and television may draw more viewers now, but poetry continues to inspire us, reveal us to one another, and teach us important truths about being human.

The reason is simple: Poetry not only reflects the heart and soul of a people, it has a wisdom all its own. There is nothing like poetry to throw light into the dark corners of existence, and make life's runaway locomotive slow down for a moment so that it can be enjoyed. Science and technology explain much of our world. Psychology tells us more about human behavior; all three succeed by following orderly rules and theories. Poetry offers truths based on intuition, a keen eye, and the tumultuous experiences of the poet. Long ago in India, for example, Urdu poets writing in the verse form known as a *ghazal* were also trying to figure out the universe. A ghazal was the technology they used to make sense of their world, and no doubt they felt as sonneteers and composers of villanelles do, that there are truths only to be learned when you're dancing in chains.

The craft of writing poetry is a monklike occupation, as is a watchmaker's, tilting tiny cogs and wheels into place. It's ironic that poets use words to convey what lies beyond words. But poetry becomes most powerful where language fails. How can we express in words that are human-made emotions that aren't? How can we express all the dramas and feelings that are wordless, where language has no purchase? Words are small shapes in the gorgeous chaos of the world. But they *are* shapes, they bring the world to focus, they corral ideas, they hone thoughts, they paint watercolors of perception. Truman Capote's *In Cold Blood* chronicles the drama of two murderers who collaborated on a particularly nasty crime. A criminal psychologist, trying to explain the event, observed that neither one of them would have been capable of the crime but together they formed a third person who was able to kill. Metaphors, though more benign, work in the same way. The chemical term for what happens is *hypergolic:* You can take two inert substances, put them together, and produce something powerfully different (table salt), even explosive (nitroglycerine). The charm of language is that, though it's human-made, it can on rare occasions capture emotions and sensations that aren't.

The best poetry is rich with observational truths. Above all, we ask the poet to teach us a way of seeing and feeling, lest one spend a lifetime on this planet without noticing how green light sometimes flares up as the setting sun rolls under, the unfurling of a dogwood blossom, the gauzy spread of the Milky Way on a star-loaded summer night, or the translucent green of a dragonfly's wings. The poet refuses to let things merge, lie low, succumb to habit. Instead the poet hoists events from their routine, plays with them a while, and lays them out in the sunshine for us to celebrate and savor.

When a friend and I were cycling the other day, she mentioned that reading poetry frightens her. "What if I don't get the real meaning?" she asked. "What if I read 'a ghostly galleon' and think it's referring to a ship, when it's really referring to the lost innocence of America?"

I was dumbfounded. Someone had taught her (and nearly everyone else) that poems work like safes—crack the code and the safe opens to reveal its treasure.

"There are many ways to read a poem," I said. "After all, you don't really know what was going through the poet's mind. Suppose he was having a tempestuous affair with a neighbor, and once when they were alone he told her that her hips were like *a ghostly galleon*. He might have then used that image in a poem he was writing because it fit well, but also as a sly flirtation with his neighbor, whose hips would be secretly commemorated in verse."

"Do poets do that?" she asked, slightly scandalized that noble thoughts might be tinged with the profane.

"I've done it," I admitted with a grin. "I presume other poets do."

I went on to explain, as teachers of the writerly arts do, that poems dance with many veils. Read a poem briskly, and it will speak to you briskly. Delve, and it will give you rich ore to contemplate. Each time you look, a new scintillation may appear, one you missed before.

The apparent subject of a poem isn't always an end in itself. It may really be an opportunity, a way for the poet to reach into herself and haul up whatever nugget of the human condition distracts her at the moment, something that can't be reached in any other way. It's a kind of catapult into another metaphysical county where one has longer conceptual arms. The poet reminds us that life's seductive habits of thought and sight can be broken at will. We ask the poet to shepherd us telescopically and microscopically through many perspectives, to lead us like a mountain goat through the hidden multidimensionality of almost everything.

We expect the poet to know about a lot of strange things, to babysit for us, to help us relocate emotionally, to act as a messenger in affairs of the heart, to provide us with an intellectual calling card, to rehearse death, or map escape routes. As many have pointed out, poetry is a kind of knowing, a way of looking at the ordinary until it becomes special and the exceptional until it become commonplace. It both amplifies and reduces experience, paradoxical though that may sound. It can shrink an event teeming with disorder to the rigorous pungency of an epigram. It can elasticize one's perspective until, to use an image of John Donne's, a drop of blood sucked by a single flea accommodates the entire world of two lovers. Few views of life are as panoramic as the one seen through John Milton's cosmological eye. Milton could write "All Hell broke loose" because he knew where (and what) Hell was; he had sent his wife and daughters there often enough, and his vision encompassed it, just as it did the constellations (many of which he introduces into *Paradise Lost*). He could write "Orion rose arm'd" because he'd observed Orion often enough when the arms weren't visible.

Poetry, like all imaginative writing, is a kind of attentiveness that permits one both the organized adventure of the nomad and the armchair security of the bankteller. Poetry reminds us of the truths about life and human nature that we knew all along, but forgot somehow because they weren't yet in memorable language.

If a poet describes a panther's cage in a certain vivid way, that cage will be as real a fact as the sun. A poem knows more about human nature than its writer does, because a poem is often a camera, a logbook, an annal, not an interpreter. A poem may know the subtlest elisions of feeling, the earliest signs of some pattern or discord. A book of poems chronicles the poet's many selves, and as such knows more about the poet than the poet does at any given time, including the time when the book is finished and yet another self holds her book of previous selves in her hands. A poem knows a great deal about our mental habits, and about upheaval and discovery, loneliness and despair. And it knows the handrails a mind clings to in times of stress. A poem tells us about the subtleties of mood for which we have no labels. The voluptuousness of waiting, for instance: how one's whole body can rock from the heavy pounding of the heart. It knows extremes of consciousness, knows what the landscape of imagination looks like when the mind is at full-throttle, or beclouded, or cyclone-torn. Most of all, it tells us about our human need to make treaties. Often a poem is where an emotional or metaphysical truce takes place. Time slow-gaits enough in the hewing of the poem to make a treaty that will endure, in print, until the poet disowns it, perhaps in a second treaty in the form of a poem. There is even a technical term for that: a "palinode." A poem knows about illusion and magic, how to glorify what is not glorious, how to bankrupt what is. It displays, in its alchemy of mind, the transmuting of the commonplace into golden saliences. A poem records emotions and moods that lie beyond normal language, that can only be patched together and hinted at metaphorically. It knows about spunk, zealousness, obstinacy, and deliverance. It *accretes* life, which is why different people can read different things in the same poem. It freezes life, too, yanks a bit out of life's turbulent stream, and holds it up squirming for view, framed by the white margins of the page. Poetry is an act of distillation. It takes contingency samples, is selective. It telescopes time. It focuses what most often floods past us in a polite blur.

We read poems in part, I think, because they are an elegant, persuasive form of reasoning, one that can glorify a human condition feared to be meaningless, a universe feared to be "an unloving crock of shit," as philosopher Henry Finch once said off-handedly. To make physical the mystery is in some sense to domesticate it. We ask the poet to take what surpasses our understanding and force it into the straitjacket of language, to rinse the incomprehensible as free of tell-tale ambiguity and absurdity as possible. That's not to say that we don't find nature ambiguous or life absurd, only that the temptation to play and land the mystery like a slippery salmon, to freeze it in vocabularic aspic, is irresistible. Surely this is not far afield from the hunting magic of the cave drawings at Lascaux.

We ask the poet to reassure us by giving us a geometry of living, in which all things add up and cohere, to tell us how things buttress one another, circle round and intermelt. Once the poet has broken life into shards, we ask him to spin around and piece it back together again, making life seem even more fluid than before. Now it is a fluency of particulars instead of a nebulous surging. We ask the poet to compress and abbreviate the chaos, so we don't overload from its waterfall of sensations, all of which we nonetheless wish somehow to take in.

Every poem is a game, a ritual dance with words. In the separate world of the artwork, the poet moves in a waking trance. By its nature, poetry and all art are ceremonial, which we sometimes forget, except perhaps when we think of the Neolithic cave painters in the *mysterium tremens* of their task. Intent on one feature of life, exploring it mentally, developing it in words, a poet follows the rules of the game. Sometimes artists change the game, impose their own rules, and disavow everyone else's. Then they become an *ist* among the *isms*. But there are always rules, always tremendous concentration, entrancement, and exaltation, always the tension of spontaneity caged by restriction, always risk of failure and humiliation, always the drumbeat of rituals, always the willingness to be shaken to the core.

Once, after a lecture, a woman asked why accomplished scientists and prose writers (such as Loren Eiseley), who turned to poetry late in life, were such poor poets. Is it easier to switch from poetry to prose than from prose to poetry? she wondered. I don't think the genre is what matters, but the time of life. If you read the first book by famous scientists—J.B.S. Haldane, Werner Heisenberg, Francis Crick, Fred Hoyle—you find minds full of passion and wonder. Those books are thrilling to read because mystery is alive in them, and they are blessed by a youthful, free-flowing enthusiasm. But in later books these same people become obsessed with politics and sociology; their books are still of intellectual interest, but they've lost the sense of marvel. Those who stay poets all of their lives continue to live in that youthful state, as open and vulnerable and potentially damaging as it can be.

I suppose what most people associate with poetry is soul-searching and fiercely felt emotions. We expect the poet to be a monger of intensity, to pain for us, to reach into the campfire so that we can watch without burning ourselves. Because poets feel what we're afraid to feel, venture where we're reluctant to go, we learn from their journeys without taking the dramatic risks. We cherish the insights that poets discover. We'd love to relish the moment and feel rampant amazement as the seasons unfold. We yearn to explore the subtleties, paradoxes, and edges of emotions. We long to see the human condition reveal itself with spellbinding clarity. Think of all the lessons to be learned from deep rapture, danger, tumult, romance, intuition—but it's far too exhausting to live like that on a daily basis, so we ask artists to feel and explore for us. Daring to take intellectual and emotional chances, poets live on their senses. In promoting a fight of his, a boxer once said, "I'm in the hurt business." In a different way, artists are, too.

And yet, through their eyes—perhaps because they risk so much—we discover breathtaking views of the human pageant. Borrowing the lens of an artist's sensibility, we see the world in a richer way—more familiar than we thought, and stranger than we knew, a world laced with wonder. Sometimes we need to be taught how and where to seek wonder, but it's always there, waiting, full of mystery and magic. I feel that much of my own duty as a writer is to open those doors of vision, shine light into those dark corners of existence, and search for the fountains of innocence.

The world is drenched with color and nature is full of spectacles. You would think that would be enough. Yet we are driven to add even more sensations to the world, to make our thoughts and feelings available in words. We use words for many reasons. As a form of praise and celebration. To impose an order on the formless clamor of the world. As a magical intermediary between us and the hostile, unpredictable universe. For religious reasons, in worship. For spiritual reasons, to commune with others. To temporarily stop a world that seems too fast, too random, too chaotic. To help locate ourselves in nature and give us a sense of home. Words bring patterns, meaning, and perspective to life. We keep trying to sum life up, to frame small parts of it, to break it into eye-gulps, into word-morsels that are easier to digest. Sometimes words allow us to put ourselves in harmony with the universe, to find a balance, however briefly, in life's hurricane. They make it possible not only to communicate with one another but to do it in a way that may change someone's life.

Isn't it odd that one big-brained animal can alter the course of another's life, change what the other sees when it looks at its reflection in a mirror, or in the mind's mirror? And do that by using the confection of *words*. What sort of beings are we who set off on symbolic pilgrimages, pause at mental towns, encounter others who—sometimes without knowing it—can divert or redirect us for years? What unlikely and magical creatures. Who could know them in a lifetime? When I start thinking like this, in *words,* wonder shoots its rivets into my bones. I feel lit by a sense of grace, and all my thoughts turn to praise.

Excerpted from *Deep Play* (New York: Random House, 1999).

Diane Ackerman is the author of sixteen works of poetry and nonfiction, including, most recently, Deep Play *(prose)* and I Praise My Destroyer *(poetry).*

Skin Deep

MEGAN FOSS

My sister died for ten years. And when it was finally over, I didn't know how to answer people when they asked how it happened. The death certificate lists respiratory failure, hepatic failure, heart failure, and kidney failure as the causes but she was only forty-nine and she didn't smoke, drink, or use narcotics, so using the doctor's explanation only leads to more questions.

Patti was ten years older than me and I have no real memories of her before she was fourteen or fifteen and I don't remember her being heavy then as much as I remember my mother talking about it. Locks on the food cabinets and the annual fights when it came time to buy school clothes. Looking at the one picture of her that remains from those days I'd guess her to be about a size 14 but when my mother took us shopping she always made Patti choose her clothes from the plus-size racks. I can still hear her saying, "If you want to be fat, you have to accept the consequences," and so Patti went off to high school in clothes that were never meant to be worn by a teenage girl.

By the time my memories really take hold she probably carried at least three hundred pounds on her five-foot, two-inch frame and if she hadn't been so incredibly intelligent, the weight would undoubtedly have been an impediment to any kind of successful career. But she moved off on her own after she graduated from high school and took the civil service test and got herself a civilian job at a Navy base. And that suited our mother just fine because then she didn't have to look at her and shudder before turning away and whispering, "I can't believe that came out of me."

Our mother never found a way to love Patti. She took every pound as a personal attack. And when Patti moved to San Francisco and went to work at Glide Memorial in the heart of the Tenderloin, our mother insisted that the reason Patti did it was that she'd become so hideous that nobody but a bunch of *ghetto trash* would accept her. She never considered that Patti believed in what she was doing. Never assigned credit for the forty-eight hours that Patti worked without sleep helping to process the Vietnamese orphans who landed in San Francisco during the Saigon airlift. Or the days she worked helping to organize the food giveaway that the SLA demanded for the return of Patricia Hearst. And when Patti started working with prisoners coming out of San Quentin, our mother said, "Wonderful—maybe one of those guys will be desperate enough to marry her."

And because I was ten years younger and I grew up hearing that kind of talk, I believed it all for a very long time. When I was young and she came to our house to visit, I told my friends she wasn't really my sister. That we were just related by marriage. I avoided going anywhere in public with her and as I grew into those nasty teenage years when the nicest of children seem to develop a mean streak almost overnight—I laughed at Patti and made fun of her and I wasn't even terribly careful about whether or not she heard me.

It wasn't until I displeased my mother with my own heavy thighs and my own promiscuity at the age of thirteen and gave her a newer and nearer target for her cruelty that I began to understand what Patti had gone through. But by then she was a thousand miles away and couldn't offer me any support.

We became close again around my sixteenth birthday—three years after I left my mother's house and went to live on the streets. I ended up in San Francisco and rediscovered Patti. And as strange as it seems, because she was over four hundred pounds then—I didn't see her weight when I looked at her. I saw her life—her glorious life that seemed to have excitement and energy spilling from every corner.

She typed the original manuscript for Leon Uris's *QB VII* and she knew Eldridge Cleaver. And when the sportswriter from back East who'd been hiding out Patty Hearst turned himself in at Glide, I got to be there with her and watch the corners surrounding the church fill up with silly-looking FBI agents in black suits that looked like the fabric would melt under the scorch of the sun. I remember walking up Ellis Street with her, past two or three groups of them, and as we approached the last couple crewcuts before going in the church, I looked at them and said, "Do ya really think you're incognito? Y'all look ridiculous." She should have told me to be quiet but she didn't. She put her hand in the middle of my back and scooted me past them, but she couldn't keep from laughing.

She had friends in every district of the city and seemed to have her fingers into everything. Later my mother would claim that all that success could only have come to Patti in San Francisco. "Only in that land of fruits and nuts would she be anything other than a hideous freak." And later—when Patti married Ben who was AWOL from the federal prison at Terminal Island, my mother's only comment was, "Well if any good thing ever comes out of her being so obese it's that she probably won't be able to get pregnant and have a bunch of nappy-headed brats."

But she was wrong. Patti did get pregnant. Ben got caught and sent back to Terminal Island to finish his time while Patti went through a pregnancy that could very easily have killed her. And later, when she wanted more children but couldn't risk it, she and Ben adopted a special-needs child. They moved out of the city to Martinez after Ben got stabbed in a holdup while he was working at a 7-11. She still worked in the city but she wanted her boys to be raised at a slower pace than the city allowed. So she got up every morning at 4:00 so she could get her children ready to meet the day and still have time for the three legs of her ninety-minute commute on public transportation.

For all the years that I spent supporting a two-bill heroin habit doing twenty-dollar blow jobs, Patti was my only emotional connection to the outside world. My parents moved without letting me know where they'd gone or what their phone number was and if I wanted to speak to them I had to call Patti and have her relay the message. Hers was the one home I could go to if I wanted to remember how straight people lived. If I wanted to see what it would be like to take a shot at normality again. I told my mother that years later and she said, "No wonder you stayed hooked. If I thought that was normal I'd probably shoot drugs, too."

I was in jail in Virginia when Patti started dying, and since my mother wouldn't dream of going to the hospital and comforting her, Ben took it all on his shoulders. She fell in her frontyard and impaled her knee on a metal stake and ten years later she eventually died from complications arising out of that injury. By the time the state of Virginia cut me loose (along with a formal request to spend the rest of my life outside its borders) she'd been sent home from the hospital. The damage had been repaired and it looked for a while like a complete recovery would occur. She'd gotten close to five hundred pounds during her pregnancy and never dropped any of it and the one danger still remaining was whether or not the leg would ever again be able to support her weight.

But anybody who thought that would keep her down was sadly mistaken. Within a few short weeks she'd resumed her hectic schedule and in what I know was frequently a state of near agony she dragged herself to the bus stop and the Bart station and into the city where she had to walk almost four blocks on that leg to reach her office. She'd changed jobs by then and worked for the California Nurses' Association and she used to say how lucky she'd been that the accident happened when it did because along with the new job she got a medical plan with Kaiser Permanente. And back then we were naive enough to think that was a good thing. We hadn't even heard of Bill Clinton and nobody was talking about a national health-care plan. Kaiser was years ahead of the rest of the country and we were terribly impressed with their efficiency and the amazing array of doctors and medical technology she now had access to. They had a huge sprawling facility above the freeway in Martinez and she didn't have to pay a penny of her medical costs. We didn't know then that she'd got herself involved with a bureaucratic monstrosity that would eventually take her life.

Somehow in the process of keeping that monstrosity running—in making sure all the forms were filled out and all the computer programs that tracked all their information kept running—they missed the infection that set in. It began on the inside of her calf below the knee. Suddenly her skin began rupturing. Ulcers formed in the flesh and grew and spread until finally there were seventeen of them. By the time the doctors began to treat it seriously, the infection had spread. It moved to the other leg and she was struggling to manage her life while both her legs were literally rotting out from under her. Ben went to remove the bandages one summer afternoon and discovered that the wounds had become infested with tiny wiggling white maggots.

It was then, I think, that she finally began to accept our mother's vision of her—began to feel like the hideous freak my mother insisted that she was. She dropped her head on her chest and sobbed. "I can't take it anymore, Mouse."

She'd called me Mouse since I was a tiny child. There was a poem called "Muggins Mouse at the Seashore" that I loved to have read to me. "Megan" sounded sort of like "Muggins" and so I became "Mouse."

"I really can't stand this," she continued. "I can deal with the pain and the bandages and the blood, but I can't stand it if I'm going to be eaten alive by worms."

I reached out and wrapped my arms around her neck and laid my head on her shoulders. She never minded the long ridges of tracks on my hands and my neck and my arms. Wasn't afraid when the splits and oozing places came in contact with her. Didn't mind the horrible way I smelled when the heroin started sweating out of my body because I needed a fix. She'd hold me and call me Mouse just the same as she had when I was a bright and happy little girl who still had a whole world to conquer. And when repeated efforts to get me to seek treatment repeatedly failed she made sure I had sterile syringes.

"You're not gonna get eaten alive," I whispered in her ear, but I understood that it was the indignity and not any real fear of the maggots that had prompted her to finally give in to her tears.

We sat there for a couple of seconds while she cried and then in a tiny little voice I could barely hear, she started singing. "The worms crawl in. The worms crawl out. The worms play pinochle on your snout." And then she started to laugh and the laughter got thinner and thinner like the skin of a balloon stretched to the point of breaking until finally she just laid quietly back on the bed with the tears draining from the outside corners of her eyes and soaking the sheets beneath her.

By then they had a hospital bed set up in the living room because if she slept in the bed with Ben and he accidentally bumped one of her legs it sent her into spasms of pain. Through it all she kept working. She kept getting on that bus and making her way over to the city and walking those four blocks. She and Ben had those children to raise and the income he got cooking in a restaurant wouldn't have been enough to afford a one-bedroom apartment in the Bay Area.

Six months later they began the surgeries. The doctors attempted repeated skin grafts to try to heal the deteriorating flesh but the minute one took, her legs would begin to rot in a new place. And then suddenly her stomach started developing large twisted knots in the flesh that were as hard as rocks. Fevers of 104 and 105 would grip her for two or three days at a time but by the time she could get to the doctor they would have subsided and the doctors would stand in front of that brave face and tell her that wasn't possible. She couldn't possibly be running fevers like that because they couldn't find a cause for it. No residue of disease could be located to offer an explanation and so they simply told her it wasn't happening.

My old man went to prison in July of '87 and when Christmas came around that year Patti sent Ben out to get me off the streets so I didn't have to be alone. They hardly had enough money to buy presents for the kids and a tree and so to decorate the house we bought balloons and crepe-paper streamers and strung them through the living room—and to the children it looked just as festive as the displays that Macy's set up in the center of the mall.

We sat up late Christmas Eve night and snuggled and sang songs the same way we had as children. It was the first real Christmas I'd had in three years and there was even a present under the tree for me the next day. It was a "Pillow Person," one of those pillows that had arms and legs dangling from it and a face on the front. They each had one and when I opened it, she said, "It's hard to think of anything to get you because—because—well, you just can't have much out there. But I thought you could leave it here and then you'd always know you had a place to come lay down when you're tired."

I went to jail in February and got clean for the first time in six years. During the months that I spent there Patti put money on my books—not much, but enough to make sure I had tobacco and occasionally the rare luxury of a package of Taffy Creme cookies. As it got closer to my release date, she came to see me and we talked about my future.

"Mouse," she said and leaned across the table to hold my hand. "You can come and stay with me and I'd love to have you—but you need to get out of here. There's nothing for you here. It'll just happen all over again—and I need you to live. I need you to be okay. In case I'm not—I need you to be okay. You're only thirty and you have your whole life still. You have to go."

I thought she was probably right but that all seemed much easier in theory than practice. "So where I'm gonna go?"

Her liver had begun failing by then and her skin had a yellow sheen to it that made her look like she'd been coated in butter. Her normally blue eyes that had turned green under the effects of the jaundice filled up with tears and she tried to smile when she spoke but she couldn't hold it. "You have to go home, Mouse."

My father had retired and it turned out that when my parents moved they'd returned to the Pacific Northwest. Patti had been negotiating with them to allow me to come there. My mother didn't want anything to do with me and I suspect, looking back, that Patti probably guilt-tripped her into agreeing. However she did it, they finally agreed and when the heavy clanking-metal doors closed behind me for the last time, Patti and Ben came to pick me up at the front door of the jail. They'd made a plane reservation for the next day, but for that last night she rented movies and we sat cuddled up eating popcorn and watched *La Bamba* and *Dirty Dancing*. They were the first movies I'd seen in six years.

And oddly, because it hadn't been her intention, both films evoked very specific memories from our childhood. Both films depicted the era in which she'd been a teenager. She'd had a huge collection of records and we sat and talked about the ones that had been her favorites. Buddy Knox singing "Party Doll" and Joey Dee and the Starlighters and "The Peppermint Twist." To the extent that our mother allowed her to be, she'd been a normal, giggling, boy-crazy, getting-drunk-and-puking-sloe-gin-fizz-all-over-her-dress kind of teenage girl. She didn't have the poodle skirt or the little sweaters with the Peter Pan collars because if she could have found them in her size my mother's belief that she could shame her into losing weight by dressing her up in frump wear wouldn't have allowed her to have them.

But she'd had parties where they put sawdust on the garage floor and danced to those records 'til midnight and no matter what my mother thought of her chances the parties had been crowded with laughing, gyrating young people. Patti had made the best out of a very bad bargain and I watched Patrick Swayze and Jennifer Grey dancing in that room full of young people to Bill Medley and Jennifer Warnes singing "(I've Had) the Time of My Life" and my breath literally choked in my throat. Had she ever had such a moment? Had there ever been anything that could qualify as that moment in her life? And then I looked at her propped up against the pillows in her hospital bed and she had tears in her eyes—but she was smiling.

"He reminds me of Johnny Darovich," she said and nodded at Patrick Swayze in all his black leather—and I nodded back.

"Yeah—he does," I said.

"Do you remember him?"

"Sort of. Mostly I remember the black leather jacket and the duck-tail." I paused for a second and then laughed. "And I remember you rushing him out the back door when he stayed too late and was still there when Jennie came home from work."

We were raised to call our parents by their first names. In some strange way, Jennie thought it spoke to a sophistication she wanted to be associated with. We hated it. We were always having to answer questions like "Aren't they your real parents?" or "Don't they want people to know you're their kids?"

Patti laughed at my recollection. "I can't believe you remember that. You couldn't have been more than six or seven."

"What I remember is that you always bought me an ice cream from the ice cream man so I wouldn't tell."

"Yeah I did. And I always got you a Nutty Buddy. It was worth it. Jennie would have died if she'd caught me with him."

"Patti?"

"Hmm?"

"I don't wanna go back." I couldn't imagine going and trying to live that way again. Trying to be what it was I was supposed to have been with people whose voices I couldn't even remember except as they'd been raised in anger.

"I know you don't. But think about why. Is it just because you're scared? I know it isn't because you want to go back out on those streets."

"Yeah—I do. It's home," I told her and felt tears stinging my eyes. It seemed like I was always crying in those days. Like the tears of ten years had just been waiting for me to finally get clean so they could sneak up and betray me to the world as a wuss.

She reached out to put an arm around me and her arms looked as damaged from the years of injections as mine did. Great pits and holes and long raw stretches along the veins. The rest of her skin had grown grey and toughened—leathery with hundreds of cracked lines that looked like scales.

It was almost impossible to remember the soft, laughing teenage girl who'd danced on the sawdust and tried so desperately and so futilely to gain her mother's love and approval all those years ago. But before I left the next morning she sat on the edge of the bed and took her hair down and it still fell in a thick cascade all the way down to her waist. She usually kept it in a tight knot on top of her head because she so rarely go the chance to wash it, and pinned up like that helped hide the grease and dirt—but the effect was to make her look even more misproportioned than she was. The small tiny face seemed deformed on top of her massive bulk. She needed some balance—something to soften.

And I'd learned living on the streets to keep my hair twisted into French braids because I got the chance to shampoo my hair about as often as Patti did. It wasn't so bad in the summer when it was warm enough to wash it in the river—but during the winter months I kept it knotted in those plaits so my dates couldn't tell how dirty it was. So they wouldn't be reminded that I was a heroin-addicted street rat. They didn't like that. Didn't like to be reminded that the money they gave me was contributing to the enemy in the war on drugs. Not having the capacity to stay clean was one of the few things that caused me shame and embarrassment on the streets. It represented a failure at some essential element of femininity and I looked at my sister and remembered back to her early years when in spite of her increasing weight she'd kept herself immaculately coiffed, dressed, and made up.

So that next morning, before Ben took me to the Bart train that took me to the airplane that took me away from her for almost eight years, I threaded Patti's hair into two perfectly shaped French braids and did her makeup. Only when I held the mirror up for her to look into, her eyes filled up with tears and the carefully applied mascara ran down her cheeks and looked like cracks formed in old arid concrete.

The only thing I had to take on the airplane with me was my Pillow Person, and it was also the only thing I had to hang on to in the first few months when I struggled to stay put—to not run back. I'd watch the evening news to find out where the drug busts were so that if I decided I wanted to go back to being a junkie I'd know where to find that kind of traffic. And I'd dream sometimes that I was back in California and had a big old chunk of dope in my hand and was heading for a shooting gallery—and then I'd look down at the cellulite in my thighs and remember how much weight I'd gained sitting in jail and I'd be too embarrassed to have anybody see me that way and I'd decide to wait until I was skinny again to get high. Fat as a defense mechanism.

When I got pregnant, I got almost phobic about my weight. And every time I went to put a cookie or a piece of fried chicken or a spoonful of ice cream in my mouth, it seemed like Jennie was standing there reminding me how terrible I'd feel if after I had the baby, I discovered that I'd put those thirty pounds back on. "You don't want to end up looking like your sister, do you?" Even when she wasn't standing there to say it, I heard those words. And it didn't occur to her as she watched the cheeks and the thighs finally thinning out that it just wasn't healthy for me or the baby to be losing weight at that point. Never occurred to her that I'd almost completely stopped eating and that when I did I immediately went to the bathroom and stuck my finger down my throat. Of course she didn't realize that at eighty-two pounds she'd finally fallen completely victim to her own anorexia either.

And I undoubtedly knew on some level that what I was doing was bad for my physical as well as mental health, but most of the time I managed to convince myself that the weight I was losing was a result of working so hard—of having a job that required a lot of physical exertion. And even if I hadn't had that lie to tell myself, I had by then become thoroughly enculturated into mainstream femininity—ingrained with the knowledge that disease, exhaustion, or even the starvation of my own growing baby constituted acceptable sacrifice if it made me thin. Molly's father left me when I got pregnant because, in his words, "You were almost too fat to be attractive before you got pregnant. I'm not hanging around for this." At first anything short of death seemed reasonable. But I finally even became convinced that death was better than being fat. In my mind, fat became synonymous with freakish, and if I ever forgot that, I had my mother to remind me of my sister whom she grew increasingly bitter about as the years went by.

Patti and I talked on the phone a couple times a month during those first years I spent in Washington, but Jennie rarely spoke to her at all. Called her on Christmas and her birthdays and Patti always called her on Mother's Day—but other than that they didn't have much contact. And I got stuck in the middle. Got stuck negotiating that awkward space between them. Trying to make Patti think Jennie ignored her and cut her out because of a dozen different reasons—but never the truth. Never because she just didn't like her. Didn't want to be reminded of her abnormality. At the same time that my life was becoming more and more normal in my mother's eyes—by the time I finally began to accomplish what had seemed an impossibility for most all the years of my life, began to be a daughter my mother didn't feel ashamed of—Patti's abnormality seemed to take on new dimensions and proportions with each passing season.

Skin Deep

By the time I got pregnant, Patti had become virtually housebound and her family's financial circumstances had been severely altered. They were now surviving on her disability and a check the state sent to Ben every month for taking care of her. That money was an extension of her disability funds. She needed a nurse's care on a daily basis and Ben had worked in hospitals on and off for most of their marriage. He didn't have any kind of medical education—no nurse's degree and not even certification as a nurse's aide, but he was accustomed to illness and bedpans and death and dying. And he loved her more than I've ever seen a man love a woman. For all that my mother thought Ben was the last choice of a woman who had almost none to begin with, I came to understand in those last years of Patti's life that it was some kind of grand design that brought him into her life.

Once or twice a year he'd go off on a crack bender and Patti would call crying and hysterical—terrified of what would become of her without him. I know Jennie didn't enjoy those calls, but every time she hung up the phone afterwards, she said the same thing. "I don't know what she expects me to do. She made her bed and now she needs to lay in it. I'm not going to send her any money. Ben will just spend it on drugs." It wasn't a reasonable argument—like I said, it only happened once or twice a year and the longest he ever stayed gone was a week. But when you're living way above the comfort level and your firstborn child is dying in an abyss of poverty, you have to find a way to justify it. And in my mother's defense, I have to say that she just didn't have it in her to imagine Patti's needs and condition. And she never understood anything about people who used drugs. She could be so repulsed by her own daughter that even from a thousand miles away she could barely bring herself to make contact—but she couldn't understand why Ben, who lived in such intimate proximity with Patti's increasing pain and dependence, had to do what he did in order to survive. Had to go away every once in a while in order to be able to stay.

While I was putting the finishing touches on my nursery and

starving myself so I wouldn't end up looking like my sister, her organ systems began breaking down. At just about that same time the doctors at Kaiser Permanente finally put a name to Patti's disease. She had elephantiasis. Ben told me that over the telephone and I immediately conjured up pictures I'd seen in books of people with limbs—and in the case of men, frequently the testicles—swollen beyond recognition. That accounted for the hardening of the tissue in her belly—it had become a giant hundred-pound rock resting on her organs.

But when I went searching for answers in books, the first thing I discovered was that the disease was virtually unheard of in this country. Its most common cause is from an infestation of lymphatic channels by filarial roundworms whose larvae are transmitted by insect bites. But these are tropical parasites and Patti hadn't ever traveled outside the western United States, and no matter how we phrased and rephrased our questions, her doctors had no answers. As we struggled to break each new piece of information down to digestible chunks, we ran into another dead end. It was when they began telling us that it was all too complicated to explain that I think we began to understand that whatever was wrong with her had her physicians for its source. Was a result of their attempts to treat that initial injury to her knee all those years before.

As each of her systems shut down, a team of doctors struggled to repair the damage but they couldn't stay ahead of it all. Her kidneys would begin to fail and they'd get them functioning adequately only to discover that her hepatic system was giving out. And by that time Kaiser had grown into such a monster that we didn't even know half the doctors' names, much less have faces to attach them to.

Patti and I continued to stay in close touch over the phone but it was Ben I turned to for real solid information about her health. But even at that I began to feel more and more distanced from what was going on with her. Ben reported the best he could, but he had a thick and melodic Cajun drawl that was sometimes difficult to understand when I was looking right at him and his voice had gotten so quiet over the years that there were times when I just agreed after asking "what?" for the third time.

Patti had begun experiencing comas by that point and on one day she'd sound alert and informative and the next her speech and thinking would be riddled with delirium. It was difficult to judge over all that distance what condition she was really in, and attempting to communicate with Kaiser was absolutely impossible. She was the patient and when she needed to communicate with them she had to fight her way through computerized message machines and just sit and wait and hope for the best. I didn't have a chance of getting a living, breathing human being on the phone.

It was sometime in '92 when Ben started talking about an operation that might save her life. Doctors from all over the world had confabbed over Patti's condition and they'd finally come up with a treatment plan. They were going to cut off that hundred-pound pile of tissue that was squashing the life out of her. An elephantiasis expert was flying in from India to do the surgery and Ben sounded hopeful, but to me it sounded like her body had been donated to science before she was finished with it. The only details I ever got about the surgery were that someone was filming it for public television and that when they took her to surgery they put her on one gurney and her stomach on another and wheeled them in together.

And initially, things looked hopeful. Her health improved but it cost her over five hundred dollars a month to maintain the medical insurance that made that possible. She could have been the perfect poster child for Clinton's health-care plan except that she was grotesque and ugly and when people looked at her, many of them, I suspect, were like my mother and thought she would have been better off not being at all. We grew more distant in the next years and I'm ashamed to say that it had as much to do with my discomfort at being caught between her and my mother as it did with the miles between us.

And then in the winter of 1994–95 my mother and father were

both diagnosed with potentially terminal illnesses within two months of each other. Cliff had developed lung cancer and Jennie had congestive heart failure. It was during those months when my father was dying and my mother retreated even further into her anorexia and an addiction to pain pills she'd developed as a result of a nerve problem in her back that Patti and I recaptured that closeness we'd shared during those years when I was on the streets and she was all I had to remind me that I'd ever lived any other way.

It was strange because she'd been gone away from home and virtually cut off from her parents for almost ten years by then and I'd spent almost seven years living five minutes away and seeing them on a daily basis—but she was the one who seemed most affected by their illnesses. Perhaps it was a luxury afforded by her distance—perhaps being three states away allowed her to feel and absorb things in a way that I couldn't because I had to look at it every day and hold myself together. I had a four-year-old-daughter and, after all those years of failure, was about to graduate *magna cum laude* with an English degree and was going to begin teaching at the same university while I pursued my master's degree.

I called Patti the night before graduation. It had come to me slowly—but I'd realized that over the last years, she'd shared far more in my reinvention than just being a comforting voice at the end of a telephone line. When I fished in Alaska that first year she'd written me two or three times a week and asked a hundred questions. When I got pregnant, she started rereading the books on babies that she'd packed away when her boys started school. And when I went back to school after a lifetime of being stupid and had to take my first algebra test, her blood pressure went up along with my stress levels. She got headaches when I took algebra and couldn't sleep when I was cramming for finals. She'd shared it all—had found a way, trapped as she was within her rotting body, to experience the world outside her own misery by looking at it through my eyes.

Four hours after graduation I packed up a suitcase and Molly and headed back to California for the first time in seven years. It wasn't a surprise trip—I'd been planning it for almost three months. What was a surprise was that while Molly and I were crossing Grant's Pass Patti spiked another one of those 105-degree temperatures and had to be rushed by ambulance to Kaiser. They managed to bring the fever down and wanted her to stay there so she could have access to IV antibiotics, but she wanted to go home. She was going to see her Mouse for the first time in seven years and it wasn't happening in a hospital.

We arrived at a little after three in the morning. They'd moved yet again. They had friends who owned a large four-bedroom house in Vine Hill that they rented to them for $1,200 a month—a steal by Bay Area standards. But the neighborhood was a ghetto by anybody's standards. When I was running those streets Vine Hill had been a labyrinth of flat-roofed, bars-on-the-windows, tarpaper houses populated by the county's second- and third-generation of color-claiming gangbangers. A modern-day hole-in-the-wall where even the sheriffs didn't go.

It had changed some. The house Patti lived in and a couple dozen others had been built in the years I'd been away and some of the yards even looked like people paid attention to their upkeep—but I knew enough about Vine Hill to make sure my doors were locked and my windows were up as I cruised the narrow, twisted streets until I found Patti's cul-de-sac.

The door was standing slightly ajar, and at three in the morning that seemed really strange—particularly for that neighborhood. But everyone but Patti had gone to bed for the night and she was afraid she wouldn't be able to get to the door so she'd had Ben leave it open for me.

One of the biggest shocks of my life came when I got inside and saw her for the first time. She looked so small. She probably still weighed a bit over three hundred pounds then, but compared to the enormous bulk she'd been carrying when I left, she looked virtually petite. It was most evident in her face. Eyes that had always looked small because of the large pockets of fat around them now looked huge and I could see her cheekbones for the first time in all the years I could remember looking at her. Her head wobbled on her neck like she was drunk, but the smile on her face—the smile on her face was like she'd just come downstairs on Christmas morning and discovered that every single item on her wish list was waiting under the tree. It covered the entire lower half of her face.

Her eyes moved from my face to my hands to my hair—and then slowly to the small fingers wrapped around mine. To the four-year-old face that couldn't hide the fright going on inside, and for the first time I looked beyond the face of my sister—beyond the love in her eyes—and saw the scene the way Molly saw it.

Stacks and stacks of bandages. At least thirty different pill bottles on the dining table beside the hospital bed. The absorbent pads spread out beneath Patti's body that had obviously already absorbed something. Her body covered in what looked like a giant pink tent and sticking out below it legs that were unrecognizable as body parts and instead looked like oozing masses of mutilated meat. Like roadkill. Crutches and wheelchairs and complex hospital equipment they used for cleaning her legs that looked like a cross between a mini hot-tub and a crock pot.

The longer Patti looked at Molly the tighter Molly squeezed my hand. And then she whispered something I couldn't quite make out. I leaned down just a little so I could hear her when she repeated it. "Jabba," she said.

Again I leaned closer and I could see she was getting frustrated because I wasn't understanding what she was trying to tell me. "Jabba," she said again and louder and that time I understood her. The monster from *Star Wars*.

Patti understood her, too, but instead of recoiling or showing any kind of hurt, she smiled at Molly and held her arms out. "I know, sweetheart. I look pretty scary."

I remembered that voice from a hundred moments in my childhood. At bedtime. When my parents fought. When nobody would play with me and I got left alone on summer afternoons. I remembered that voice and it was as if something in Molly inherently recognized it, too. She dropped my hand and walked directly into Patti's arms. "You're Mommy's sisser," she said.

Once Molly got settled on the bed beside Patti she looked around the room and then up at Patti and in a completely matter-of-fact four-year-old voice asked, "Are you gonna die, too?"

"Molly," I said and moved forward, completely unsure how to deal with her responses and her questions.

But Patti put her hand up and whispered over Molly's head. "It's okay." And then she turned to Molly. "Who else is dying?"

"My gramma and my grampa."

I think it was then that Patti finally accepted that Cliff, at least, was going to die. We talked about it the next day and she was still convinced that Jennie would come through the surgery her doctors had suggested and go on for another ten or fifteen years. I argued with myself about whether or not to try to prepare her for the very real possibility that that wouldn't happen. At that point Jennie was still refusing to have the surgery.

I tried to explain it—but even to my ears, accustomed as they were to my mother's increasing eccentricities, her reasons for not having the surgery sounded bizarre. Ben was standing in the kitchen snapping green beans while he kept an eye on a big skillet simmering Swiss steak on one burner and an equally large skillet snapping and popping with grilled onions and sliced fried potatoes on another. And it struck me that if there was anything good—anything at all—about Patti's predicament, it was that she probably never ever worried anymore about her weight. She probably ate and enjoyed—as much as she was able to enjoy anything—Ben's wonderful cooking.

It was a strange irony that his cooking was very similar to my mother's. They'd both come from the South and had tendencies toward the deep-fried and high in fat. Huge plates of crispy fried chicken or catfish. Thick, golden-brown French onion soup with melted cheese and flaking crusts of sourdough bread floating on top. Fritters and cornbread dripping in butter and honey. Pecan pies and peach cobblers. Jennie would set the platters on the table and everybody would dig in. Everyone but Patti. Jennie would already have served Patti's plate and Patti would sit and stare at all that homecooking in the middle of the table and then down at the cottage cheese and broiled fish or naked hamburger on her own plate. There was no cottage cheese in her fridge while I was there and she could finally eat what she wanted free of guilt. Could eat because she was hungry and it tasted good.

"So why she doesn't want the surgery?" Ben asked from the kitchen.

"She claims she's not having the surgery because she'd have to take her dentures out and she says she'd rather die than have anybody see her without her teeth."

"Oh bullshit," Patti said.

Ben came out from the kitchen and stood with a fist on each hip and his arms bowed out at the sides—and his mouth literally hanging down on his chest. In the years I'd been away, I'd forgotten how old he was. He'd turned fifty-eight that year—but even with the increasing strands of gray in his hair and knowing that he'd had a heart attack and now had his own set of dentures, I couldn't ever think of him being much above thirty. I suspect that had to do with those occasional crack runs. And in spite of the heart attack he was still built like a brick shithouse. Great huge biceps and pecs. The skin that was the same color as the glazed walnuts Jennie always ordered from a specialty catalog at Christmastime stretched tight across his arms as he stood there just gaping at me.

"I'm not joking," I insisted and it was a strain to keep laughter from coming out. "She means it. I've listened to her argue with the damn doctor about it."

"There's got to be some other reason. There's got to be," Patti said shaking her head.

How to make them believe that. How to make her believe that. Sitting there in a physical condition that repelled most people who came in contact with her and clinging to every tiny second life allowed her. How to make her understand that my mother's fear of looking old and ugly during surgery could lead her to make a decision that would cost her life when Patti battled for each new day in a body most people would claim wasn't worth inhabiting. Looking at Patti and thinking about my mother—it seemed to me that we'd all been trying to have that conversation for our whole lives. And I wondered how in the world I would survive with both of them gone. The self-hatred and self-destruction that my mother had taught me. The desire to survive and believe that Patti had given me. In their extremes they were all I knew about how to be a woman.

Patti got sicker while we were there. I got to experience first-hand what it was like for her to need her doctors. She had to dial a phone number and then access another phone line and then she waited on hold for over forty minutes just to be able to record a message. Her fever escalated four degrees while she waited on the phone and not a doctor in sight.

Once they'd written her up and filmed her surgery and decided she no longer had publishing appeal, they'd go for twenty-four or forty-eight hours without returning her calls. They treated her like the roadkill she resembled. I could almost hear them saying, "Can't somebody get that shit off the road?"

She grew childlike while I was there. Couldn't remember half the events in her life and when Ben tried to tend to her needs she'd bat at him with her arms and scream. She tried to lift herself off the bed because she claimed she needed to go to the store and collapsed in a puddle of blood and putrefaction on the floor. We managed to get her back up on the bed and Ben gave her enough morphine to keep her quiet and sedated for a short time.

Shortly after she fell asleep Ben broke down in tears. It was the first time I'd ever seen him cry and another indicator that things really were as bad as they looked. She—we—had lived with her disease for a lot of years and if, in the beginning, it seemed like she couldn't survive, over time it had come to seem like she just couldn't die. But the quivering in Ben's jaw signified defeat.

"We can't go on like this too much longer," he said. "We're broke all the time. By the twentieth of every month we're going to the food bank. And the damn doctors don't do nothing but make shit worse."

He stood up then and pointed out toward the garage. "Come here. I got something for you to see."

I followed him outside and toward the side door of the garage. He pulled a key out of his pocket and put it in the lock. "You can't get in here from inside anymore," he said as he pushed the door open.

I was about to ask him why when it became obvious. It was a two-car garage and packed floor to ceiling and wall to wall with boxes that had never even been opened. There was a small walkway between the stacks that he'd obviously used to get more stuff in there but it was barely passable. "What is all this shit?"

"Hospital supplies. They come every week. I've called a hundred times and told them we don't need them but it's in a computer somewhere and they keep on coming."

"What kind of supplies?"

"Betadine. Bandages. Shucks. All kinda shit. Half the time we don't have enough money for food cause we gotta pay that damn medical insurance while they keep sending us all this shit we don't need."

"Can you sell it anywhere?" If there was a market out there for that kind of shit he would have had the connections to move it.

"I wish."

"What are you going to do with it all?"

He just shrugged his shoulders and backed out and locked the door behind him.

Over the next twenty-four hours she got sicker while we waited for the doctors to call back. A nurse had called twice and told Ben to use his own judgment. If he thought it was bad enough they should call an ambulance. But in her lucid moments Patti wouldn't hear of it. "Noo—I don't want Molly to see that. I can wait 'til they go." Her words slurred and I thought it was probably just as scary for Molly to be watching her deteriorate as an ambulance would have been—but oddly, Molly seemed more okay with the situation than either Ben or I did. And in the end, Patti waited until we left to go to the hospital where she stayed for almost four weeks.

Patti had prepared for Cliff's death as much as she could and so when that happened she handled it relatively well. But after that Jennie quit speaking to her altogether. They'd argued over funeral arrangements. Patti tried to convince her that, for the sake of his brothers at least, there should be some kind of service and Jennie took offense at that and simply wouldn't speak to her again. She thought it was terribly intrusive for Patti to suggest anything and after that I rarely raised my sister's name in the presence of my mother because Jennie'd let loose with a stream of invective that never failed to make me shudder.

Six months after my father died, Jennie finally agreed to have heart surgery. I'd given up my house and moved in with her, hoping that between the two of us we could afford to hang on to her house. I'd tried to get her to move in with me and Molly. My house was cheaper and that way Molly wouldn't have been uprooted from the home she'd lived her entire life in, but Jennie wouldn't have anything to do with that idea.

In the days before her surgery was scheduled I tried to get her to call Patti.

"I don't want to," she'd snap at me.

And finally I got up the nerve to pose the *what if* question. "You're her mother. What if you die and she doesn't get to say good-bye?"

"That's her problem and I don't want to talk about it."

The last words she ever said to me were in the car in front of the hospital. She wouldn't let me go in with her and had already laid down the law as far as visiting was concerned. The first twenty-four to forty-eight hours after surgery she'd be on a respirator and there would be *no* visitors until she had her dentures back in, and that would be after the respirator was removed.

She only weighed seventy-four pounds that day in the car when I said good-bye and she said the words that drove me nuts for months. "I do so regret your life."

She died in the hospital fourteen days after her surgery. The respirator never came out and I never got to talk to her again. It was during those two weeks that I tripped. For the first time in seven years I slipped. Those words she said stole my sleep and infested every empty space my mind had left. So many interpretations. Was she apologizing? Or was she telling me she regretted my existence? The two poles drew words and theories to them and I watched them ricochet back and forth until I thought I would surely go mad from sleep deprivation. Then I found two bottles of morphine she had stashed in the bathroom and life became relatively peaceful for a while. I still couldn't sleep—but the words slowed down. And then she died.

I'd basically known that was going to happen from the third or fourth day. She pulled out her feeding tubes and laid there and starved herself to death. The doctors were stunned and amazed. They called me into a conference to explain to me that her living will prohibited them from force-feeding her and they all looked terribly perplexed. I wasn't. I'd been watching her starve herself for a long, long time and it seemed entirely appropriate that she'd use hunger as her instrument of suicide.

But Patti—Patti kept thinking it was all going to work out and when I had to call her that Sunday morning and tell her that her mother was dead, her moans and her repetition of the single phrase—"I never got to say good-bye"—turned something in me to stone. Whatever grief I might have experienced at my own loss turned into cold hard little stones that rattled around and around in my head. So I took more pills.

I think there were a hundred of them all together—probably more than enough to hook most people. They may have hooked me. I don't know. I don't really remember. Those next two or three months are still a blur. The only tangible evidence that my life turned in those months was on the scale in the bathroom. I started eating. I ate and I took pills and I ate and I took pills, and when I ran out of pills I went to a dealer I'd known for three or four years and bought a small shiny ball of heroin. I didn't think one single time about the five-year-old child who was depending entirely on me for every single one of her needs. I took the dope home and into my mother's bathroom and dropped it in a spoon with the handle bent so that I wouldn't lose a single precious drop when I held my lighter under it and cooked it.

And then I looked in the mirror. Fat. I could hear my mother's voice from that year when my thighs first got heavy. "Fat fat the water rat." You can't support a decent heroin habit on a graduate instructor's pay, and fat hookers just don't make good money. I'd made the best money on the stroll in my day—five hundred bucks on good nights. I could live with going back to hooking. But I couldn't face being fat in public and streetwalking's a very public existence. I wrapped the dope back up in its plastic and foil and put in the bottom of my jewelry box, promising myself that it would be there when I lost the weight I'd gained.

Patti and I talked on the phone at least once a week in the fall and winter of that next year. Sometimes I could understand her—sometimes she was a child again and wanted to know where her record albums were.

In her lucid moments we talked about what I was going to do next. In a few months I was going to have my master's degree and I was torn between trying to go on for an MFA and going back to California to be with her. But even in her childish peevish moments she knew what she wanted me to do. "Keep going, Mouse. Keep going. Look at you. You're going to do it all."

So I started applying to grad schools. And the day I was offered a fellowship in the writing program at the University of Iowa, Patti and Ben spent money they didn't have sending me flowers—creamy white roses.

It was almost four weeks later that she called and I knew she was calling to say good-bye. Her words ran together and then she'd stop speaking and gasp for breath. "I have to go now, Mouse. I have to go now but you have to go on—you have to keep on keeping on." Keep on keeping on. It's a prison term. It's how you learn to do your time.

"Wait," I said into the phone. "Wait. Wait. Please don't go yet. Please. Wait for me—I'll come. I'll be there tomorrow."

"I wish I could, but I can't. I have to go now. I love you forever, Mouse. Go on to Iowa. Finish the book—Ben'll be here for you. Don't let me down, Mouse."

Then the phone dropped and I could hear voices in the background. "Hey—hey—somebody pick up the phone." I was hollering and then I tried to whistle—but I've never been able to whistle.

Finally Ben picked up the receiver and I was initially surprised by how calm he sounded. "Hey there."

"What's happening—what's going on?"

"The ambulance gonna be here in just a minute or two." He paused then. "There it is there—I can hear the siren. We gotta go, Sweetie. I'll call you later."

"Can I call the hospital?"

"Yeah, but we going to Walnut Creek."

"Why ya going to Walnut Creek?"

"Kaiser Martinez closed down. I gotta go. Call over at Walnut Creek in about an hour." And then the click. I held the phone out in front of my face looking at the numbers and buttons—at the receiver as if waiting for it to explain the conversation it had just conducted.

It seemed like the final irony and the final tragedy that Patti had outlived the institution that had been such a player in the nightmare her life became. The building had been at least ten stories—the parking lot measured in acres. The health plan of the future—managed care for every need. Tits up in ten years.

And I was as angry at Kaiser in that moment as I'd been with my mother the day I had to tell Patti she was never going to get the chance to say good-bye. They'd turned her disease into a bureaucratic battle zone—but as bad as it was, it had been familiar to her. When she went there the nurses knew her and treated her kindly. They understood the unique needs of her condition. Now she was going off to die with strangers who would recoil at first sight of her. People who hadn't watched and admired that amazing strength that kept her going when it seemed impossible. Doctors who wouldn't feel any responsibility for their part in this debacle—this ludicrous failure of medicine and money. And while all categories of institutions have much in common—when you've spent as many weeks and months of your life in the same one as she had, this new place would be strange and alien. Their systems had failed worse than hers and they were sending her off to die without benefit of any familiarity of place.

She went into a coma in the ambulance on the way to the hospital and never regained consciousness. When I spoke to Ben later that night, he still sounded hopeful—but I knew. I knew from her phone call. For days he sat by her bed—barely sleeping. Barely eating. He told me the only time he moved was when she coded and they brought in the crash cart to shock her back to life. And when he told me that I was horrified. Thought that he'd lost his mind. Just couldn't face life without her and so he had them keep resuscitating her.

But the truth was even more horrifying. It wasn't that Ben couldn't let go. It was Patti who'd left the orders for resuscitation. They were to take all steps necessary to maintain her life until June 14—the day of her oldest boy's graduation—because on the day she died the funds that had been supporting her family would be cut off. She had—in the midst of that poverty in Vine Hill—managed to raise a young black man who was going to graduate and go to college. And in today's world I can't imagine a greater accomplishment. But she was afraid after everything they'd been through, that if he lost his mother and his home, he might not make the final stretch. And so for two weeks they shocked and injected and jolted that poor tired body back to the status of a bleep on a heart monitor so that her son could get to graduation.

On the thirteenth day I borrowed money from one of my professors and booked a flight to Oakland for the next day. I couldn't stand the idea of what was happening to her. I wanted to see. I don't know quite what I wanted to see—but I had to see. The aura of unreality that had wrapped itself around what remained of my family seemed to beg for closer inspection—for definition and tangibility. To be seen.

Late that night—a little after two in the morning—I called the nurses' station and asked them to ring her room so I could talk to Ben. I didn't have anything in particular to say—I just woke up and felt the need to call. But he'd gone home to change and take a shower. So I asked the nurse if she'd go in Patti's room and take the phone to where I could hear her breathing. There was a whoosh like the wind used to sound blowing through the trees by the river on its way out across the delta followed by a few moments that sounded like children's feet padding across a kitchen floor. The respirator blowing air and then the plastic accordion in the ventilator collapsing. I listened for at least five minutes and the nurse—bless her—didn't say a word or do anything to interrupt. And then so quiet I never knew if it came from inside or outside—*Good-bye, Mouse.*

She died an hour later. Ben kept his family and his home together and I suppose if my mother was still alive she'd say he probably did it selling drugs or doing burglaries because she couldn't possibly have understood the drive for life and love that kept that family going forward for so many years.

Clifton did graduate and currently attends Diablo Valley Community College. I went from size 7 jeans to size 16 and that ball of heroin is still in the bottom drawer of my jewelry box. Every once in a while I take it out and unwrap and smell it. Looking for that sweet-like-brown-sugar-and-bitter-like-black-coffee-both-at-the-same-time smell. But it's lost its potency over the months.

It amazes me sometimes when I look at it. Memories of being raped by strangers and living life behind bars and the fear of AIDS were never enough to keep me clean—but not wanting to be seen as fat by the people I grew up with could. It must be similar to what Patti faced when her ten- and twenty-year class reunions came up.

It doesn't seem to matter so much now what my mother meant that day in front of the hospital. It took a long time to be able to write about my sister because I knew it would mean telling those things about my mother that make her look like the monster. But that's not how I see it. She was as much a victim of our culture's obsession with beauty as Patti and I were. She must have had demons of her own that made the ones Patti and I faced look like the Easter Bunny in comparison.

And I don't mind being chubby anymore. I understand that I have a different relationship with food than most people. When most people think about being hungry, what they're thinking is that it's time to stop whatever they're doing and sit down and eat. When I think about being hungry I think about there not being any food. I think about going five days without a bite to eat.

But for a while after I caught that glance in the mirror, I went back to puking up my food after every meal. And last spring, when my husband only had two months left to do at San Quentin and promised that this time he was finally really going to make it up to Washington to see me, I panicked. Binged and purged and starved myself so that I could look like the girl I was the last time he saw me all those years ago. It didn't work. Didn't drop a pound. And the day before his release when we were making his airplane reservations, I decided I had to tell him. That it was only fair to tell him how fat I was before he wasted money on an airplane ticket and broke parole by leaving the state.

"Darryl, I've gained a bunch of weight," I told him.

"Ah—you were always a big girl," he came back with.

"No—I mean I've really gained weight. I'm like a size 16 now." And then he laughed and it went on and on. "I don't think it's funny, Darryl," I said and my voice cracked at the end with tears.

"Aw Girl—come on. You should be a size 16. Hell—you should eat as much as you want. I don't care if you're a size 20. You did your years being hungry. It's your turn to eat. What's the point in staying straight and having money for food if you gotta feel like shit about eating it?" And I thought for a minute about tribal cultures where fat was a symbol of social status. Represented achievement. Having enough. Food as a source of life rather than death.

It really was so very simple but until Darryl reminded me I'd forgotten. He was right. And perhaps what saves me from allowing my relationship with food to take my life is that I had those years where we lived from day to day and never knew when or how we'd get enough to eat. Perhaps it's the memory of that very primal relationship we had with food that's allowed me to make peace with my cellulite. And I wondered as I said good-bye to Darryl and hung up the phone how different Patti's life might have been if anybody had ever told her what he told me. Told her that it was her turn to eat.

Megan Foss is currently finishing her MFA at the University of Pittsburgh, where she teaches freshman composition. She was the recipient of the Rona Jaffe Women's Writers' Award in 1998 and the Iowa Arts Fellowship in 1997. In addition to teaching at the University, Foss teaches at the Allegheny County Jail and serves on the county's Committee on Drugs and Alcohol. She and her eight-year-old daughter, Molly Jo, have now made Pittsburgh their permanent home.

The Preacher Says

MALCOLM CASH

Loving can be a heavy cross. But first I will go as far as I can.
—BORIS PASTERNAK

The white boy asked me, "Are you named after Malcolm X?" Upon hearing the question, I stared at him: It was the first time anyone had ever asked me if I was named after Malcolm.

As I looked in the white boy's face, trying to see the angle of his question, I asked myself: Why should I be named after Malcolm X? Is every Black boy in America asked this question?

Yes: I knew of Malcolm, but to my fifteen-year-old mind, Malcolm's image and fame were an orbit of anger, a paragon of what not to be. Further, Malcolm was out of the realm of my religious upbringing. And at that time, this was no small order of calling. Even as we all had our Blackness in common, my tradition taught that the divine order still had a calling and lushlife of who would be redeemed and saved, and Muslims—Black or non-Black—were not a part of the elected.

Yes: I was fifteen and Black in America. I was old enough to count dead Black bodies, and mature enough to see the ways of white folks; thus I understood Malcolm's rage. Still for me, this knowledge was not a foreground to be named for Malcolm X.

Like many Black youths of that time, I had seen Malcolm's smiling and contorted face on documentaries. I had heard his mimicry of the white man as the devil (not the embodiment of evil: *the devil*), and even with a shaky knowledge of African-American history, I knew he had been violently assassinated in front of his wife and children as he prepared to give a speech.

Knowing this, why should I be named for this legacy? Was the white boy asking me a different question under the guise of inquiring about the origins of my name? Or maybe it is not him at all. Maybe the timbre of the question lifted a veil of color and consciousness I had been blind to. Perhaps the boy's probing was taking me in a new direction, pointing toward a possible pathway I had never considered, but felt somewhere deep within.

What I do remember is I very much wanted to dismiss the boy and his intrusion, but even as I walked away from him, his query lingered in my mind. The more I pondered the status of my name, and remembered Malcolm's face on that screen, the more I began to feel an unsettled stillness that would not abate.

After school I boarded the bus to head home. The air was hazy and disquieting. It felt like it might rain, and I was anxious to get home to finish my chores and get out in the streets with my boys. Yet as the bus approached home I could not take my mind from the boy's query.

I suddenly found it necessary to consider the two sides of the past and present, and where my name fit in the equation.

Before this afternoon I had never given the origins of my name one thought, now I needed to know. The more I reflected on the representation of a name to a history, of a gain to a loss, of the inner possibilities of who I might be *if I were named after Malcolm X,* the more I knew that if I wanted to quell the motion in my mind I would have to ask my father about the source of my name. I could have easily asked my mother, and she would have given me a direct, factual answer: *Yes, you are named after Malcolm X; No, you are not named after Malcolm X.* And while I did want a factual answer, my spirit longed for a truth which, I sensed, would go beyond the facts. In essence: to know my

The Preacher Says

true name I would have to confront my father about my identity, and even then I knew this confrontation might contain the sum of my quest, but the substance would go beyond his answer.

I don't remember how much time elapsed from my encounter in school and me asking my father if I was named for Malcolm X, but I vividly remember that my inquiry opened up a new world for me. My father was not the kind of man who talked a great deal to his children, yet he had a demeanor of openness about him. This paradox stemmed from the fact that he was verbose to a fault, yet in his verbosity the personal character of his life, thoughts, and dreams were shielded from all of the candor, laughter, and chatter.

It was a Sunday afternoon, and my family had returned from morning church service when I finally decided to ask my father about my name. At the time my three brothers and I were still living at home, but our house was uncharacteristically quiet. I was almost rueful as I approached my father's study. The door was slightly cracked, and I could see my father sitting at his desk, reading the Bible. I timidly tapped on the door. When my father heard the knock, he slowly looked in my direction. He signaled me in.

Silence. My demeanor made it clear that I had something to say. He waited. We were still in our church suits, and I was anxious to know how he was reading the silence between us. I gestured at loosening my tie to buy time, half-opened my mouth, but no words came out. I angled my body so our eyes wouldn't directly meet, but before I could complete my turn our eyes met. I had never looked my father directly in the eye, and this holding of our eyes flexing the air with tension and questions and mystery drew me still, and in the stillness my father found an opening space to start the dialogue: "Yes?"

He uttered the word in the tone of a question because he could see I was having a difficult time getting out whatever I had come to ask him and my silence made it clear that I had come to ask a question, not make a statement. My nervousness was apparent as I fidgeted with my hands, then pretended to suddenly be interested in the design of his office, and the pictures on the wall. I looked at the pictures like I had never seen them before, which, considering my state of mind, I might not have, for surely they looked unfamiliar at that very moment.

My father is a Pentecostal minister, and in the Pentecostal tradition preachers rarely write their sermons down on paper. The faith is *lived*. And to truly live, you must *speak the Word*. As we sat in his study on that Sunday afternoon, my father was waiting for me to speak. Taciturn I was not, but at *that moment* I turned to the images on his wall as a way of clearing my thoughts. More important, the pictures told a story I knew and needed at that hour. There was a picture of a white Jesus directly above his desk, and to the left of this picture was a photograph of my father preaching his first sermon. The caption above the photograph read, "First Sermon, January 1966, Church of God in Christ." In a palatable silence I gazed at the photographs. My eyes fixed on the picture of him as he was thirteen years earlier. His eyes followed mine and locked in step the picture of him holding his Bible, eyes full of an infinitessimal mission and pleading questions. Though my father loved to talk, he also knew the virtue of patience. Though he did not use his study to *write*, he deeply valued his time alone in his office the way a monk valued a monastic library. This room was his temple for reflection. Though he would often bellow a prayer or sermon anywhere in the house, it was in this room that he daily sealed himself to encounter the voice of God. After dinner he usually went to his study to take care of church business, meditate, and prepare his thoughts and sermons within his mind. At that moment I was hoping the face on the wall would ask my question, and then I could retire to my room or go ride my bike. The Jesus photograph would be my magical entry to knowing the answer without having to utter a sound. But I knew this was not possible, so I mustered up my bearings, and finally spoke.

"Dad, am I disturbing you?" I said, my mouth dry.

His eyes reeled around the room, still following mine. "No, I was just reading my Bible."

"Well, may I talk . . . I mean, may I ask you a question?"

"Sure."

Now I had no more reasons to hesitate, and the weight of what I had come to ask was upon me and, frankly, not being accustomed to holding conversations with my father I awkwardly blurted my question out: "Dad, did you and Mother name me after Malcolm X?"

It was finally said, and after I asked him, I felt an inward peace. It was clear to me that my question surprised him on one level; but as he raised his eyebrows, it was equally clear that he had anticipated this question for a long time. Judging from his unruffled stare, I would have thought he had never heard of Malcolm X, but I knew better, so I waited through the brief and charged silence. And the silence was made more dramatic when my father began to wipe his dry eyes.

He then opened his Bible and stared at the pages as if he expected the book to speak for him.

As I waited I grew anxious, yet somewhat amused, because even at that age, I knew of my father's flair for the dramatic.

Physically my father is heavy and big in stature, but small in height. Even at fifteen I could nearly stare him in the eyes. And three of my six brothers tower over him. Still, his manner of carrying his diminutive height imparted a sense that he was in charge at all times in our house. Being raised in his home I had watched (not only heard) him preach innumerable times in church, at the dinner table, in the park, in the car, and nearly any other place where he could fashion and weave a sermon around some point or idea that seemingly was not remotely connected to the church until he finished drawing it out. He often told his stories and parables in such an idiomatic way that his chosen subject was reinvented with a skill that bordered on the illusory. Knowing this, I was prepared for my father's love of suspense and his flair for the spectacle, especially if he believed the panoply was for a life-transforming purpose. So I waited. Anticipating some form of drama, I steeled myself for the unexpected. I really didn't believe my father could say anything that would catch me fully off guard.

When he finally began to talk, my father kept his back partially turned from me so I could only see a shadow of his face.

"1963 was one of the coldest winters we had in Lorain. I remember it well. One reason is at the time I was working at Ford Motor Company. And when I say working, I mean real working. Nothing like today, when people say they going to work, then spend eight hours washing cars, answering phones, or selling chicken. Back then a day at Ford was like a week at most jobs today. At Ford you were on your feet twelve, sometimes fourteen hours a day with one lunch break, and two short fifteen-minute spells for relief. Many a day the work line was so hurried, you didn't get a break.

"Back then wasn't hardly no women in the plant, and you didn't see too many little men either. To work at Ford you had to have constitution and steadiness. In those days they didn't stop the line less life or death was at stake. Only exception I know of was the day President Kennedy was killed. On that particular day I was working the afternoon shift, and just as I turned the crane to hook a back wheel on the '63 T-Model, the line suddenly stopped moving. I immediately got nervous because I figured somebody on the line done got hurt bad. I'd been at Ford for almost ten years and I'm telling you, ain't nobody just up and shut the line down without a good reason, cause union or not, that's asking for trouble. But before I could call out the man's name in front of me, I heard this loud wail. I didn't know where it came from, but it was clearly a man's voice with a high snatching sound to it. I had heard many screams before, in many kinds of places, but his cry pierced the air something furious. His holler sounded like a wounded animal that was trapped for sport and could see the shadow of its killer coming upon it. Hearing this, I naturally thought we had a big emergency up front, then I heard someone say out loud, 'No! They can't kill the president!'

"At first I thought I misheard what he said. Then the cry got

The Preacher Says

louder, and I saw the shock on the faces of the men in front of me, and I knew then what had happened. Course I'm as shocked as the next person. I slowly lowered the crane and headed to the TV lounge like everybody else to hear the news. All I was thinking to myself is if they shot the president, then any of us could be next. 1963 was a time of violence throughout America. Considering how we have always been treated in America, I never was surprised to see them beating Blackfolks on television, or to see our churches being bombed like they done in Birmingham. Even still, it was something else to see somebody actually up and kill the president in broad daylight. After it happened I was as stunned as the white men, and though I didn't cry out or mourn in public, I was as sad to see it happen as anybody else. You were born two weeks to the day he was shot, so me and your mother gave you Fitzgerald for a middle name . . . in honor of Kennedy."

His brief pause, and the downcast look when he said, "in honor of Kennedy," showed me an aspect of him I had never seen. My father, who before now had never exhibited a political consciousness, nor preached the social gospel of Malcolm X or Martin Luther King from his pulpit, now furrowed a cleavage of awareness and mourning that caught me off guard. As I listened to him speak I could feel the cumulative weight that Kennedy's death had brought him. The involuntary prolongations in his voice bore a melancholy of remembrance more than a calamitous outlook on those times. The more I listened, the clearer it became: The murder of the president touched my father on a very personal level. Fifteen years later his disfigured voice and uncommon demeanor showed the lingering shock from the assassination and I sense that Kennedy's death had been a pitiable loss of a former kindled hope. But my father was not one to wallow long on any subject or event.

"Two weeks after Kennedy was killed, I was at work when my foreman called me off the line. Like I said, they didn't shut down the line for no reason, so I had to find me a quick shift recovery man before I could let go of my work. I got Bob Johnson to cover for me, and went to the foreman's office. I had let my supervisors know your mother was home pregnant, so I pretty much could guess what he was calling me for.

"When I finally made it to his office, he winked at me and said, 'Sam, you got a emergency at home. Get someone to cover for you for the rest of the day.'

"I winked back, and let out a hearty laugh. By now I was happy as a lark. I found a replacement and called home. Sammie Jr. told me Mr. Johnson had already taken your mother to the hospital. Turned out that Mr. Johnson didn't take your mama to the hospital at all, but took her to Dr. McGown's office. But I didn't find that out until I rushed over to the Elyria hospital and they said they didn't admit any Sylvia Cash that morning. When the nurse told me that I rushed home, and who do I see but Mr. Johnson, sittin' on the porch waitin' for me. I jumped out the car and hollered, 'Mr. Johnson, where's Sylvia?'

"He stared in the sky, then said, 'I was home and one of your boys ran over to get me . . .'

"I interrupted him 'cause he was talking too slow, 'Yes, yes, Mr. Johnson, but where's my wife?'

"Mr. Johnson said, 'Mr. Cash, I'm tryin' to tell you. Little before noon your boy came rushin' up on my porch like a wild geese, clamoring, "Help, Mr. Johnson, help. My mother having a baby and my daddy at work, and mother need a ride to the hospital!" Naturally I rushed over to your house, and sure as we standing here, Mrs. Cash ready to make way. So I hurry up and rush her in my car and start to take her to the hospital, but she insisted on me taking her to Dr. McGown's office, so I did. Well, 'bout time we got there it's near noon, and I ran over to open her door, and when I did she stood up, then she bent over quick like, and the next thing I know, the baby done popped right out on the sidewalk.'

"When Mr. Johnson said you just popped out I just froze in my tracks and glared at him. I thought he was trying to tell me you were dead. I looked at him and screamed, 'My baby just up and fell on the sidewalk!' He must have sensed what I was thinking, because he quickly told me you were fine.

"Now I just looked at Mr. Johnson like he was crazy. A part of me wanted him to thank him for taking your mother to Dr. McGown's, but the other half of me wanted to box him upside his head, telling me your baby exploded on the street, dead in the middle of winter. But I just asked him, 'Where's Sylvia at now?'

"'Well, Mr. Cash, I reckon Dr. McGown done put her in the hospital by now.'

"I stared at him for a split second, trying to decide whether to thank him and cuss him out, or just thank him. I just thanked him, and set out to look for you and Sylvia.

"By the time I caught up to both of you, you were up in a Cleveland hospital doing fine. I tell you I was scared at the time, but thinking on it now, I'm not surprised at how you were born. Seems natural that you came like you did, because later I was to find out that you had a call on your life while you were in your mother's womb. And that being the case, the little knock on your head back in the winter of '63 is nothing compared to what's in front of you...."

I confess: my father's story greatly astonished me. He had surpassed himself on this one. As I thought about his story my mind kept going to the words of my grandfather before he died: "Son, you might know the curve is coming, but if it thrown right, don't matter if you know it's coming, because you still can't hit it." My father's story was a wicked curve ball, and I was behind in the count.

My father had given me this tale in a matter-of-fact manner, with no pretense that he was making a grand announcement of any kind. As I turned the story over in my mind, I was trying to draw on my inner resources and seek the understanding I had been prepared all my life to hear. The habitual turn of my small round face toward the pictures on the wall of my father's study could not stretch out the deeper meaning of his story. I knew that my father's tale was a partial answer to the question of my name, but more than an answer, his chronicle was an opening for me to follow him to some place I was becoming very fearful of.

Sitting in his study, I wanted an unambiguous answer instead of cryptic signs to skirmish through. Yet I knew my father, thus I understood the next step was to wait. And listen.

"I was naturally happy because your mother had safely delivered our seventh child. But I was also cautious because now I'm seeing my seventh child, but in my mind you got a half-halo and half-child fixture about you. I'm looking down at your face in the hospital crib, and while I'm admiring my newborn, I'm really wanting to know if your future is going to be like that preacher said it would be. . . ."

He timed the turning of his head to see if his revelation was in concert with my rising head. I was now looking at him in the eyes for the first time in my life, looking at him differently than before. I forgot fear and dread and confusion. I was solely in a state of wonder, and the nightfall in his own eyes revealed that he knew he had me.

"Preacher," I muttered. I caught myself beginning to stare at my father as the rapture of his calculated revelation stirred some fear and excitement within me.

"What preacher?" And before he could answer: "A preacher said what about who?" The assured look on my father's face reminded me of how when I was younger he would whistle in a loud, melodic way when it was time for dinner, or church, or he just wanted to check on us. And whether my brothers and I were playing basketball or racing on our bikes or sledding in the snow our bodies would almost respond in a natural rhythm with his whistle. It was strange how we never spoke about it among ourselves but in the tenor of his whistle we felt a certain love, so we looked forward to hearing it. When he whistled for us our friends would often attempt to tease us with the taunt, "Daddy's calling, you have to go home." We laughed, and they thought we were trying to lighten the blow of their taunting, when in fact we were laughing at them, for what they heard as a closing down of our play we heard as a love signal from our father to us, and raced home in merriment.

Now, in his study, there was a warm twinkle in my father's eyes. I was taken aback by this information, which felt like an unveiling *and* a love signal similar to his whistling. As we sat there we both knew his ploy had worked: I now needed to hear more to see if this was another of his idiomatic currents to hold your attention, while what followed might be mundane or lighthearted; or was this dramatic whispering a conscious shifting to a pathway toward a deeper truth that might help answer my question.

"You see, son, around late '62, I suddenly became real sick. Somehow I just up and lost my equilibrium with my whole body. Would stand up and tilt right over to the other side. Doctors couldn't figure it all, and it seemed as if I might never walk again.

"Within two months I had to get a walking cane, and I couldn't work. I couldn't understand what was happening to me. After six months or so, my condition became so bad that I ended up in the hospital off and on. Before I went in for the last spell, your mother became pregnant with you. Sometime in the summer of '63 I was in the hospital in Cleveland, and one day a strange man walked in my hospital room. Came in as calm and collected as if he had known me all my life.

"When he first walked in, I thought I recognized him as an old running partner from my younger days in Youngstown. But the closer he got, the more I realized I had never seen him before.

"At this time I was already mad as a bull because I'm lying on my back, and can't move without pain. When I looked at him in that brown pressed suit, with his hat dangling at his side, I could sense he was from the South. He definitely wasn't a doctor, or family, or a friend, so what he doin' in my room? Before he could open his mouth, I'm all on him.

"'Man, who are you!?'
"He didn't say anything at first, just stared at me like he feeling sorry for me, and that got me even madder.
"'I don't know how you got in here, but nigger you better find the door out quick as you came in.'
"Knowing my mood and words were only fits of anger, the stranger looked at me as I vainly struggled to rise, then he finally spoke.
"'My brother—'
"Just hearing the word 'brother' from this strange man made me cut him off. With all the strength I could muster, I shouted, 'I ain't your goddamn brother. Don't come in here with that Civil Rights talk. This ain't Georgia.' I knew he didn't mean anything by it, but lying on my back, I suddenly had visions of that old Southern countryside your Uncle Ralph and I had to work all them years in Garnet, South Carolina. I shut him out of my mind and really start to yell at somebody else. 'Man, I been on the back of the bus. I toiled the cotton fields. I worked that tired land. You weren't my brother then, so don't go claiming me now. You hear?' The emotionless expression on his face never changed. I couldn't tell if he was listening or not, and that made me even madder. I wanted to sit up and sock him in the mouth. Who was he to walk into my hospital room and call me brother? He wasn't my brother? Ralph was the only brother I knew after my mother took us south.

"When I was four, Mama had a falling out with my daddy, and next thing we know, me and Ralph boardin' a train with Mama from Youngstown to the country. She wasn't there no more than a good year before she up and suddenly died in the backcountry. Did this stranger know that? Did he know how Ralph and me was separated from our brothers and sisters for years, and had to sneak home just to get out the South? Naw, he didn't know it; couldn't know it. So he was lucky I was down for the count, and couldn't move, cause otherwise I

The Preacher Says

would have busted him in the mouth for walking in calling me 'brother.' But since all I could do then was get loud, that's what I did.

"'I been south, man. Lived it. You hear me: lived it! Now I'm free of them crackers, so you can go back to where you come from with that. Man, you better know where you at before you come bustin' in here calling somebody brother. This is Cleveland, not Georgia.'

"Despite my anger and rudeness, the stranger kept a soft voice, and continued to observe me with compassion. Then he said, 'As you will have it. But sir, I've come to deliver a message. It is for you to decide how you take it, or if you will receive it at all.'

"'You come with what? A message. A message from who? Man, what nonsense you talkin?'

"'My brother, God has sent me, thus I am here. I am going to tell you what I came from Chicago to tell you. Then I shall leave.'

"At first I could not answer or comprehend. 'God?'

"'Yes, God.'

"'Man, if you don't get the hell out of here talking to me about somebody's God and I can't even walk. I knew you were a fool when you came in. Now I know for sure. God! Ahhhhh!'

"Truth is, I was confused. After I come back north from Georgia in '48, I took to the streets. When me and your mother first got married I made a living as a pool shark, and could out hustle anybody this side of New York. Being in the streets taught me to see any hustle miles before it hit, so I knew this peculiar man wasn't a hustler. Still, I couldn't catch his angle. This God talk was blowing me away, and at that moment the loss of my physical equilibrium was nothing compared to my emotional unbalance. But I wasn't going to let him see me sweat.

"The man got real quiet and waited for my next outburst; but I suddenly became more composed, and actually started to feel better. I turned back over in my bed, then raised myself up so I could see his face better. He was deeply black, and wore a neatly pressed brown suit.

229

He was kinda tall, slim, and looked real neat. I start to look him over real good now. My calm told him I was ready to listen. Then he began to talk in a real slow Mississippi accent.

"'Sir, the Lord has sent me to tell you that the child your wife is carrying is a boy. He is your seventh child, and he is called from the womb to proclaim the truth, and preach unto all nations. He shall be like Jeremiah, ordained to speak from birth, and like Jeremiah, he too will rebel against his calling. But preach he shall, because he is sanctified by the blood, and it is for you to raise him in the Word. My brother, it is for you to be a leader unto men, so that your son may know the way. Thus saith the Lord.'

> Yes: Thus saith the Lord.
> I heard the Lord
> He heard my cry
> Come unto me, and pray."

This song and the preacher's proclamation were the manifest proverb of the faith I had witnessed all of my life. I had heard the song played in church, seen old dark women dance to it, wailing in midnight tarry services; had watched Black men beaten down by life release proxies of anguish, refined and moved beyond dreads of death and sealed with a bond of love that always ended with: "Thus saith the Lord."

And the shadows did not die after the prayers, but after the temple doors were closed. At home, on more nights than I can recall, I laid in bed and heard my mother praying to God in song, reciting scripture, bellowing praise, usually concluding her call to God with a punctuated and mirthful "Thus saith the Lord." When I heard my mother's piercing cry in the night—and daylight—it was as if she had followed St. Anthony into the African desert, and with the bygone saints was beckoning God to heal the binding wounds. It was as if her wail was an epigraph of time itself. And as I listened to her, my heart was hardened

The Preacher Says

toward the God that never seemed to hear her, to answer her prayers with a better life.

And now, after a lifetime of hearing "thus saith the Lord" as a natural inscription of whom we were as a family and a people, I was being told its original context for my father. Though he been raised in the church, and heard many sermons and witnessed many tarry services before this preacher came with his oracle claims, this encounter was his first experience of truly reflecting on the interior dimensions of a faith which to now was a episodic and halftone divergence from his emotional life. In a vivid and eventful way I began to hear the beginning sketches of an answer to my question. But I still couldn't reconcile the preacher's proclamation to my own life.

"I got real quiet then, because unless he got a hustle for real, or he knew Dr. McGown, how this man from Chicago know your mother was pregnant? And how he know Sylvia and me got six other children? I could tell by the way he looked away from me that he knew he had my attention.

"Now I really wanted to know who he was, so when I asked him who are you this time, we both heard the crack and restrain in my voice. The preacher saw I was paying attention now, but he only answered, 'I am a man sent to tell you the Word, and I hope you have an ear to hear.'

"I was stumped. I got nervous, and I'm sure he could see it on my face. I wanted to ask other questions, but he placed his arm over his coat, and told me that he had delivered the message, and had a train to catch back to Chicago. He placed his hand on the door, but instead of leaving, he stopped in the doorway, then turned around and frowned at me. He just stood there for a few moments. It almost seemed as if my quietness upset him. Neither of us said anything. But he had a hurt look on his face. I had seen that face many a morning down on the cotton farm in South Carolina. Sometimes one of our older uncles needed help, but he wouldn't ask you, he just looked at you in a certain way, and you knew to go over and lift the heavy bucket, or lead the mule, and when you were through, the uncle couldn't say thank you, he just looked at you in a certain way, and his eyes thanked you, and you went back to picking your cotton ration for the day. As the preacher stood in that hospital room, I saw my uncles' questioning eyes in his facial expression. It was like his face was pleading with me to heed his word. I could tell he couldn't figure out my inner response to his mission, so he put his hat on, and walked out the room.

"When he left I found myself pouring in sweat and feeling like I needed some air, and fast. Now at this time I wasn't in the church, but I didn't mock God either. Your mother was deep in the church and would politely ask me to go, and a few times I did, but mainly I danced around the edge because I just couldn't see myself falling out and speaking in tongues, and waiting on the Lord to make things right. But that night I just couldn't brush the strange visit aside.

"I kept asking myself: Why? Why me, and how on earth did he know my wife was carrying, let alone that this coming baby is our seventh? Years later when I started studying the Word, I came to know the spiritual significance of the number seven, but at that time I was only thinking in worldly terms. And truthfully, on that night my thinking was all confused. Later your mother came to visit, and Sylvia knew me well enough to see that underneath my calm something was wrong. After about an hour, I hadn't said much, so she asked, 'Sam, what's bothering you?'

"I turned away from her so she couldn't see my face because I had a sudden and strange urge to cry.

"'Bothering me? Nothing.'

"'Sam.'

"'Well yes, my back is hurtin' like hell, and it's hot in here, and I want to go home.'

"'I see. Well, I remember when we were in Savannah, and things were going real bad between us, and I had to call Daddy to drive all the way from Youngstown to get me. You remember that?'

"'Yes. Why?'

"'Because I remember you couldn't face Daddy when he asked you, "Sam, why I had to come all the way down here and get my daughter?" You hid your face from him the same way you hiding it from me now. I know something wrong, but if you don't want to talk on it, that's fine by me. I just don't like being left out of your troubles when I need to be included. That's all.'

"I knew she meant it, and I knew she was right, so I told her the whole story. Never did figure out why I kept having the urge to cry, but I held back my tears, and warily looked at her as I told her about the preacher's strange visit. Well, maybe I shouldn't say it that way, because your mother believed the truth of the story the minute I told her. Being deep into the church, she believed anything that sounded like it was a message from Heaven. Knowing this made me want to dismiss the preacher's story even more, but in the back of my mind something made me hold on to it enough to halt my total doubts. Oh I continued to disbelieve him for a while, but a year or so after he left, I got my health back, then gave my life to the Lord. Soon thereafter I felt the call to preach myself. And through the years, it didn't feel like God, but something I can't name helped me to know that one day you would come asking me about your name, and I'd have to answer you by telling you the story of the man from Chicago."

The Book of Jeremiah says: "Before I formed thee in the belly I knew thee; and before thou came out of the womb I sanctified thee." For my father, Jeremiah's prophesy and the nomadic preacher's visit are intertwined revelations. For him, the preacher's vision was akin to the tarrying services he saw as a child in South Carolina. In the services the saints would gather by the altar—or by the river—and someone would slowly lift his or her voice in prayer or song, and for hours they would offer supplication and remembrance to God, asking for an intervention and a sign of the gift of mercy and intercession in the affairs of the heart and man. For my father the preacher brought a gift of intercession for both of our lives. When he became a preacher himself, his spiritual conversion wrought a new understanding of the Chicago minister's words to him in the hospital room. He now was telling me this story so that I could complete the circle, which of course meant that I would accept my calling to proclaim the gospel as it was prophesied that I would.

In the end, my father said yes: I was named after Malcolm X. Unlike my middle name, which they both decided, my first name was my mother's doing, and he saw no harm or significance *to it*. For my father, the *truth* was embedded in the report sent to him through the itinerant minister from Chicago, not the nomenclature of two dead men.

For years my father loved, shadowed, fostered, and could only imagine me and my future through the lens of what the preacher had said to him as he struggled to reclaim his own life from a mysterious illness. When I first heard the story I did not link the telling of the tale and my father's own sickness. It is only now, twenty years later, that I see the cushioned nexus of the two conditions: my father came to believe the words of the preacher because shortly after the minister left my father physically was healed, and for him, this recovery became the grounding for his discovery of God.

I was born in 1963. My father was saved in the biblical sense in 1965, and began to preach in 1966. This trajectory caused him to lift his own eyes to the heavens and claim his own salvation. His road from orphaned child to farmer to pool hustler to husband to father to working-class preacher posed its own answers to him about the power of God, and how, indeed, God might send a backwater preacher with a revelation for his son's life, and thus: his own.

Even as my father outwardly accepts my own sense of duty and desire to write, I feel the strand of a silent exchange of waiting and wonder between he and I. It is a creative holding and strong stillness, bound in the memory of a wandering preacher, and wrapped in the sounds of a fading whistle from another time which has passed, but is not forgotten.

The Preacher Says

Malcolm Cash is the father of a wonderful ten-year-old daughter. He is an essayist and poet from Lorain, Ohio, and will complete his MFA in Creative Writing at the University of Pittsburgh in 2000. His major areas of interest are Africana studies, religion, literature/drama, politics, and public speaking.

The Poor People's Campaign

PETER S. BEAGLE

1. The Southern Caravan

They really were poor, by the way. People keep asking me about that, as though the depth of their own compassion depended upon it. It seems to be very important to ascertain that the members of the Poor People's Campaign, the muddy, ungracious dwellers in Resurrection City, were "representatives"—comparatively well-off messengers from the genuine poor back home. That's the polite way of putting it.

In a sense, it's true. The lost poor, the people long drained of the energy either for hope or for fury, for anything but staying alive—no, they didn't come to Washington. My friend Mr. Collins W. Harris, who owns the land he farms, and lives comfortably by the dire standards of Crenshaw County, Alabama, never expected it to be different.

"The people who ought to be with us, the ones who need help the most, they won't move to get it. You can't make them move. I know a woman down near where I live, she was born in a cow pen, and she lives there now, and she'll die in that cow pen. You couldn't get her to think about living nowhere else but there. In my community it's no good telling people how to do—you have to show them. You got to let them see you being what you talk about. So I just had to go on up to Washington."

But the people who did come to Resurrection City were properly

The Poor People's Campaign

poor, by the standards of anyone who is likely to be reading this story. I do want to get that cleared up. When in doubt as to the exact degree of deprivation, teeth usually provide a convenient index. Your true poor old man most often has a collapsed mouth: hard, slick blue-gray alternating with blazing splotches of infection; empty, except for a couple of tallowy lumps. The young ones—the girls especially—tend to have curved holes in the sides of their teeth, and soft bluish spots, almost transparent. They get sick easily, too.

Remember that poor people frequently lie about their condition, not only to reporters and interested visitors, but to one another. "How much money you think I got in my pocket right now? Yeah, well, I got as much as I need, man, as much as I need." The women will talk much more openly on that subject than the men and boys. The women's wounds are elsewhere.

"We eats grits and we drinks that Kool-Aid," she said. I never knew her name; she was a big old woman from Marks, Mississippi, who lost her shoes marching in the rain. "Grits and Kool-Aid and dry beans. I got my daughter and my three grandchirren living with me, and two of them little chirren ain't never had a piece of pork or a chicken in all they lives. My daughter gets fifty-four dollars and eighty cents a month from the welfare, and there ain't a job in town would pay her that much. It just seems like nothing ever changes. For a while these few years, with Dr. King and President Kennedy and all, I was having some hopes that my grandchirren might be going to have a better life than I have had. But it just seems like nothing ever changes. When I was a little girl they wasn't no welfare, but sometimes you could kill a pig, eat pork all winter."

The Poor People's Campaign was born—partly, at least—out of those three desperate words: nothing ever changes. Dr. Martin Luther King Jr. announced the Campaign in December of 1967 as an extended program of demonstrations and possible civil disobedience in Washington, D.C. He spoke of "dislocating" the city, of tying up transportation, sitting-in at government offices, boycotting the schools, filling the hospitals and the jails—all the established methods practiced and perfected against the Bull Connors and Jim Clarks in such stations of the cross as Montgomery, Birmingham, Selma, Albany, Grenada, St. Augustine, in the days when the South was a lone, mad outlaw, and freedom meant voting and integrated restaurants. "These tactics have done it before," he said, "and that is all we have to go on."

But that was long ago, a generation. Then he had been able to compel the federal government to protect the constitutional rights of Southern blacks; now he was calling for a revolution—for a guaranteed annual income, for the abolition of slums, for free food and medical care for the poor, for the creation of millions of meaningful jobs. In that one sad, foolish, lovely word, "meaningful," lay Dr. King's real radicalism, his challenge to a conviction as old as America: that the poor have no right to enjoy themselves. They may live, but they must never be allowed to forget that they are being punished.

Dr. King's plan was to establish a grand coalition of poor people—black, white, Mexican-American, Indian, and Puerto Rican—and to bring them to Washington in April: some three thousand to begin with, and thousands more later. They would build a shantytown on public land (it was then to be called "The City of Hope"), and they would tell their story and be their story, making their need, their anger, their sickness, and their beauty visible on the six o'clock news, day after day, for as long as it might take to shame a nation at dinner into seeing them. I don't think the plans were ever much clearer than that.

He spoke often of the Poor People's Campaign as the last chance to avert civil war and the fascist dictatorship that he feared must follow. But it seemed even then that he expected the campaign to fail, in terms of achieving its objectives, and that his real hope was to expose America's suicidal selfishness to itself and the world, beyond anyone's skill to cover again, or to forget. Reject these, tear down their shacks and run them home, and America will never again be able to lie about what it is. In no other country could that be conceived of as a victory;

The Poor People's Campaign

but then, no other country has the particular stake in its vision of itself that America has.

On April 4, 1968, a few days before the Poor People's Campaign was to have been launched, Dr. King was murdered in Memphis.

The Reverend Ralph David Abernathy, Dr. King's closest companion and associate, succeeded him as the head of the Southern Christian Leadership Conference and leader of the Poor People's Campaign. More beside than behind him stood a rank of brilliant individualists—Hosea Williams, James Bevel, Andrew Young, Jesse Jackson—all with more familiar names and more flamboyant personalities than his own. Abernathy is a heavy man with a sad face. He may have been the best man Dr. King could have chosen as his heir, or the worst. I don't think it ever mattered.

The Poor People's Campaign was made up of eight contingents converging on Washington from different sections of the country. In early May I joined the caravan of buses coming up out of the Deep South, starting from Edwards, Mississippi, and winding through Alabama, Georgia, the Carolinas, and Virginia—the world of preachers and mules and tarpaper made to look like bricks—Martin Luther King's world. I'd been there before, for a little while, in the summer of 1965. Much in the land had changed a great deal in only that short time, but not this world, not to my eyes. It took me a good while to feel the difference.

The Southern Caravan was overwhelmingly black, of course. I think there were eight whites out of perhaps 450 marchers. But in Fayette County, Tennessee, three summers ago, the only safety and comfort was to be surrounded by black faces, black shanties, broken black roads, to wriggle as deep down as possible into the body heat of the ancient black life. In a day or so, on this return, it was like that again, even to the slowing-down of my New York voice, my stumbling hunger to be friendly as unchanged as the landscape. And I was at once embarrassed and relieved to find it so.

Sometimes there were eight or ten air-conditioned Trailways buses;

239

more often we rode in tiny, stuttering crates with the names of high schools and Baptist churches painted on their sides. The black communities of each city we stopped in paid our way on to the next, as they fed us fried chicken, took us home to spend the night, and wished us a somewhat overeager "Godspeed." SCLC's taproot is the black Southern church, and the church can still command in Greenville, South Carolina, and get hundreds of box lunches fixed, and find money where there is no money. This is not the case in Chicago.

The oldest man I met was seventy-six, according to the middle-aged friend who was always with him. Toothless head as naked as a kneecap or an elbow; the flesh used up, fallen away around the high tendons—nothing left to him but bones, black skin, and a terrible sweet smile. I never heard him speak. The other man helped him to dress and undress, washed him, shaved him, talked quietly to him in the chaos of the church dinners and the rallies on the basketball courts. "I take pains with him," he said. "Because I know God will bless me if I take pains with him." He was a tall, slow man himself, still strong, but starting to bend, starting to wear down. The two of them were next-door neighbors in Birmingham. "I got to carry him back home directly after we get there, cause he can't be sleeping out in no shack, his age. But he just wanted to go so bad. He's been real sick, too, with his stomach."

There were others nearly as old: women like huge, soft towers of starch; men as gristly as snapping turtles, their ages not measurable in years but in degree of defeat. But the majority of the Southern marchers were very young, ranging from junior high school age into the early twenties. Riding the buses with them felt like going off to summer camp. The young men drank peach wine openly, though it was forbidden, and stayed up all night fooling around with the girls, and always had one more knife that they didn't turn over to the campaign marshals. In Fayette County they were like this—foolish, big-talking, blooming into unimaginable bravery.

Three years before they were much more isolated, much less

aware of other blackness, other poverty, other worlds. Now they know all about Watts and Hough and Rochester; about Chicanos boycotting the Los Angeles high schools and Dick Gregory going to jail with the Indians in Washington State—even about Harry Edwards's proposal that blacks refuse to compete in the Olympic Games. They knew about SNCC and Stokely Carmichael even then in the southwest corner of Tennessee; but now, away down in Marks, Mississippi, they know who the Black Panthers are and the Brown Berets. They aren't afraid of white people anymore, and they know that they frighten whites, and for a while this discovery will make all others secondary.

Sitting on a tree stump somewhere in South Carolina, waiting out the third bus breakdown that day, Wilson Talbert, a lean, neat nineteen-year-old from Selma, showed me a snapshot of his family and told me, "When I graduated high school last year, I found there was just three kinds of jobs I could get. Porter, garbage-man, waiter. That was it. That's all they got for black boys, stay in school or don't stay in school. They just gone draft you in the army, anyway, whatever you do. Ain't much to wait around for, is it? It used to be I didn't know to want anything better, but now I do. If I find a good job in D.C., I'm staying on up there—if not, I don't know. I'm not looking to get in no trouble, but you get to thinking about it, you don't know where to stop."

The young girls on the buses were in school or unemployed; most of the older women were on welfare. Grace Pitts, who got on the bus at Charlotte, North Carolina, was twenty-three years old, but she looked older, except when she smiled. She had a beautiful face, finely made and balanced, like a kite or a guitar. Grace was unmarried, but she had three children by two men. She lived on welfare, and such money as the oldest child's father gave her from time to time.

"I don't like being on the welfare. But we eat just the same food as when I'm working, so I think it's better for me to be home with my children. I know I'm not poor like some of these people—" (Collins Harris had chided her mildly for telling a reporter the amount of her allotment, which is three times what she'd get in Mississippi or Alabama) "but I'm poor. We aren't starving, but we don't ever get ahead, not one step. I'm going to Washington because I can't stand to think that it's never going to be any different. I know some of these women lived worse all their lives, but I couldn't stand it."

For all the new awareness, many of the marchers had never been more than fifty miles from home in their lives, and they grew homesick and fearful as the buses wound north. I remember big, intense Jesse Williams, who stood up in the front of our bus as we neared Virginia to warn all the girls, "Look, sisters, from now on you got to be watchin' yourselves all the time with these city boys, or you likely to wind up floatin' face down in the river somewhere. I mean, we just play like we bad, but up here they ain't playin'. You got to watch yourselves."

Henry Lee Williams, his younger brother, had spent almost every day of his sixteen years in Marion, Alabama. Small, dark, square-faced, his eyes as shy as Jesse's are fierce, he talked most of the time about a café where he loved to eat. He's known the woman who runs the place all his life, and she cooks the best chicken in the world. "You ever go down to Marion, you tell her you a friend of mine, and she probably charge you a little less. She don't cook just for the money, she's a real nice lady. I wish I was there right now, me and my friend Arthur."

I think it was in Charlotte that the rumor spread that everyone was going to have to make up five good reasons (some said ten) for going to Washington, in order to answer the reporters properly "when they come on the buses lookin' for a fool." If there was such an edict, it was never followed through; but the story was believed, because SCLC was always doing things like that, or announcing them anyway. Rumors and official information proved accurate about the same percentage of the time.

At sixteen Henry Lee was already a veteran of the dogs and the jails, of being beaten up because it's fun. ("Every time that club miss my head, I hear it come down on the sidewalk—whock! whock!") He knew why he was going to Washington, but it panicked him to have to

The Poor People's Campaign

put it into words. This is what he came up with, finally, talking about his reason for dropping out of school.

"The books was all tore up. You be working on a problem, turn a page, and the next page might be gone, just tore right out. I couldn't work with no messed-up books like that. You know, a black student, he probably worry more than a white student about somethin' like that, about not finishin' a problem, spellin' a word wrong. They take it very serious. You want to get it right, and sometimes you get mad."

The caravan's nurse, Nanny Washburn of Atlanta, rode on our bus. Reporters in every town always picked up on her, because she was white, and because her blind son was traveling with her. They used to describe her: faded and arthritic, eating her sunflower seeds and going on in a voice like a gnat, "America is a sick nation, so sick, and when the revolution comes we gonna have to put all them Congressmen in the mental asylum." No story ever mentioned that she had beautiful hazel eyes, luminous and perfectly clear: mermaid's eyes.

Nanny is a witness, Nanny is the Ancient Mariner. She was a labor organizer in Georgia in the twenties and thirties, when that was synonymous with being a Communist and a nigger-lover, in the endless Southern night, when nobody cared. There was no civil rights movement then; there were no sit-ins, no boycotts, no movie stars buying full-page ads in the Sunday *New York Times,* no college students coming south for the summer, no federal troops in the schools, no voting acts in Congress, no cases before the Supreme Court. The Ku Klux Klan flogged, castrated, and murdered, and nothing was done, nothing was expected to be done. Nanny was there when nobody cared, and now she has no conversation: only a story.

She was frighteningly humble, this Southern white woman who had been hit on the head with gun butts. "I want you all to tell me when I say something wrong or offend anybody," she was forever reminding us all. "I'm no intellectual, you know. I can talk to the people, cause I'm one of them, but you be sure and correct me when I say something stupid. I want you to correct me, cause I got so much to learn." Nanny Washburn, sixty-eight years old, with a dead husband, a blind son, and a blind daughter who died.

My best friend throughout the Campaign was Collins Harris, who came from "somewhere near Grady, Alabama." He turned fifty-eight in Resurrection City; he'd be almost ninety years old now, if he's alive. You might very easily have seen him in newspaper photographs in 1968 or on television: cameramen always zeroed in on him. Collins was the man wearing an old straw hat the color of bottom-leaf tobacco, with a frayed purple band around the crown that said FREEDOM in gold letters. He had a white mustache, and a calm, solid way of standing still and looking around him. His dark brown skin was almost entirely unlined: only his curiously mischievous eyes were old. There were little skims of yellow in the white, and the outlines of the irises were beginning to blur. You would have remembered him.

We met on the bus, on the second day out of Macon, when I sat down next to him and he offered me a slightly questionable apple. I turned it down. Collins twitched a sardonic eyebrow and asked, "No? Why's that?"

"I'd really like the orange," I said. Collins smiled.

We traveled together from then on, sharing food, clothing when my knapsack got lost, and occasionally a bed—traditional American relationship between the white boy and the older black man. It is long gone now, with the world that produced it, and I wonder where the white boys will go to study competence and grace in the world.

Collins is a farmer, but he has made a living as a welder, a carpenter, and an auto mechanic. He has been married twice; he has children and grandchildren and children again, the last two adopted a few years ago. He shaves with a floppy straight razor. He believes in God, but not very much in ministers. There was a minister in Durham, North Carolina, who voiced some fear that the Klan might retaliate for his opening his church to the Poor People's Campaign. Collins was disgusted. "What's the use of a preacher who ain't got no more faith in God than that? That man got no business preaching to me."

The Poor People's Campaign

He was with Martin Luther King from the beginning, the Montgomery bus boycott of 1955. Collins never talked much about Dr. King, just as he never sang or clapped during the marches, or applauded the speakers at the evening rallies. "I can't be bothered with singing lies," he said once. "I don't sing or pray less I mean it." But one evening in Norfolk, as part of the entertainment, a local boy got up and recited the "I Have a Dream" speech in a ghastly perfect imitation of Dr. King's voice. I was chilled, horrified—I didn't realize what I was hearing, as I came to understand after several more recitations in more churches by children so proud to have Dr. King alive within them. But when I turned to say something to Collins, he was crying, without making a sound.

As long as the caravan was moving, it was all right. There were fights and hysterics, and every possible kind of logistical foulup (buses and people got lost with the same ease as luggage); but even so, the spirit of the caravan was alive and hopeful. The best moment came when we marched five miles through Greenville and it rained so hard we couldn't breathe. The water was over our ankles, and we put our arms around the nearest shoulders and went on, laughing, gasping, pulling off our shirts, singing a dozen songs at once, totally disorganized but overcoming. The young man who led the march was a cripple on crutches, but he walked all the way, with two friends wiping the rain out of his eyes. They tried to make him get into a car, but he fought and cursed them so hard that they let him walk.

"We shouldn't have stopped for dinner," Collins said later that night. "We could have walked all the way to Washington." Then he laughed and nudged me, but I already understood that Collins is never just joking.

We never really got to Washington, not together. The Southern Caravan ended in Fairfax County, Virginia, nine miles from Washington. Resurrection City had been under construction on the Mall, by the Reflecting Pool, only since May 13—less than a week—and there was a shortage of food and housing for new arrivals. Our group was broken up and scattered through several private schools and Unitarian churches. We remained in those "holding centers" for three days. It was a bad time. The momentum of the march was completely dissipated; there was nothing to do but sleep, eat, and watch television. Litter piled up in the antiseptic dayrooms where we spent almost all of our time; drugs made their first appearance, and fights were popping everywhere. People started being sent home in batches—worse, they began to leave on their own, out of boredom and homesickness. Robert Hanson, the crippled march leader, was robbed of all his money and wept helplessly in the bathroom. "You try to be nice," he kept saying.

The SCLC staff who came out every day to hold the nonviolence workshops that were originally supposed to precede the campaign were as appalled by us as any white social workers might have been. From saying that we were the only people who could save the soul of America, they began to imply that we were being held in Fairfax County not because Resurrection City wasn't ready for us but because we weren't ready for Resurrection City. The character of SCLC—and the story of the Poor People's Campaign—is contained in that inversion.

They were afraid of our failing them, rather than the other way around. I think of the young SCLC girl—bright, pretty, certainly hip—who asked each of us in turn to give his or her definition of nonviolence and refused to comment on the answers, or to reply to any questions herself except with another question. Everybody got mad, and so did she finally. She snapped, "Look, I didn't come here to answer questions. I'm the one who's supposed to be asking them."

On the morning of May 22, ready or not, we were driven in private cars to Arlington Bridge. From there we walked to Arlington National Cemetery to visit John F. Kennedy's grave. We sang "We Shall Overcome" very quietly, and stood silent for a little while, and then we walked back down to the bridge and over it into Resurrection City.

"Well, I'm home," Collins said. He was as calm and slow and easy as ever, but when he took my hand, his own hand was trembling.

2. Resurrection City

The rain wasn't what ruined it. The weather was dreadful, of course: not only during those three-day spells when the whole camp turned to a shimmering red-clay gumbo, but also in the brief intervals of dank heat that dried the ruts between the wooden shacks ankle-deep and sucked a sick, stinking fetor up out of the mud. Garbage wasn't collected; the truck that serviced the chemical toilets couldn't operate in the wet. It was cold, and there was nowhere to go to be warm. People stayed in bed all day, or sat by smoky trash fires. Mosquitoes actually started to breed in the flooded areas where the children liked to float around on big pieces of scrap wood.

The day we arrived on the Washington Mall, we were issued bedding and enough plywood and hardware—but no instructions—to start constructing simple A-frame shelters. Collins, as befitted an experienced carpenter, took twice as long to choose our materials as anyone else in the shivering, bewildered crowd and then set about building us a house. I can't call it a shack. It had a foundation, a level floor, a real door that stayed shut, and even a couple of basic bedframes for our splotchy gray mattresses. There was no insulation, of course, but there were no drafts either, and no leaks, which made it quite possibly unique in all those rows of hutches and coops and lean-tos bounded by Constitution Avenue and Independence Avenue, the Washington Monument–Lincoln Memorial, where Collins and I washed up most mornings. By neighborhood standards, we were living in a mansion.

Perhaps Dr. King's greatest disappointment in Resurrection City would have been that it was so disproportionately black. The Appalachian whites (who included Myles Horton, founder of the famous Highlander Folk School) were isolated in one swampy corner of the camp; the few hippies had their own quarter. The various black contingents quickly settled into semi-independent city-states called "Boston," "New York," "Watts," "Atlanta," "Baltimore," "Philadelphia," and so on, each choosing representatives to meet with the other delegations at the proposed City Council. You could always tell where you were, walking the duckboard streets of Resurrection City, depending on the graffiti adorning the sloping roofs: New York and Philadelphia ran to BLACK POWER, Atlanta was SOUL POWER, while Watts rather surprisingly favored quotations from Gandhi and Dr. King. Many of the Baltimore shacks were emblazoned with detailed scenes of Africa, Egypt, and children playing happily in some green anywhere. And the rain fell endlessly, endlessly on it all.

But the rain wouldn't have mattered if the campaign had been moving. Boredom and confusion—not paid agitators from SNCC, as we kept being told—were the saboteurs of Resurrection City; but at the first flicker of direction, the slightest hint of real confrontation, the marchers surged together and functioned perfectly well. They picketed the Department of Agriculture in the rain, day and night; they spoke their minds to everybody from jumpy cops with two-foot billies to Attorney General Ramsey Clark; they went to jail for singing and praying in the streets on Capitol Hill. The SCLC leaders were annoyed about that, because it hadn't been planned in advance. Spontaneity made them as nervous as it did the Washington police.

It was all like a badly rehearsed ballet: a *pas de deux* between two strangers with no sense of each other's rhythms, ambition, and limitations. In such a dance, there are moments of frantic improvisation, but what is happening is still a ballet, with rules, and an ending, and few echoes beyond that ending. Anyone who expected something different shouldn't have gone to a ballet.

Could it have been any different?—if Dr. King had lived, perhaps? Surely not in terms of what was achieved. I'm amazed that they squeezed as much as they did out of Secretary of Agriculture Orville Freeman: more money for the federal food-stamp program; six new commodities added to that dole; emergency food distribution in about 250 poverty-stricken counties, and the standard programs established in 331 more. For this was Richard Nixon's sullen hour, and the congressmen's mail was running two and three to one against the Poor People's Campaign. It couldn't have ended any differently, but it didn't have to be the staged, dishonest mess that it was. Even with all that rain.

SCLC never truly decided just what Resurrection City was supposed to be. In the earliest rhetoric, it was going to be an instant slum, a deliberate embarrassment beside the beautiful Reflecting Pool. "We're going to bring all our troubles to Washington—all our rats and our roaches, our sick folks, our hungry babies. We're going to show those people up there just how we have to live, in the richest country in the world." By the time we got there, it had been reconceived as a City of God, "where you don't pay no taxes, and you don't go to jail," a magical exemplar of the humane society. At the end, it was an island. Nobody beyond the frail boundary fence—and not everyone behind it—cared about Resurrection City.

Most of what the newspapers said was true; if they lied about some things, they missed a few others. There were guns in Resurrection City—I heard shots twice at night—and there were knives and a hell of a lot of liquor. Pot was easy to come by, and I knew at least one woman who was on heroin. There were rapes, shakedowns, attacks on tourists and reporters. Robbery was so common and unpunishable that most people quit bothering to report it. Of the SCLC marshals who patrolled the camp, half were thieves and bullies themselves, while the rest ran themselves almost insane without reward or encouragement. Dr. Abernathy and Hosea Williams kept on talking about those paid agitators.

Yet I never felt in danger in Resurrection City; and if I didn't love it, there were people who did. I remember a fierce man named Ray Robinson saying, "The moment I step outside this city, even just to walk over to the Reflecting Pool, I am dehumanized, man. Dehumanized. And I don't get human again until I'm back in Resurrection City with my friends. I have to make myself go outside, when I go."

Mrs. Mary Frances Thornton, a tiny, demure lady like one of those foot-high African antelopes, stayed on week after week with her ten-year-old son, though she hadn't meant to remain so long. "I like it here," she said. "There's nothing happening here that's any worse than Selma. I live in one room there, too, and it smells worse than anything in Resurrection City. Now here I've made some real good friends, and the SCLC—" which she pronounced "Elsie-Elsie," like most people— "they feeding us much better than we ever ate in Selma, and nobody messes with me and Ernie. They talk about closing down Resurrection City, because of it being a health hazard and all, but nobody ever says they should close Selma down. That's what they should do, close Selma."

Yet the Southern Caravan—the contingent Mrs. Thornton and I traveled with—was the only one deliberately broken up and scattered throughout the campground. I have no idea why this was done. Many of the Mississippi and Alabama people were ill at ease among Northern blacks and began leaving, a few at a time. Young Henry Lee Williams was gone in a week, and Wilson Talbert left soon after. I don't think the two men from Birmingham—the old man and his friend— ever made it to Washington.

But a surprising number of men and women from the Deep South hung on through the cold rain, the aimlessness, and the trouble, walking 'round and 'round the Department of Agriculture; standing up in committee rooms to address polite, worried white men as distant as Martians; taking their food back to their shacks to eat in the quiet; sitting out in the sunlight on folding chairs, fussing leisurely for hours about some text in Matthew. They were home.

Grace Pitts and her children stayed to the end, and Nanny Washburn walked with her blind Joe wherever people were walking that day, passing out vitamins and saying, "It's wonderful, it's just wonderful. I'm just so glad I lived to see it." A half-crazy girl from

The Poor People's Campaign

Charlotte, whose fits of crying and fighting on the bus made her an immediate scapegoat for the other women, became something of a saint in Resurrection City when she stood up at a rally to announce that the welfare people wanted to take and put that loop inside her, so that she couldn't have any more children. "I got something wrong in me there," she said. "It's hurting me all the time, but I am not going to no hospital and let them doctors touch me and put that loop in me." Women started to cry, listening to her.

Collins Harris just went on being Collins Harris: unhurried, undeceived, yet everlastingly hopeful. Many things about Resurrection City distressed him, especially the ways of the Northern city kids; but when I think of him, I see him ambling after a marshal who was dragging a boy in a gang jacket toward the plywood "City Hall," meaning to get him sent home. The point isn't that the boy hadn't done what the marshal said he had, and that Collins made the marshal turn him loose, but that Collins cared enough to move. He never seemed to think much about whether he should move or not.

Whatever he thought about SCLC's direction of the campaign, Collins remained completely loyal to Ralph Abernathy. Guerrilla talk bored him; boycotts, sit-ins, cooperatives, and political pressure were his reality. "These kids running round hollering black power, black power, talking bad about everybody, calling Mrs. King 'Ol' Hattie,' I want to know where's they program? You got no damn program, don't you come bothering 'round me. I don't mind going to jail, I wouldn't care about getting killed, but not for no fools."

I used to watch him at meetings of the pointless, powerless City Council, listening silently to furious monologues about how Detroit and Philadelphia got issued everything first, while New York, located a long way from the dining tent and out of earshot of the rickety public-address system, was having to buy and cook its own food, and we want our cooking gear back. The hippies would suggest that we live like our Indian brothers, in tribes, entrusting our decisions to those elders who were mystically connected to the old tribal wisdom. "I think we're getting too strung out behind this whole organization thing. Like that's the white man's bag, this categorizing thing." Council meetings went on like that for hours.

At last Collins would get up and talk one more time about the need for us to be like bits of sand and stone, mixing together into the common mortar of a new society. "If you can't be a rock, be a pebble, be a little chunk of gravel. It all makes mortar. I'm trying to be some cement, myself." I remember when he first came up with that image, studying an old brick wall. He loved good workmanship.

But there was no mortar in the Poor People's Campaign. Except for the Appalachian whites, none of the other delegations ever lived in Resurrection City. The Indians stayed in St. Augustine's Episcopal Church, the Mexican-Americans in the private Hawthorne School. Until very near the end of the campaign, we were told almost daily that "our brown brothers" were about to move in. We demonstrated with them a few times—at the Supreme Court and at the Department of Justice—but they weren't fooled.

"We have to read the damn papers to find out what you people are doing," a Mexican-American acquaintance told me. "And when we get something going by ourselves, you just walk right in and take it over, go home when you feel like it. We're having a rally or something, your guys come on and push our guys off the stage. Hell, we can't work with you, how we gonna live with you? You got no respect for us, no more than the Anglos, you think we can't tell?"

Originally a triumvirate of equals—black, Indian, and Mexican-American—was to make decisions for the campaign, but the closest that plan ever came to realization was an occasional hurried conference between Ralph Abernathy and Reies Lopez Tijerina, when the New Mexico Chicano leader had been complaining too loudly about SCLC's domination. But SCLC never could share power much. I remember what a friend of mine who worked for SNCC in Mississippi said about them three years ago.

"They move into an area where we've been organizing, and it's like the circus coming to town. They won't work with the local people like we do—it's just a couple of rallies, a couple of speeches, couple of marches, a few heads busted, lots of headlines, and they're gone again, and we have to start all over. Nothing we can do about it, either. They got Martin the Ace going for them."

They don't have Martin now. One woman in Resurrection City said of Ralph Abernathy, "Dr. King could talk for twenty minutes, and I wouldn't understand one single word he said, but it didn't matter. Dr. Abernathy, he talks for two hours, and I understand every word. But I guess I don't care."

His situation was tragic, but he kept finding his way into absurd, pitiable messes, caused mostly by a reluctance to trust his followers with the truth. The resentment engendered by his staff (and most of SCLC's people) living downtown at the Pitts Motor Hotel might have been much less intense if Abernathy had simply explained that he couldn't possibly run the campaign from Resurrection City. But he let himself be acclaimed mayor, and he had volunteers—Collins was one—working every day on a big plywood house, which he never lived in. The low point came on the evening when he was called to the camp after there had been a couple of really bad fights. He promised sadly that if everybody got themselves together and behaved, he'd see to it that they got more fried chicken for dinner. Abernathy never made a speech in Resurrection City without promising chicken or filet mignon.

The speeches poured down on us as unceasingly as the rain. The SCLC had been born of the black Southern church and drew its strength from that soil, and the Poor People's Campaign ran on the rhythms and language of the church: on images, on metaphors, on slogans banged out over and over. Jesse Jackson's shouts of "Soul power!" and his morning ritual: "I may be poor, but I am—somebody! I may be hungry, but I am—somebody! I may not have an education, but I am—somebody!" James Bevel's signature vision of white society as a dangerously sick, mad patient, and the poor as doctors and psychiatrists. Ralph Abernathy promising to smite the Pharaohs of this nation with plague upon plague, until at last they let our people go. And, always, the image of Martin Luther King as the murdered dreamer whose dream cannot be killed; as Joseph among his envious brothers.

> And when they saw him afar off, even before he came near unto them, they conspired against him to slay him. And they said one to another, "Behold, this dreamer cometh. Come now therefore, and let us slay him, and cast him into some pit, and we will say, Some evil beast hath devoured him, and we shall see what will become of his dreams."

Hosea Williams, SCLC's direct-action leader, had the most striking image in his repertoire: the black dawn cities, with thousands of people hurrying way across town to haul the white man's garbage before he gets up, to start cleaning his house and fixing his meals; of mothers leaving their children to raise the white man's children. Hosea is the one who was always warning, "Tomorrow we are going to jail, brothers and sisters, tomorrow we are going to give the cops a chance to use those billy clubs. The picnic is over."

But it was never anything more than a ballet, a trivialization of real hunger, and real injustice, and real, sleepless pain. Once in a while things flashed out of control for a moment, like the time a delegation from the entire Poor People's Campaign met with Ramsey Clark, having spent the previous day demonstrating outside the Department of Justice, demanding to see him. The grievance at issue was a Mexican-American concern, but the Resurrection City blacks took over, standing up one by one to sock it to Ramsey Clark just because he was there and white, and their lives are hopeless, and his department is unfortunately named.

Lila Mae Brooks of Sunflower County, Mississippi—where Senator James O. Eastland was drawing $13,000 a month for not growing anything on his land—shouted at Clark, "If we don't get no justice, man, you better be gone from here. You done sat down for too long. You done got fat back there. You letting the world know that you ain't a man."

Hosea himself was very quiet, murmuring only, "We ask justice to help us redeem the soul of America." But back in Resurrection City he chewed out Lila Mae Brooks and the other delegates furiously. Over and over he kept saying, "You got to ask the man for what he can deliver. I was ashamed of you today, shakin' your finger at him."

But the day before, Hosea had been out there for seven hours, calling Ramsey Clark a criminal and a Pharaoh and a white god, and threatening to tear his playhouse down. People like Lila Mae Brooks don't understand about ballet, about symbols, about the uses of rhetoric. They thought it was all for real.

In the evenings I sat with shadows around the trash fires that gave Resurrection City the look of a Civil War encampment; or I drank sweet wine between cold plywood walls, with the rain thudding on the plastic skylight. Somewhere around the Baltimore shacks, the kids would be beating on garbage cans, on bottles and metal pipes, drumming out the same rainy riff for five or ten minutes at a time, and then breaking flawlessly to a new phrase. There would be a candle blowing, and someone asleep in a corner.

"It's bullshit, brother, you know that. They ain't done nothin' right since we got here, and it wouldn't make no damn difference anyway. Johnson ain't gone give us nothin' that matters. No way."

"You hear they tryin' to kill Abernathy?"

"Yeah, that would do it, man. I ain't sayin' I dig Abernathy so much, but that would have to be it. Black power all the way then."

"I called my mama last night, and they ain't had one welfare check come in since I left there. Somebody said they was gone do that to anybody went to Washington, but I didn't believe it."

"Your mama! Willie Evans from Dearborn, his mama called home and she found out somebody had done ripped the roof right off her house. Just skin it right off, man, like you skin a banana. Just skin the whole roof off."

"Goddamn, they want it to happen! They want it to be the fire, and people gettin' shot up and killed. And they gone get it like that, too—I don't see no way 'round it. I know it's comin'."

A friend of mine called them the moribunds: the young men and women who were so sure that they were going to be killed very soon. I remember how many of them wondered aloud often whether they would actually be able to shoot at their white friends when the time came.

Cleveland Red, who might be seventeen or twenty-five, told me one evening that it was the Mafia behind all the trouble between black and white, behind all the trouble in the world. "We got to stop them, man, you and me. You telling me we gone let five thousand of them turn three billion of us around?" He never pretended to be nonviolent. "Shit, I been violent all my life, only I never called it that. You don't think about it, you just like a damn fish in the water. And they tryin' to tell me about that Gandhi."

There was a lovely black woman from Newark who used to bounce up in front of me on the skiddy duckboards, demanding, "How are you today, my brother? How are you really holding out?" Her name was Dolores, and she had high cheeks and long, clean fingers. She was an astrology nut and called everyone by his or her zodiac name. Once she said to me, "Your race is finished, your time is over everywhere. I'm talking astrologically now, not politically. Even if you started to do right, it still wouldn't make any difference to the stars. Your cycle is over, that's all. Exhausted."

I liked her very much. I said, "Please don't call me 'you' like that."

"I know, I'm sorry," she said. "But I have to do that, or else it just gets impossible."

On the night of June 4, Collins and I were roused in our shack by the rusty splutter of the public-address system coming to life. We came awake swearing, "—Two in the damn morning, and they still play-toy-ing around with that damn thing—" and then the words began to sink in. "Senator Robert F. Kennedy has been shot in Los Angeles."

Robert Kennedy's murder marks a dividing line in the history of the Poor People's Campaign. In that week, Resurrection City's population—three thousand when we arrived on May 22—fell to about five hundred; in that numb and silent week, with a moratorium on all demonstrations, the last of the campaign's energy trickled away. When the demonstrations resumed, they had contracted to a twenty-four-hour vigil at the Department of Agriculture, protesting Orville Freeman's refusal to recommend that food stamps be issued free of charge. It was at that time also that Ralph Abernathy was apparently forced by the SCLC staff to withdraw his support of Bayard Rustin—vulnerable as both as a leftist and as a gay man—as the organizer of the June 19 "Solidarity Day" demonstration. The date, celebrated as "Juneteenth" among black people in Texas, was chosen because it wasn't until that day—in 1865, more than two years after the Emancipation Proclamation—that slaves in Texas finally learned that they were free.

The Broadway and Hollywood visitors still came to Resurrection City, and that church money and assistance that only Martin Luther King's people could have mobilized kept coming until the end. Living conditions did improve somewhat: SCLC managed to get electric lights, sewer lines, and a couple of drinking fountains installed, and a well-equipped day-care center constructed. But the sense of having been abandoned by the campaign leaders grew just as steadily. There were at least three invasions of the Pitts Motor Hotel by different groups from Resurrection City, demanding angrily that Abernathy and his staff move out. They did at last, just before Solidarity Day, but by then it meant less than nothing.

The organizers, the brilliant, charismatic heirs of Dr. King—Andrew Young, Jesse Jackson, Hosea Williams, James Bevel—all withdrew, little by little, not so much in the body—after all, they worked terribly hard, and stayed up all night holding conferences, and at the last Ralph Abernathy went to jail for twenty days—but in spirit. The withdrawal of the spirit has nothing to do with the activities of the body; in fact, there is often an inverse relationship. And the further away SCLC drew from embarrassing, hopeless Resurrection City, the more desperately they put on the messy people who stayed there. The saddest lie was the one about the "waves of marchers" all across the country, ready to move into Resurrection City if and when it was emptied by mass arrests. There was another about alternate camps being established in Virginia and Maryland.

There isn't much to say about Solidarity Day. Very few people knew who Bayard Rustin was, nor Sterling Tucker (his replacement, recruited hurriedly from the Washington Urban League), but many—the young especially—sensed that the difference didn't matter at all to the Poor People's Campaign. Dolores the astrologer said it early. "They'll make a jillion speeches, and sing 'We Shall Overcome,' and pledge to go home and work in their own communities. And then they'll climb right back on those buses. No, it's over, brother, all that sociable stuff. It's over."

Some 50,000 people showed up on June 19, representatives of all the old alliances: the labor unions and the college students, the intellectuals, the clergy, the concerned middle class; Peter, Paul and Mary, Eartha Kitt. Hubert Humphrey made an appearance, and was booed. Eugene McCarthy was cheered. There were a jillion speeches, many of them quite good. But it was a very hot day, and there were few places where people could sit down and still hear the speakers on the steps of the Lincoln Memorial. By the time Ralph Abernathy spoke, it was nearly six o'clock—time for the buses to leave—and the crowd had frayed to 10,000 at most.

The night before, I had sat for a long time with four middle-aged black men on the raised porch that one of them had built in front of his shack, listening to a record of Martin Luther King's speeches. Nobody said anything, but as each side ended they turned the record over to play the other again. I thought of that, listening to Abernathy.

The Poor People's Campaign

"I intend to stay here until justice rolls out of the halls of Congress, and righteousness falls from the Administration, and the rough places of the Government agencies are made plain, and the crooked deals of the military-industrial complex become straightforward." Dr. King was lucky to die when he did. It could have been him up there, telling lies with his heart breaking, instead of on that long-playing record in the night.

I left Resurrection City the next day. The camp's federal permit was due to expire on June 23, but I never thought the police would come in. I didn't understand ballet as well as I thought. Dolores's stars predicted it all, doubtless: not only Ralph Abernathy's big solo—the last march to the Capitol to be arrested—and the equally important ensemble of the thousand policemen stomping down the snow fence and flattening the shacks; but the kids throwing rocks at the cars cruising around their island, and the cops blanketing the place with tear gas at three in the morning. That wasn't part of the dance; but then classical ballet, classical theater, isn't much in vogue today. They have this thing now where the audience gets up on the stage.

The last time I saw Collins Harris, he was adding a whole new section to the shack we had lived in for four weeks, to make room for more people. He had already made a table and a clothes closet, and he talked about putting in a little stove. When we said good-bye, he said, "Well, Pete, I enjoyed just about every moment we spent together, and the few I didn't, they wasn't your fault." I heard later that he got ten days in jail.

Peter S. Beagle is the author of the novel Tamsin, *and of such other books as* The Last Unicorn, A Fine and Private Place, *and* The Innkeeper's Song. *He studied with Monty Culver and the late Edwin L. Peterson Jr. at the University of Pittsburgh, graduating in 1959. At present he lives in Davis, California.*

How Butterflies Grew Wings

KEELY BOWERS

My mother wanted to be a writer. She kept a green folder with writing in it in a box in our cellar, on the top shelf of the metal cabinet above her dresses wrapped in plastic. Her Freeport High School yearbook was up there too, musty smelling, with petals of dried roses caught between its pages, and folded notes from her high school boyfriend, Jimmy Burden. She showed me the box when I was nine, on a cloudy weekend when she decided to clean out the cabinets and instead ended up reading cross-legged on the hard cellar floor.

In the folder were poems and themes she wrote in high school English classes, and they were marked with red, teachers' ink. They were about "Sorrow" and "A Time Machine" and "My Mother" and a lot of other things. She read them to me on the floor while I listened, my nightgown stretched like a tent over my knees. She read as if she stood beneath lights, stagestruck, lifting her head and placing one hand on her chest during the most moving parts, demanding my attention. She read about a woman struggling toward her lost lover across a desert landscape, a woman with a fear-gripped heart and "fatigue-clenched eyelids," and when she read that line she stopped.

"You know," she said, "the teacher made fun of me about that. About the fatigue-clenched eyelids. He laughed, and he wanted me to show him what that looked like. But I mean, can't you just imagine it?"

she asked me. "This woman is *dying* of exhaustion under the *scorching* desert sun, can't you just *see* her eyes like that?" and I nodded quickly. My mother squinted her eyes and tried to show me what the woman looked like. "And her lips," she said, touching her own lips gently, "they were parched and burned from the sun's rays, and the backs of her hands," she said, touching the back of my hand on the floor, "were blistered and raw—I mean, can't you just see it?"

"Yes," I said, still nodding. And I could see it. I could absolutely see it all—the sun and the blisters and the cracked lips and even the clenched eyelids, and I thought the story was wonderful. I wanted her to read me more, so we spent the morning and part of the afternoon under the dim cellar bulb while the furnace hummed behind us.

"Everyone else made their time-machine poems about the future," she said. "Stupid robot and spaceship poems and cars that fly. But see, I made mine be about the past." She read to me about the time machine that would transport her to Camelot and castles and brave knights on horses, sorcerers, and princesses awaiting their loves. And when she would finish each piece she would grin and blink her eyes at me, waiting for my response. I would tell her it was good and look closely at her, try hard to see my mother as a high school girl at a desk, pushing her pen carefully across a page.

She showed me her senior yearbook pictures, how she was voted Best Actress in *Rebel Without a Cause,* and there was a picture of her sitting on the edge of a director's chair. She wore a striped sweater and a white ribbon around her hair, which was shiny and black. Her hands perched tensely on her knees like restless birds about to take flight. She was smiling, but her eyes were not. They were small and tired and dark-looking, and she told me, "It's not a very good picture."

She read to me the signed messages from her friends, who all said things like "Good luck" and "To a funny girl" and "Remember all the good times." But then she read one by a girl named Barbara, who said she was off to New York to become a poet, and she hoped to see my mother soon in the Village. My mother explained to me that Greenwich Village was where beatniks hung out. When I asked her what beatniks were, she told me they were writers who were poor and looked like hippies. I asked her if she had wanted to be a beatnik in the Village, but she told me no, that really she had wanted to go to Scotland and live on the moors and write—like the Brontës, she said, and she talked about high sea cliffs and fog-swept fields and waves crashing against rocks where maidens had leapt.

At that time, my mother had never been farther from our home in Kittanning, Pennsylvania, than Niagara Falls, where she and my father had honeymooned. There were places she wanted to see, like Arizona and Paris and Africa. There had even been talk of our moving to Egypt, something about phone lines and recruiting men. My father worked for the phone company, and over supper one night he had only mentioned it. My mother had called all her friends and talked about it for days, telling them breathlessly, "Guess what! Looks like we might be moving to Egypt!" She had wanted my father to hurry up and put his name in or sign up or do whatever he had to do. Pyramids and camels and desert and the mysterious Nile she had talked about. She had told me she played Cleopatra in a high school play, and that people thought she looked like Elizabeth Taylor back then.

There were no pyramids, no tickets to Egypt, but just before I turned eleven, in December of the next year, we went to California. My father had business in San Francisco, and my mother and I got to go along, leaving my little brother with my grandparents.

My mother was thrilled, and she bought new clothes for the occasion—sundresses and bright shorts and yellow high-heeled sandals. "Don't these look like California?" she said to me at Kaufmann's, holding up a pair of overalls with little green palm trees all over them. She bought them for me, along with a pair of orange sunglasses, and it all went into the giant plaid suitcase, which we had to struggle to close. But in San Francisco it was blustery cold and gray, and the new, bright clothes stayed packed. We wore coats with our hoods up, and my mother swore up and down the piers at Fisherman's Wharf our first day there. It was cold at the beach, too, and foggy, and she swore about the dog turds in the sand, crossed her arms, and glared as my father snapped pictures. I got an earache. After that, she and I stayed at the hotel in San Jose while my father attended his telephone company meetings and seminars.

The hotel restaurant had burned down a few days before we'd arrived, so my mother and I had to find another place to eat breakfast. We would walk down the long hill of the hotel drive and cross ten lanes of traffic, my mother clutching her purse and squeezing my hand and yanking me across the highway to the little islands in the middle where we would wait again, and then dash again to another island, and finally to the other side.

When we entered the restaurant my mother found company in the friendly waitresses, who filled both of our cups with black, steaming coffee. Within about ten minutes my mother had told them all about us—how we were from a town near Pittsburgh and we didn't have ten lanes anywhere in Pittsburgh like that, how she had expected California to be warmer, and how the view from our hotel-room picture window was the lousy remains of that fried restaurant. My mother and I would take our time, eating stacks of pancakes and sausage while she told her new friends how afraid she was about getting us back across that sea of speeding cars.

We didn't take a bus anywhere, or a train. We certainly didn't venture into San Francisco ourselves—not without my father. So we sat by the hotel pool every day, which was contaminated and roped off. Pieces of burnt material lay at the bottom of the deep end like the bodies of dead fish, and signs told us, "No Swimming." It was too cold anyway. We were the only ones out there, so we had our choice of the white deck chairs. We lay in the sun in sweatshirts and jeans with our hands pushed into our pockets, and business men looked strangely at us on their way to their rooms.

There beside the pool I showed my mother the story I was writing. It was an assignment for school. I was in the fifth grade, and we were to write what my teacher had called a folktale, a story about how an animal had gotten to be itself. I was trying to write about rabbits and why their noses twitch and was having a hard time with it, so I asked her. My mother took my tablet and read it, and she shook her head. "Rabbits? No, no, you can do better than this. Forget rabbits. Now let's see, just let me think a minute." I scribbled on the arm of my chair, disappointed that she hadn't found anything in what I'd written.

"How Butterflies Grew Wings," she said suddenly, sitting upright.

"That's dumb," I said. "Lisa Walton is doing that. It's already taken." Lisa Walton went around humming. Lisa Walton wore pink dresses and walked on her toes.

"So what?" my mother said. "All the more reason! Yours will be the best."

She told me what to write. She started with, "It was a damp and dreary day in the Land of Nothings and Nobodys," and she made up a character named Camden the Caterpillar, who would save a fairy princess from a spider by spinning its silk around the spider's legs. Camden would be rewarded by the princess's magic—the fairy princess would make Camden and all caterpillars change from homely earthbound creatures into beautiful winged ones, and my mother used words like "cumbersome" and "majestic" and I complained, told her I couldn't use words like that or they'd think someone else had written it, but she wouldn't back down. "'Cumbersome' means clumsy. Anybody asks, you tell them that. And 'majestic' is full of power and beauty and magic. Like those mountains over there." She pointed at the brown peaks in the distance that looked flat against the sky. "Now you know what they mean so you can use them." I was still doubtful, sure that Mr. Trudgin would see right through it, sure he'd call me up to his desk and question me suspiciously. But I wrote it all down.

Later that evening my mother would hurl a bucket of ice against the wall of our room and demand that my father put us on a plane back to Pittsburgh. She would tell him she'd had enough of goddamned California, that it was nothing but a goddamned burnt restaurant and beaches of shit and he could shove his goddamned phone company meetings. My mother and I would take the red-eye flight home that night without my father, four days early. My mother would have to scrape the ice off the windshield of our car in the Pittsburgh airport parking lot without gloves, and she would curse my father even more, while I watched from the front seat. But that afternoon in the chilly sunlight, our last day in California, with the wind on our ears and our noses running, my mother's imagination was set loose and running, and she conjured words from an enchanted place I couldn't see and held them out to me in her palms, still glowing.

Mr. Trudgin thought it was wonderful. Lisa Walton did not. Mr. Trudgin read my story to the class while I sank down low in my chair, embarrassed and thrilled, and he told me I ought to send it to *Highlights* magazine, or *Jack and Jill*. I raced home after school to tell my mother, and she took me out to celebrate at the Rusty Lantern, the restaurant on the river where she worked as a hostess. She told her waitress friends there that I had written a story that was going to be published, and I just smiled and sucked on my straw and began to believe, somehow, that it *was* my story.

The summer before I started high school, my father's company transferred us to Williamsport, a small town in the mountains of central Pennsylvania. My mother missed her restaurant friends desperately. She scraped the dirt-brown paint off the cheap woodwork in our new house until she was raging mad, and my father stood helpless in doorways. She threw a jelly jar at him. It exploded on the blank kitchen wall like a purple star, and she shouted at him to leave it there, just like that, because that's what she thought of this goddamned house and this godforsaken town. I ran quietly up the stairs to my room. She cried and shouted at the same time, and my heart felt squeezed tight as a fist. She threatened to snatch up my brother and me and move us back so fast it would make my father's head spin, so help her, God.

Then my mother found a job as a unit secretary in a hospital. She gave up her silky hostess dresses and high heels for a blue and white smock and uniform pants. She went through a period of training that exhausted her. She told frightening stories about dying people, about a man's brain running out on his pillow when they attempted to change his bandages. The man had shot himself. My mother smoked cigarettes and sipped hot tea when she came home, held her head in her hands. I helped her memorize medical terminology at the kitchen table late at night, quizzed her on the meanings of *-ectomy* and *-itis* and *-otomy*, pointed out diagrams in my own physiology textbook. I thought I might like to be a surgeon, or a coroner like the TV character Quincy, or a scientist who spent long hours gazing through microscopes at maps of tissue samples and collecting valuable data for research. My mother was happy about this. Biology had actually been her second love, she told me, next to writing.

In my room at night, I wrote poems in a plain blue diary that I locked with a tiny gold key. From my window I watched the radio tower flash red signals on the mountain, and I dreamed up stories. I wrote about a runaway girl who finds a runaway boy living under the radio tower in the woods, and they swim naked in the moonlight and ride his motorcycle through the streets of town like mystery lovers. I tried to imitate my mother's descriptive language and drama.

At one point, encouraged by my English teacher, I decided to submit a story to the high school newspaper. I labored over the story for days, carried it around in my spiral notebook. I stared at it on the crowded school bus waiting for some kind of magic to lift my story off the page, but it was always awkward and wrong-sounding, the sentences stiff and flat like grounded kites no matter how hard I ran with them. I kept tearing the story out. Then, pressed for time, I secretly searched the downstairs closet for my mother's folder of writing. I found a Halloween story she had written about being followed through the neighborhood by a ghost. I stole it all, but I made it my neighborhood. It came out in the school paper, but I never showed my mother. I wanted to pretend it was mine.

It was the only kind of attention I sought. If my mother was queen of the stage in high school, I was the opposite. I avoided notice, moved silently through the crowded hallways as if I were invisible. I ate my lunch between dusty stacks in the school library with my nose pushed into a book. I could never style my straight hair to look the way it was supposed to, so I stuffed it into a ponytail every day and forgot about it. My mother held my appearance under close scrutiny, wrinkled her face at me. She told me I should really put rollers in my hair, tweeze my bushy eyebrows, wear shadow to draw boys' attention to my eyes. I was inept at makeup. I wore thick black eyeliner only, which I thought made me look mysterious, and I wore cowboy boots and jeans every day. My mother told me I looked trashy. "You should always wear shadow to match your eyes," she insisted. "We both need to wear green." I refused. Green shadow made my eyelids look like I'd colored them with fat green chalk.

My mother would stand before her bathroom mirror and paint her eyes like Cleopatra's, pluck her eyebrows into thin feathered arcs, brush her cheekbones with bronze sparkly powder that made her look like she'd been to a Caribbean island. She would never leave the house without her eyes, without lipstick carefully applied, and fragrance surrounding her in a cloud, nearly visible. She didn't let the drab hospital smock cramp her style. She bought long stylish earrings to match her navy-blue uniform pants, and she painted her nails crimson. My mother walked the sidewalks of town under an imaginary spotlight, and she expected the same of me.

When I was in college my mother proudly put my picture in the Sunday paper under the title of "Kid of the Week," something parents in Williamsport did for their younger children's accomplishments, like little Billy's first home run, not their college kids, which was especially humiliating. The caption said I was at Pitt studying to be a doctor and making the dean's list, and what a wonderful person I was. My mother the press agent. I desperately hoped everyone I knew in that town had somehow forgotten to read the paper that day. I was already pushing science to the edge of my desk, squeezing by with a *C* in the last chemistry class I would ever take, my interest in science giving way to my desire to write.

My mother told me her story in the spring, toward the end of my junior year of college. My father was away fishing, and I was spending the weekend at home for my mother's birthday. I asked my mother about her high school boyfriends, about Jimmy Burden in particular, and why she hadn't ended up with him. I knew how special he'd been to her, knew his name was scribbled on the labels of her old 45 records in her slanty teenage handwriting. I knew it was Jimmy Burden she dreamed about when she blasted those scratchy records and ironed my father's shirts. I asked her what he looked like. I asked her if she had thought about marrying him back then and why they had broken up. We were in the kitchen, just finishing the supper dishes, and my mother made coffee.

"I had a baby," she told me. Just like that.

I waited, dumbstruck, while she got up to get more coffee. She said, "I always worried you'd meet up with and marry your half-brother, like they do on the soaps."

"It was Jimmy Burden's?"

"Whose else?" she said, raising her eyebrows at me.

She told me everything. She told me about the summer she spent in Pittsburgh when she was seventeen and pregnant, at a home for thirty unwed mothers. My grandmother didn't want the neighbors to know. She told me about the room she stayed in with the window overlooking the hot city street and the cot against the wall with the yellow blanket, the other girls she met, some who were farther along, some not so far. She told me about the rules, how they were to dress, how they had to wear skirts and nylon stockings in the sticky heat, weren't allowed makeup or nail polish. She told me about the chores, how she had kitchen duty for a while, which meant getting up in the dark before everyone else, but she kept overcooking the eggs, so they moved her to cleaning duty. She told me she would lie down on the floor on the far side of a bed with her broom underneath and sleep that way, until she heard the housemother's heavy footsteps coming down the hallway. Then she would quickly move the broom back and forth. She said it was like punishment.

We stayed up half the night at the kitchen table, and my mother talked and smoked cigarettes, blew the smoke out the screen door, and outside rain tapped against the wooden porch railing. She remembered everything, every detail. She remembered the leaf-green color of Jimmy's shirt the first night they went out, and the raspberry ice cream she had the last day she ever saw him. She told her story with urgency, as she tells all her stories. She makes you listen. She doesn't want you to forget.

"Mum would come pick me up in Pittsburgh sometimes on Saturdays and take me home to Slate Lick for the day," my mother said. "It was funny. She'd drive the car down through the grass and pull right up to the back porch so the neighbors wouldn't see me getting out of the car. I would have to hurry up the back steps. She told everyone I was in Washington, D.C., with my aunt. She even made me write phony letters to my friends and tell stories about what I saw in D.C. so no one would be suspicious. Sometimes I resented it, and then sometimes I had fun with the letters, making up stories about a place I'd never seen and bragging about sweeping romances with strangers I met on trains. I would give them to Mum, and she would send them to my aunt, who would mail them to my friends from there so the postmark would be right."

I asked her what Jimmy was doing during all of this. She said she didn't hear from him. He planned to go to college, she said, so he didn't want to marry her. But she said she waited for him to call. She told me she listened to dedications on the radio station at night and sat on the windowsill in the dark after lights out, waiting for a breeze. She watched cars pass and heard the city sounds. She wore Jimmy's class ring around her neck on a long chain underneath her blouse. She wrote in a diary. She wrote Jimmy letters but didn't mail them. He never called. One night, she said, she sat on the sill for a long time, put her hand on her belly and felt the baby moving. She sat that way, and then she pulled Jimmy's ring off the chain and threw it down to the street.

"Do you hate him?" I asked her.

"I never hated him," she said.

She told me she wished she had kept the writing she did in that room. "I wanted to put it behind me," she said. "But you know I wish I had it now. I think it would be good to read what I wrote." She told me that soon after she'd left the home, she met my father and married him quickly, hoping to replace the child she'd lost.

While she told me this, I imagined Jimmy Burden as she'd described him, with his red hair and lifeguard tan and blue Chevy convertible, driving fast along the river with his radio and his buddies and his college plans, approaching escape velocity. I wanted to hate him, even if she didn't.

Back in Pittsburgh, a week before that semester let out, I wrote her story. It was the first time I had ever written something so real and called it fiction, and I remembered the details as she had told them, made the story a first-person account and tried to slide into her skin, looked out at the Pittsburgh street from my dorm-room window above Fifth Avenue and tried to imagine she was looking at it from a small room in summer in 1966. She had lived here, I thought, and I had never known it. She'd had a baby she'd had to walk away from, down the front steps of that home in October to my grandmother's waiting car, the baby left in a room behind her and the summer far gone. What was she dreaming about then, during the car ride home to Slate Lick, I wondered. Her life must have seemed as wide and empty as the yellow fields they passed, unraveling on all sides.

But things would come together. My grandmother would see to that. She would get someone to give my mother a job at the phone company as an operator, and my mother would sink safely into routine, earn a paycheck, eat lunch at Mike and Lil's with the other office girls everyday. There wouldn't be any talk of college—my grandmother didn't see it as a choice for women. My mother would meet my father at the phone company and try to slip out of dates with him. But he was persistent. He would drive the thirty miles into the country to get her, come sleet or snow, she always said, rolling her eyes. And at night in my grandmother's house, she would dream she heard her lost baby crying and she would wake up sobbing in the dark, clutching at the sheets.

From my dorm room I watched the lights on the avenue change to flashing, and the weight of my mother's story fell like a bundle into my arms. I felt responsible for telling it right, for seeing everything she wanted me to see, but our dreams were not interchangeable. The story would be hers, but it would be my conjuring, my own view from my window holding me firmly in place.

My mother came to stay with me once when I was in graduate school. I was teaching the morning she arrived, and I told her to meet me on the fifth floor of the Cathedral of Learning after I had let my class out. She was very excited about this. She would see the building I taught in and meet the people I talked about, and she was careful to get directions. She worried about what she should wear and asked me for suggestions over the phone, told me she didn't want to look funny, told me she wanted to look like a graduate student, so maybe she'd wear a long denim skirt and gauze blouse and her Indian jewelry. "Would that look okay?" she wanted to know. "I mean I wore this outfit to the mall and one of the sales girls told me I looked like a *poet*. It just made my day. I told her my daughter is a writer and that you and I like to wear gauzy clothes like this."

"I don't wear gauzy clothes," I told her, annoyed and sounding like a punky fifteen-year-old, resisting the parallel she was trying to draw between us and the image she had of what poets look like. We argued for a while about what kind of clothes I wear, and when we hung up I felt guilty, thinking I'd hurt her feelings.

I was busy that weekend finishing a story for my manuscript, and while I typed in the living room, my mother ran the sweeper, dusted, mopped my bathroom floor. "If you'd keep up with the dusting it wouldn't build up so much," she said. I lifted my feet so she could sweep underneath me. "You don't have to do all this," I told her, knowing that, of course, she did. She is forever putting things in order, cleaning, rearranging. She vacuums the footprints off the carpet in her own house and yells at my father for walking on her freshly swept floors. He is supposed to use the throw rugs as stepping stones to get to the couch and not let his feet touch the carpet.

"You just go ahead and write and don't worry about what I'm doing," she said. Then she wanted to know what I was writing about, and I told her a little about what was happening in the story. She asked me more questions. She began offering suggestions. First they were melodramatic. "Well," she said, "what if Valerie needed a kidney transplant, and the mother had to give her a kidney? *That* would reunite them." Then she said, "Or maybe Valerie kills herself, and the mother finds her, and the coffee cup Valerie had been drinking out of is *still* warm? Now that would be something! Can't you just see her standing there, holding that warm cup, gazing out the window at the rain?"

I laughed, I covered my head, I yelled at her to stop. I said that no, of course, I couldn't write those things, that those things were awful and she argued a little, and then she went back to vacuuming. But for the rest of the morning she kept wandering in between cleaning tasks and offering me more suggestions, toning them down a bit to make them more acceptable to me, but still pushing for suicide. "No," I said. "There will be no warm coffee cup. And no 'fatigue-clenched eyelids' either."

"Hey!" she shouted, resisting a laugh and pointing her finger at me, "I was a good writer, damn it."

We took a walk through Shadyside that weekend. My mother wanted to see the house she'd stayed in when she was seventeen. When we found it, it appeared abandoned, with its vacant porch and dark windows and vines snaking up the orange bricks. "Yes," she said. "There it is." She pointed to the window that had been hers, on the second floor. I imagined her up there looking out, and I imagined Jimmy Burden's ring hitting the ground at our feet, looked down at the sidewalk as if I expected to find it there.

"I remember the day I walked down those steps," she said. "See, you went in the front door when you first got here and you came through it when you last left the place. In between you had to use the back door." She pointed at the large window on the ground floor. "And the baby was in there." She told me she cried so hard coming down the steps that she couldn't see. She told me my grandmother shouted up the steps at her, told her, "You want him then, go get him, goddamn it!" My mother had paused only a moment to imagine she might really have a choice, the sidewalk blurring and turning colors through her tears. Everything must have stopped for her just then, just for that instant when she saw the shimmer of a possibility and just as suddenly watched it vanish, knowing the decision had been made for her months ago.

Sometimes my mother sees my life as romantic. There is the idea of being a writer. She tells people, "My daughter is a writer." She took one of my story titles, "White Dove," and put it on the license plate of her new car, thinking it would bring me luck. She refers to her car officially by that name now. "Gotta go wash White Dove," she'll say. Sometimes she calls me on the phone excitedly offering title suggestions for my novel. But sometimes, too, the reality of my situation is too much. Then I get a different kind of phone call.

She wants to know what's taking me so long to finish the book, and when it will be published, and when I will have a respectable income and buy a house, and have children, a washer and dryer, a new car like hers. Because no matter what she once wanted to be, she became something else, and life with my father has given her certain expectations and a strong safety net. When I gave up science she understood. "I had an awful time in chemistry," she told me, accepting my decision because she believed it made me similar to her. And she embraced my desire to write because it had once been hers, and along with it all the romantic images that to her suggested a free spirit and independence and the ability to make a mark on the world. I would be like her, and I would pick up the dream where she had dropped it, and she would cheer from the sidelines. But the images she has clash with the life she knows, and the idea is safer than the real.

In my aunt's pool in Kittanning last summer, the three of us, my aunt, my mother, and I, floated on rafts in the sun. When I told them my boyfriend, Jon, and I were going to California at the end of August, my mother asked me, "Why would you want to go there? If it were me I'd go to Colorado or New Mexico. California sucks, don't you remember? Did you tell him you want to go somewhere else, is he making you go to California? Why don't you tell him you want to go somewhere else?"

But I told her that it was decided, that *we* had decided, and that we'd be in San Francisco for ten days. My aunt asked me if we were eloping, and I laughed. "Not yet," I told her. "I'll let you know."

"You'd better not be," my mother said, and I got out of the pool and sat on the edge, letting my feet dangle in the water. Beyond my aunt's tidy backyard is a wide field and an odd clump of trees in the distance on a hill. When I was a kid I saw those same trees from the swingset in our backyard, and when I swung high enough, my feet reached the tops of them. I was thinking about this and wanting to change the subject of our conversation when my mother said, "Neither of you is in a position to get married right now."

"We're not getting married yet," I said, impatiently. "And what do you mean 'position' anyway?"

She turned to look at me from her raft, shading her eyes with her hand. "And you know it would be a terrible, terrible thing if you got pregnant. You have nothing to offer a child."

My aunt began to defend me, said what kind of a thing is that to say, but I laughed out loud and told my mother, "You *would* say that," and pretended to be untouched by it.

I only thought about it later, when they all left—my parents, my aunt and uncle—for the Wheeling greyhound races, and I sat on the back porch watching lightning bugs dart over the grass.

Jon is a writer and a musician, which is a difficult subject between my mother and me. In her eyes, he's not dependable. He's a drummer—not a good catch, so I should toss him back and try for someone else. She still points out pictures of attractive men in Eddie Bauer catalogues, men she would like to see herself with—men in smart-looking business suits and men standing on boat docks wearing fishermen's knit sweaters and posing ruggedly for the camera. "Now," she'll say, "you would look good with somebody like him. Doesn't he look outdoorsy?" because image is everything. Image is the dream and the romance and the mountain seen from a distance. It is California before you get there and the pyramids of Egypt and writing on the moors. It's the man in the catalogue picture who, of course, isn't what he appears to be.

At my aunt's house, alone in the quiet, I hung up my towel and rinsed my glass in the sink and dried it and put it away. I didn't want to leave a trace. Her house is as spotless as my mother's, where everything has its place and everything has been carefully planned. And while I cleaned up and got ready to drive back to the city I felt caught in the web of my mother's contradictions. When she was twenty-nine she had two children in school and a husband managing a company and a house surrounded by flowerbeds. To my mother, my life looks awfully disordered.

Before my trip to the West Coast, I visited my parents in Williamsport. I dug out the yearbooks after supper one evening, my father's, too, this time. In my father's yearbook all the seniors were asked what their plans were, and my mother puzzled over the girls' aspirations. They planned to be married. They planned to attend beauty school. They planned to be secretaries. "How boring!" she exclaimed, putting her hands on her hips. "Can you imagine saying something like that? If they had asked me, I'd have said something a lot better than that. I'd have said I planned to travel extensively and be an archaeologist, or be a writer in Arizona, or become a doctor and treat sick children in Africa. Who in their right mind would say that they just planned to be married?" She never hinted at knowing that though she would have said those things, she would never have—couldn't have—done them. And again I got to see my mother sitting in the director's chair, only this time I knew why her eyes were dark and tired, and I imagined her walking around the school halls hiding her pregnancy, getting sick in the girls' room, failing chemistry because she couldn't concentrate—my mother who looked like Elizabeth Taylor and held the hearts of boys.

In the box with the yearbooks was a single piece of my mother's writing left from that folder she once had. She had gotten rid of the rest somewhere along the way when she was cleaning, and for some reason held onto one. It was the piece called "My Mother," but she grabbed it out of my hand before I could read it. "What's that doing in there?" she said, and she read a little to herself.

"Let me see it," I said, but when I reached for it, she frowned and tore it up before my eyes.

I yelled at her. "Why'd you do that?"

"It's stupid," she said.

"It's not stupid!"

"It's awful writing."

"I can't believe you just tore that up."

She was embarrassed. She didn't say it, but she thought I'd make fun of it and say it was bad—now that I'm older, now that I'm a writer myself. But I would never have done that. I would have seen myself as a high school girl at a desk, struggling to write what was most important to me.

I called my mother from California, and I talked to her on the back patio of the house we were staying in. The sun had left its red tracings across the sky like streamers, and my skin felt heated warm from the beach and the wine I'd drunk. California had dazzled me. I felt charged and awake, and I wanted to tell her how we'd rented a car that could handle curves as well as White Dove and raced down Highway 1 under a blue sky with the wind whipping our hair. I wanted to tell her how we'd explored rocky beaches where waves crashed and touched starfish in tidal pools, how we'd fallen asleep under a warm blanket in the sand. I wanted to tell her how we ate seafood omelettes and shrimp chowder in wharf restaurants with friends who drove up to meet us from Los Angeles, and though we were broke, we drank wine in cafés in North Beach and walked hand-in-hand through the foggy city each night, danced under flickering neon, drove over bridges and through avenues of lights. I wanted to tell her all of this, but I stopped. My words broke against a barrier reef and scattered when I realized she didn't want to hear this story.

She would rather have heard that the weather was gray, that the car had broken down in the rain, and that Jon and I had screamed across the road at each other. She would rather I had crashed a bucket of ice against a hotel-room wall, hurled a vase, demanded we fly back this instant. She would rather have heard that she was right, that Jon is the wrong man and California is beaches of shit because this she would understand—with this story we would be allies again, drawn together like we'd been by the pool in San Jose, co-conspirators dreaming of escape.

I heard her turn the stereo down, and she asked me, "Is everything all right?" Her voice was worried, sensing disaster, ready to come to my rescue. And when I began to tell her excitedly what we'd done, what we'd seen, with the whole hot and heaving West Coast rushing out of the twilight at me, I felt her pulling away, felt something click shut in her response, and I fumbled. There was silence. "So," I said, changing my tone, "how are you?"

She told me about an argument she'd had with my father, and how she was considering applying for a job in a doctor's office and leaving the hospital, and how, since it had been hazy the past few days, she couldn't get much sun, and she told me she was surprised to hear we had any sun in California because, didn't I remember, it was usually ugly. I heard her light a cigarette.

"So everything's okay?" she asked me again, still thinking I must be covering up, sweeping my dirt under the rug.

"Things are fine," I said. I resisted the urge to tell her the kind of story she wanted to hear. I told her I had to go.

After we hung up I imagined my mother sitting on the stool by the back door in her kitchen, smoking. She would finish her cigarette and dash it out, and she would turn her music up again, loud enough for the neighborhood to hear "Earth Angel," "Tonight You're Mine," and "Jimmy Lee." She would sway in front of the sink while she finished the dishes, wiped the sink dry. She would step outside into the dark to unclip her bathing suit and towels from the line and fold them neatly over her arm, while the music slipped through the screens behind her like memory, and vapor trails of jet planes crossed the sky overhead, and up on the mountain, the tower glowed red like a signal fire.

Keely Bowers received an MFA in fiction from the University of Pittsburgh. She teaches writing at Community College of Allegheny County and is currently at work on her first novel.

As I Was Walking Down Carson Street
A South Side Childhood

RICHARD F. PETERSON

Since I left Pittsburgh for good in 1965, the working-class South Side of my childhood has gone through a remarkable metamorphosis. Once distinct because of the pungent odor from the Duquesne Brewery and the black soot from the Jones & Laughlin steel mill, the South Side has become a cultural wonderland of trendy art galleries, antique shops, bookstores, and coffeeshops. Where steelworkers and Gimbels truckdrivers sat on barstools at Kalki's and Kotula's, drank their shot-and-beer combinations and sometimes mixed them into boilermakers, poets now gather for evening readings at City Books and yuppies descend from the suburbs to shoot weekend pool at Shootz Cafe and Billiards. Carson Street and environs, once populated by beer joints and greasy spoons, are now dotted with Pittsburgh's finest restaurants. If upscale Pittsburghers are looking for the city's best overall restaurant, the readers' poll of *Pittsburgh Magazine* recommends the Café Allegro down on Twelfth Street. If they want to sample the best French menu in Pittsburgh, the poll suggests Le Pommier at Twenty-First and Carson. The best European—just go up a block to the Mallorca at Twenty-Second and Carson to the spot where Bianchini's used to offer a daily luncheon special of a hot sausage sandwich and a draft of Iron City to less discerning South Siders of a past generation.

Richard F. Peterson

Along the banks of the Monongahela River, where I played hooky in the late 1940s and early 1950s from Humboldt Grade School and South Side High School, my childhood haven of overgrown weeds, washed-up debris, discarded junk, and the forgotten bottles of winos has been replaced by River Front Park with its public benches, picnic tables, and boat docks. In the same river where I waded out from shore on the industrial sludge caked on the river bottom and twisted my feet into the greasy gel to see if the waves from passing coal barges could dislodge me, families launch themselves out in recreation boats of various shapes and sizes, while the current generation of tanned, athletic-looking Pittsburgh boys and girls of summer power by on their jet-skis. Even the ballfields of my youth at Ormsby and Armstrong playgrounds and the football field at South High Stadium have undergone a strange and wondrous change. On all-dirt playground fields so dry and dusty in the summer that city workers oiled them, grass now grows in the outfield. And on my old rock-hard high school football field, the memories of lopsided games lost to Westinghouse, Peabody, and Allderdice are buried under a layer of artificial turf.

This virtual disappearance of the grimy, working-class South Side of my childhood hardly seems the stuff for a fondly written memoir about growing up in Pittsburgh in the late 1940s and the 1950s. In *An American Childhood* Annie Dillard did observe—"It was a great town to grow up in, Pittsburgh"—but Dillard's Pittsburgh of the 1950s was the Point Breeze world of country clubs, dance schools, and family servants. I can share in Dillard's memories of playing on cobblestone streets and streetcar tracks and taking class trips to the Carnegie Museum, but the boys of her American childhood, the "Central boys," destined in the 1950s to "inherit corporate Pittsburgh," were not the companions of my youth. My companions were Dillard's "oddball boys, none of whom has inherited Pittsburgh," and my childhood world of play was characterized by forbidden explorations of the rag factory and scrapyard that bracketed Merriman Way, where I grew up under the shadow of the decaying and doomed Brady Street Bridge.

As I Was Walking Down Carson Street

My field trips were furtive adventures with oddball boys into the darkened bins of Gimbels' warehouse or through the sprawling dunes of the Iron City Sand and Gravel Company as well as those secretive outings along the railroad tracks that wound their way past Levenson Steel and took us down to the river where we waded out and swam in murky water so filthy with industrial slime and human waste that we had to shower at Ormsby's public pool to rid ourselves of the evidence—the strong reek of chemicals and the dark streaks running down our bodies—of our day at the South Side waters.

Yet, as I was walking down Carson Street during one of my recent visits to my mother and realized how difficult it had become to find a confectionery, dairy store, or movie house, let alone a beer joint or greasy spoon from my childhood, I wondered how much local history was fading out even as the South Side's new cultural vitality and diversity were now so prominently on display. Of course, as I looked for reminders of my South Side childhood, I did recognize that my concern for history was cloaked in the usual midlife nostalgia for the landmarks of one's lost youth, and I also realized that I should have been more delighted than I was with the stylish shops, clever bookstores, and classy restaurants that better fit the academic character I had begun to cultivate when I went away to college over thirty years ago. Nevertheless, like a discontented and disconnected South Side Proust, I decided to search for things past not only in my own distant and fragile remembrances but in the lived histories of those who had never left the South Side.

Like a good scholar, I spent time in the archives at the Carnegie Library and the Historical Society of Western Pennsylvania, but only when I bumped into Mary Jane Schmalstieg, a self-styled local historian, at the South Side Chamber of Commerce and listened to her talk about Mass at the old churches—Lithuanian St. Casimir's, Polish St. Adelbert's, German St. Michael's, and Ukrainian St. John's—did the ethnic character of the South Side and my own background come back to life. I read through guidebooks and histories for a sense of community and local color but only when I hung out on the corner of Nineteenth and Carson and listened to my old softball buddies and drinking companions express their contempt for the current generation of weekend warriors who binge at fashionable Mario's and Margaritaville's and leave their urine and vomit in the back alleys of the South Side did the old feelings of working-class pride and respect for community become palpable. As for my own memories of the South Side, their connection with past generations became apparent when I sat at the kitchen table and listened to my mother talk about the time her father ran the old Rex (called the Strand in those days), with its silent movies, door prizes, and bingo games, the same Rex, now restored to show art films, where every Saturday afternoon I watched Frankenstein double bills and cliffhangers featuring Zorro, the Green Hornet, and Captain Marvel.

Yet of all the historical reminders passed along to me—Mary Jane Schmalstieg's yellowed copies of the *South Side Journal*, my somehow grown slightly smaller softball jerseys emblazoned with the names of teams representing everything from the Club Café to Local 1272, my mother's black-and-white snapshots of my Little League days and the annual South Side picnic at Kennywood Park—a box score sent to me from the National Hall of Fame Library of a baseball game played in 1948 between the Pittsburgh Pirates and the Cincinnati Reds became the emotional key to the memories of my childhood on the South Side. I'm fond of telling my academic friends, when talk turns to our previous lives, that I grew up at a time and place where you either stole hubcaps or played ball and that the only perceived road out of the South Side of my youth was over the Brady Street Bridge to either Juvenile Court or Forbes Field. It was playing pickup ball in Ormsby's bandbox or Armstrong's elongated field that kept me and most of South Side's oddball boys out of trouble except for the occasional shoplifting of comic books, baseball cards, or candy bars. And it was hitchhiking out to Forbes Field to pay a buck to sit in the left-field bleachers and watch the woeful Pirates of the 1950s which gave us the hopeless hope of playing someday against the hated Bums from Brooklyn instead of becoming a bum on some streetcorner on the South Side.

My trips to Forbes Field were so important to the emotional life of my childhood that, while attending a recent baseball conference at Cooperstown, I decided to ask Tim Wiles of the National Hall of Fame Library to find that 1948 Pirates-Reds box score because I believed it was the first game my father and I attended together. After all, if I wanted to recover my South Side childhood, no memory would be as emotionally perfect as going to my first major-league game with my father. Yet no memory is more dangerous, more likely to be clouded over with emotion and transformed by the mind's eye into a moment or image of what we wanted our childhood to be like—our home team should have won the game, our boyhood hero should have hit a home run, and our father should have stuffed us with hot dogs, peanuts, and Cracker Jack. How else were we to grow up, believing that, even on the South Side, justice, courage, and love prevailed.

Realistically, however, if the likes of a Mickey Mantle actually hit a home run every time a kid like Billy Crystal went with his father to his first Yankee game, Mantle's baseball heroics would have rivaled the larger-than-life feats of Pecos Bill, Paul Bunyan, and that steel-bending Pittsburgh folk hero, Joe Magerac. But Mantle struck out far more than he hit home runs, hobbled out to center field on bad legs, ruined his health with drink, and even, now and then, lost a big game, as Pittsburghers found out to their delight in 1960, my last fall in the city before going off to college at Edinboro. But, while I remember dancing in the streets of downtown Pittsburgh, poor Billy Crystal on Ken Burns's television baseball series conjured up the tragic image of his beloved Mick crying in the clubhouse. And, while I still delight in using my memory of a shot-and-beer working-class city embracing a ballclub and each other as an example to my doubting literature students of an epiphany, Stephen Jay Gould warns his friends on the Burns series never to bring up Bill Mazeroski's home run in the seventh game of the 1960 World Series if they want to remain his friends. The problem with my memory of that buried Pirate-Red game of 1948, beyond recalling enough details to give Tim Wiles a chance to find the treasured box score, was that what I remembered about the game seemed to outglow Billy Crystal in emotion and exaggeration. In my nearly fifty-year-old recollection, the game was played in the spring of 1948, making me nine years old at the time, the Pirates won the game 8–4, and Ralph Kiner, the Mantle of my South Side childhood, hit not one but two home runs off Ewell Blackwell, a tall, lean, side-winding righthander who had an intimidating reputation for throwing at batters and once said he knew Ralph Kiner didn't like him: "I could tell he was scared, and like most right-handers, he'd bail out because my fastball would break toward the batter." The home-run king of my youth scared—just say it ain't so, Ralph: "Ewell Blackwell was a scary pitcher because he was mean and would throw at you anytime. Your legs shook when you tried to dig in on him because of his sidearm delivery. Yet I hit more home runs off Blackwell than any right-handed batter" (the quotations appear in Danny Peary's *We Played the Game*).

Well, I learned from oral history that Kiner was scared, but he did hit a lot of home runs off Blackwell, the baseball-slinging villain of my youth. And, when I opened an envelope from the National Hall of Fame Library a few weeks after my visit to Cooperstown, I discovered that Kiner actually had hit two of those home runs off Blackwell in a game played on May 2, 1948, and won by the Pirates 6–4 (not 8–4 as I remembered it). When that box score arrived from Cooperstown, I felt as if I had received a gift from the baseball gods, thanks to Mercurial Tim Wiles, a magical summons to go back to the day when my father took me out of the South Side to my first big-league game at Forbes Field. Here were the ballplayers to conjure up a perfect memory of my childhood—not only larger-than-life Ralph Kiner, but local heroes like Frankie Gustine, Wally Westlake, and Danny Murtaugh as well as an aging Dixie Walker, traded to the Pirates from

As I Was Walking Down Carson Street

the Brooklyn Dodgers because he hated playing on the same team with Jackie Robinson.

There was even a delightful surprise waiting for me on the page of box scores copied and sent by Tim Wiles. In the brief write-up of the Pirates-Reds game played on May 1, 1948, the day before I saw my first game, a Pirate pitcher with the wonderful baseball name of Fritz Ostermueller had "hurled the rampaging Pirates into first place, one half game ahead of the Giants." That meant that the Pirates, doomed to be the doormat of the National League throughout most of the 1950s, were in first place on May 2, 1948, though they were to finish fourth that year. I also discovered in the May 2 write-up that Blackwell had already beaten the Pirates twice in 1948 and had won every game he pitched against them in 1947; but the baseball gods had decreed that Kiner would hit two home runs on May 2, 1948, in his first two times at bat and the Pirates would finally beat that mean son-of-a-bitch Blackwell and stay in first place—all, of course, because I had taken the magical journey from the polluted South Side to palatial Forbes Field for the first time.

With the write-up and the details of the game in front of me, I could now imagine standing with my father at the entrance to the Brady Street Bridge, under the billboard advertising Duquesne Pilsner, the prince of beers, as we waited for the 77/54 Bloomfield to turn the corner up at Carson Street and take us to Forbes Field. I could feel myself jostled about in the overcrowded streetcar (there were over thirty thousand fans at the game) as it clattered its way across the bridge, swayed onto Forbes Avenue, passed high above the river and mills until it crossed under the Boulevard of the Allies, only to begin its crawl through Oakland traffic, past the Juvenile Court building, past the Strand with its movie posters for a Gene Autry matinee double bill, until it finally reached Bouquet Street where I lined up in front of my father and waited impatiently until it was my turn to step down from the streetcar.

In my mind's eye, I can see myself crossing Forbes Street with my father, following the host of fans toward the ballpark as everything around me explodes with sound. Vendors cry out to the crowd to buy miniature bats, autographed baseballs, Pirate pennants, and glossies of Kiner, Walker, and Rip Sewell. Others want me to try on a brand-new Pirate cap, just the thing if I'm going to sit in the left-field bleachers, or demand I get my Pirate scorecard and pencil right here instead of waiting until I get inside the ballpark. And once we reach Bouquet and Sennot, where the wondrously seductive odor of the grilled hotdogs at Tom and Jerry's floats through the air, I look up for the first time at Forbes Field, at its towering white clay facade, its array of high-arched entrances topped by large awnings, and its green-painted steel girders holding the massive three-tiered concrete oval in place. And most amazing of all, I hear the sounds of batting practice as I stand with my father at the entrance to Forbes Field.

But that's the moment, the very moment when the sounds of baseball beckon me to the pleasure palace of my youth, that my memory takes an odd turn. Rather than paying our way into the ballpark, my father and I cross over to the Home Plate Café. Instead of passing through an underground world of rusted beams and pillars to our general admission seats along the first-base line, we enter the gloomy atmosphere of the Home Plate Café and sit down on bar stools. Instead of gazing out at all the green grass and open space, at the giant scoreboard and red-bricked outfield wall as I listen to my father talk about the fabled history of the ballpark and complain about the Greenberg Gardens, I sit at the bar and stare at hanging photographs of the clumsy figure of Honus Wagner leaning over to shake hands with Ty Cobb, of a smiling Pie Traynor, crouched over, ball and glove in place, waiting to tag out a runner, of the Waner Brothers, "Big and Little Poison," sitting one behind the other, bats in hands, as I wait for my father to finish another glass of beer and take me to the game.

My memory of sitting in the Home Plate Café before my first Pirate game is as vivid to me as sitting in the general-admission seats behind first base during the game, but that box score, the Hall of Fame validation of my perfect childhood memory, tells me I'm simply wrong, that I never entered the Home Plate Café on May 2, 1948. The single game I remember so vividly as being played on a glorious Saturday afternoon was really played as the first game of a doubleheader on a gloomy, rainy Sunday. As for the missing second game: "Rain that fell throughout the first contest prevented nightcap." I clearly remember Kiner and Blackwell, but not the rain and certainly not Sunday because if my cherishly remembered game took place on Sunday, then the Home Plate Café had to be closed because of Pennsylvania's blue laws. In the remembered Sundays of my South Side childhood, I watched my father drink his beer and play poker with his oddball companions at the Duquesne Social Club, while I listened to the Pirates on the radio and played shuffleboard bowling.

My memory of attending my first big-league game with my father, while almost perfect when it came to the details of the game itself, had tricked and then misled me into the Home Plate Café, but with good reason, I suspect. At the very least, it should have alerted me to the collective nature of memory, that going to Forbes Field over the rest of the season and seasons to come must have included regular stops at the Home Plate Café before and probably after Pirate games. It also should have warned me that if I wanted to return to the South Side to retrieve other memories, my father's drinking would be waiting for me at the emotional center of even the best moments of childhood.

Because we lived in the upstairs of a house owned by my father's parents, I remember spending every Christmas supper of my childhood in my grandparents' downstairs kitchen. I remember looking forward, after spending a cold day in the drafty and poorly heated upstairs rooms, to the nearly stifling heat from my grandfather's coal-burning stove and the strong odors of my grandmother's cooking. Christmas supper, prepared by my grandmother Petrauskas, was always an array of delights and horrors from the old country. Besides the traditional ham and richly buttered mashed potatoes, my favorites were the *balandeliai*, wrapped in cabbage leaves and soaked in tomato sauce, and the *kugelis* with its rich taste of bacon and potatoes. My grandmother always wanted me to try everything, but I could never eat anything as foul-smelling as my father's favorites, like the marinated herring and the jellied pig's feet, and I was not going to put horseradish on my ham even if it would grow hair on my anemic-looking chest. It was enough that I took one of the tasteless pieces of the *plotkele* blessed by the priest at St. Casimir and, after a nod from my Protestant mother, swallowed it as my grandmother wished everyone "*Su Sventom Kaledom.*"

But my most enduring memories of Christmas supper with my grandparents never end happily or merrily. In spite of my grandmother's toast, something always goes wrong. My father, after drinking all day, either starts in about my picky eating—I should be eating with my mother's Johnny Bull relatives instead of with the Bluetails—or about my mother's job at Rodger's—she's gone all night waiting tables and sleeps all day—or about getting some respect from his family—things are going to be different once he's working again, just wait and see. By supper's end, my grandfather has walked away in disgust from the kitchen table, my grandmother is telling her son "for shame," and my mother is telling me to go with my father so he doesn't break his neck walking back upstairs.

Just as going with my father to Forbes Field is the most joyous memory of my childhood, walking back upstairs with my father after another ruined Christmas remains the most grievous. But there are memories of other journeys, mostly while walking down Carson Street, that seem more routine, more innocuous, and some even pleasant enough, unless altered by the circumstances of the time. There were always those walks with my father and mother at the beginning of each weekend to the Arcade Café for supper unless my father never made it home on payday from his job pumping gas and greasing cars at some Gulf or Atlantic station on the South Side. Then Friday's walk became a humiliating search, block by block, beer joint

As I Was Walking Down Carson Street

after beer joint, as my mother bitterly observed that one day my father was going to run out of gas stations on the South Side, but he was never going to run out of beer joints.

There were also those weekday walks down Carson, first to Humboldt Grade School on Nineteenth Street, where I leered at dirty pictures in the schoolyard without really knowing what I was leering at. It was in the dingy halls of Humboldt, torn down in 1958 and replaced by Phillips School, named after a Pittsburgh civic leader who led the fight in the 1930s for the sterilization of the unfit, where my classmates and I misbehaved at air-raid drills and had to listen to our sixth-grade homeroom teacher, with cheeks like painted turds, tell us we were unfit to be Americans. If we were worth the bother, she'd march us right down to the Arcade to see *I Was a Communist for the FBI* instead of those stupid monster movies at the Colonial and the Rex. Not only was the FBI movie made on the South Side, it was a good warning about the threat of Communism, especially right here in Pittsburgh with all our steel mills, and a good lesson why even oddball children had to behave in school and grow up to be good citizens.

There were also those later and longer walks down Carson to South High on Tenth Street where in junior high I cut my woodshop class to peek at the girls through a crack in the door of the indoor pool, though I never really saw anything. And it was in senior high that my oddball companions applauded *Blackboard Jungle* for being so cool, though it wasn't, as we claimed, modeled after South High; but gave the finger not the thumb to James Dean in *Rebel Without a Cause* because he played a whiny, rich Central boy. After school and after the movies, there were those strolls to Lipori's or George's, where I listened to oddball girls swap dirty jokes with oddball boys, while the only openly gay student (a "queer" in those days) made everyone nervous by playing Doris Day's "Secret Love" over and over again. It wasn't Arnold's and *Happy Days,* but neither were the nights hanging out in the shadows of the loading dock at Gimbels' warehouse where unfit oddball girls talked dirty and knew what they were talking about, and a game of Truth or Dare was the portal to sexual discovery.

A South Side childhood afloat in working-class alcoholism, whirled about by the political paranoia and sexual confusion of the 1950s, and nearly sunk by chronic job loss hardly seems worth remembering, except perhaps as a reminder of the risk of looking back and a warning never to return. Yet, as important as it became to leave the South Side, I have never been able to shake free of my sense of alienation and loss after I left and have never felt at home except when I return to the South Side. I have spent decades of my life studying, teaching, and writing about literature, but when I lose my temper I still swear like a drunken steelworker and when I teach I always feel close to slipping into that lazy, comfortable Pittsburghese way of clipping off the ending of words and flattening or sometimes even inventing words to suit the occasion or the event.

There are three later South Side memories, of departure, loss, and return, that illustrate why, for some of us, the way out of our childhood also turns out to be the road back home. My memory of departure goes back to the spring of 1961, five years after graduating from South High. I was walking back to the South Side after working all day Saturday as a stockboy at Gimbels Department Store in downtown Pittsburgh. There was nothing eventful about the day at work or the walk home until I started over the Tenth Street Bridge and noticed a small boat circling in the water as two men dragged thick lines in the water. A few minutes after I went over to the railing, I watched the men pull the body of a young man to the surface. I knew drownings were common enough in Pittsburgh's rivers, and with all the bridges there would always be jumpers. They even leaped from bridges, like the ones at Mission Street on the South Side and in Schenley Park, that weren't over water. I also knew about young men and boys who hadn't jumped but still died because of the river—about the B-25 bomber crew that crashed upriver and was never found, about my mother's brother Charlie, who died after swimming in the river on a hot Fourth of July. But after the shock of seeing the matted hair and the pale, bloated face and watching the soaked, dripping body, formally dressed in white shirt and black slacks but oddly absent of shoes and socks, being pulled into the boat, all I could think about, as I walked down the bridge's incline to the South Side, was the horror of swimming in the river and bumping into a corpse floating just under the surface of the water. I also remembered what it was like to be submerged in water so murky you couldn't see your hand in front of your face, and I wondered if the young man had panicked and struggled against the river's green, poisonous cloud before he drowned.

My reasons for going away to college that fall had far more to do with wanting to play college basketball than seeing a drowned corpse but that moment on the Tenth Street Bridge is far more vivid and memorable as an image of departure than any industrial or park district game I played against local ex-college players like Pitt's All-American Don Hennon. Just as five years later, it was another death, that of my father, that turned a marriage and graduate school from thoughts of a new life into feelings of loss and exile.

My father died a little more than a year after a bakery truck he was directing out of the driveway of yet another South Side gas station rolled over and crushed his foot. When my mother phoned me at Kent State to let me know my father was back in the hospital, her call was different from the one she made to Edinboro a year earlier. There was no shock this time, no strained voice telling me my father was probably going to lose his foot. Instead of hearing about the pins holding my father's foot together and the threat of gangrene, I listened to my mother's tired voice tell me she had put my father in the hospital because he stopped taking care of himself and finally just wouldn't get out of bed.

As we walked up to South Side Hospital, my mother told me what the doctor had said to her. My father was depressed about losing his foot and needed medication and treatment. The doctor even wanted to know if there was any history of mental illness in our family. My

291

mother also warned me that my father was so bad he might not say anything or even recognize us. But when we got to the hospital ward, my father did seem to recognize us and did say something when he saw me, though it was only the phrase, "Apples, peaches, pears, or plums."

Those were the last words my father ever said. By the next morning, he had slipped into a coma and a few hours later he was dead. While my mother and I sat in the private room where my father had been moved and where we had listened to his death rattle, I couldn't explain to her why the doctor had said my father wasn't right in his head when any fool could see he was dying; but I could explain my father's last words. The day before, when my father saw me, he had remembered a game of ball I played as a child down on Merriman Way where the players would take the name of a fruit. Then one of the players would grab the ball, yell out, "Apples, peaches, pears, or plums," throw it straight up into the air, and call out the fruit of another player. That player, if he caught the ball on the fly, would repeat the ritual; but if the ball hit the ground before he caught it, he would yell out, "Freeze," take aim, and try to hit one of the players with the ball to put him out of the game.

As I listened to my mother's anger, the same anger that would sustain her when the local priest tried to prevent my father's burial in his parents' plot at St. Casimir's Cemetery, I realized my father had probably drifted back the day before to his own playing time and chanted the words of a game we had both played in our childhood down on Merriman Way. I could imagine my father hearing again the name of his fruit called out by his brother Tony or Joky and running after the flung ball before it bounced crazily on the alley's red bricks. If he ran fast enough, he could catch the ball on the fly, yell out, "Apples, peaches, pears, or plums," before tossing the ball high into the air and calling out the name of Tony's or Joky's fruit. If the ball bounced or was dropped, he had to race down the alley to get safely beyond throwing distance before one of his brothers yelled, "Freeze," and tried to put him out of the game.

Over the years I have come to associate my memory of a drowned young man with my decision to leave the South Side, but the memory of my poor dead father and my angry, grieving mother is the reminder that I'm still my father's son and my home will always be the South Side of my mother. Norman Mailer once wrote that "to return to an old neighborhood and discover that it has disappeared is a minor woe for some but it is close to a psychological catastrophe for others, an amputation." My father and I have both experienced the pain of amputation; and my mother and I have suffered through psychological catastrophe.

Not long ago, my wife and I drove back into Pittsburgh on a summer Saturday night just as fireworks started to explode in the sky above Three Rivers Stadium. I remember the look on her face when I told her I was glad Pittsburgh was finally going out of its way to welcome me home. But as we drove past a well-lighted Three Rivers Stadium, past the trendy Station Square, and headed into the swarm of traffic and people that had descended upon the South Side's thriving new nightlife, my memories and emotions connected me to a ghostly ballpark filled with my best memories, to a dead father made vulnerable by the struggles of a working-class life, and to an enduring mother waiting for me and still faithful to the South Side of my childhood.

Richard F. Peterson teaches at Southern Illinois University. He is the editor of Crab Orchard Review *and the SIU Writing Baseball series. His current project is "Growing Up with Clemente," a memoir about Pittsburgh in the 1950s.*

Ghost Story

JAN BEATTY

> The child senses that a woman tore him from herself, alive, covered with blood, and sent him rolling outside the world, and he feels himself an outcast.
>
> —JEAN-PAUL SARTRE

When I was growing up, I found my most profound sense of home in books—not the Great Books, but the cheesy mysteries of '60s popular culture—not the sweet inquisitive Nancy Drew, but the less refined Hardy Boys. As a young child, I read the entire series, I lived in them. There is no other way to say it—I *was* Joe Hardy. I would run from the house on summer mornings to hide in the apple orchard behind the neighbors' houses, so I could read in the trees all day to the sound of my mother's voice calling for me. I never answered. Freedom, freedom, the great pleasure of not responding, while dissolving into the new life these books gave me. I went on to assume many identities in the first ten years of my life. I wore black boots and a holster with pearl-handled guns. I pretended to be Paladin. I would pass out "Have Gun Will Travel" cards with a deadly serious conviction. Other days I'd beat up the boys on the playground, then run to church and pray that God wouldn't take my life, sentencing me to everlasting fire. I was fierce in my quest for identity—I needed a life to enter, a face to look like, a story to be in, so I made new stories each day.

How does the idea of "story" first present itself in the life of a child? At what point does one's original narrative begin? Once the child leaves the world of the mother's body? Or before that, in the womb? We've all heard (or heard about) the familiar voice of the mother: "When I was pregnant with you, all I wanted to eat was butter-pecan ice cream. . . . When I brought you home from the hospital, you were all wrapped up in a blue blanket. There was a beautiful full moon that night. . . ." It seems that there would be an indescribable comfort in the knowing of these details—that there was a witness to your arrival, someone who cared enough to pay attention to the first paragraph of your life.

The mother is the only one who can illuminate the tearing and rolling that Sartre talks about. Sure, the doctors and nurses were there, but the mother has access to the primal experience of birthing in a way no one else can translate. I didn't know whose body I was "torn" from until I was in my early thirties. I was adopted at the age of about two months (I'm not sure exactly how old I was). I don't know the concrete details of my arrival, the first few chapters of my life exist as blank, unpeopled pages in my psyche. As a human, this sense of loss has been and continues to be profound. As a writer, does this void affect the way in which I conceptualize "story"? Does not knowing my literal beginnings affect my imaginings and approach to the idea of narrative?

As far as I know, I was born in Roselia Foundling Home in 1952, a home for unwed mothers in Pittsburgh which was run by the Sisters of Charity. As far as I know, which is not nearly far enough. There are ghosts all over the story of my beginnings. No one can be pinned down. Roselia doesn't exist anymore and the records are sealed. A birth certificate takes years to get. The names on the birth certificate don't want to be found. They deny the story. The story itself becomes a ghost.

How does the adopted child conceptualize home out of this ghost world? How do our dreams and imaginings reflect patterns of space and sound in the physical world? In a 1994 interview the esteemed nature writer Barry Lopez talked about these elusive connections:

Jan Beatty

> You begin to put the world together in terms of the sensory perceptions that were regularly reinforced in you as a child. . . . Unconsciously, when I structure an essay, I, probably without realizing it, am working with the way I imagine wind moves in trees, and how one thing moves to another organism through air—very simple things like that.[1]

I know that in real life things are hard to pin down, everyone has a different recollection of happenings, love is lost and found everywhere. But consider this for a moment:

> *After the tearing and rolling, you are an infant*
> *somewhere. In a crib, in a roomful of cribs?*
> *Someone is taking care of you. You don't know who.*
> *Who is the person who picks you up? Is it a woman?*
> *Is it a nun? There is no story in sight, no same*
> *loving face, blood of my blood face. The smells,*
> *the feel of the rolling and tearing are gone—gone*
> *where? No face who has your face. No way of*
> *knowing who is who, what hands are these?*
> *Why are they different every time? There is no*
> *bonding taking place. The story is fractured here*
> *and forever after. Then strangers come to gaze*
> *at you, touch you, wonder about you. They decide*
> *to pluck you out of there and* make you theirs.
> *These strangers will take your name away and*
> *hide it. The government will cooperate. It will*
> *take months and months for this baby trade to be*
> *completed—a baby in exchange for money. Meanwhile,*
> *someone is feeding you. Is it a kind person? What*

---

1. Barry Lopez, *Prosody*, WYEP-FM 91.3 (1994).

*do they smell like? (You will never know these
hands again.) You will be taken to a strange place.
People will start calling you the lucky one, the
chosen baby, no one sees that your story is gone,
that you are being handed off like a football.
From now on, everyone will pretend that your
first story never existed, they will act and want
you to act as if you are one of them—their blood,
their faces, their world. You know that to survive,
you will have to do this, you will have to pass. But
your new "mother" has dark hair and brown eyes,
your "father" has dark hair—their noses are not
like yours, your white blonde hair shines sickly
like the odd light in a bad painting. Later, you look
at your cousins, they have beautiful long eyelashes—
all of them—the same. You value how others
resemble others—you long for it. In first grade
you refuse to make a family tree. Your "parents"
and teacher suggest you make one based on your
new family. You refuse.*

Whenever I have talked with people about my adoption, in almost every case, they want to move on to the "good" news—the part where I search for my birth parents, get a job, go to college. What is that about? Human nature, curiosity, wanting to see how the story progresses? Or, more likely, their inability or unwillingness to stay with discomfort? The problem is, as an adoptee struggling to speak about original loss, that move toward the happy ending once again reinscribes erasure of the "first" story. I have presented them with an irregular story, one that disrupts the myth of the beautiful, happy American family. Maybe even now you're thinking: *At least you had a good home, you could have stayed an orphan, or been stuck in an abusive environment.* And there would be some truth in what you say, but the move to gratitude is a problematic one. In her book, *Journey of the Adopted Self,* Betty Jean Lifton talks about the psyche of the adoptee: "As children, they feel controlled by adoptive parents who cannot or will not tell them what they need to know. Gratitude is the unspoken currency they are expected to pay. Once they move out of the adoptive home, they are determined never to go into emotional debt again."[2] Even now, as I write this, it's as if I can feel you wanting me to be grateful, that old familiar feeling of someone wanting to amend the story to focus on the "nice" parts. I'm feeling like a ghost again.

So, back to the rolling and tearing. What would happen if I tried to write the pre-verbal history of myself? I'd have to lie, make up stories—the same thing other writers do. But is there a difference in my conceptualization of "story" because I have no access to my own beginnings? What about formal structure and connections made in my poetry? Is the structure of a stanza of poetry, for example, a product of my relationship to that "lack" of original narrative? Consider the movement of this excerpt from my poem, "Boneshaker":

> . . . *Tonight I'll tell you the lie of the story:*
> *It was sky blue. A sitting room with one rocking*
> *chair and your hands, large and soft, cupping*
> *my head of no hair. And every time you whispered*
> *to me your voice a warm stream of air and*
> *no one else was alive or dead. And when you*
> *whispered goodbye, it sounded like every other*
> *word and that warmth never happened again. Then*
> *there was nothing, and then nothing, and nothing*
> *for a very long time. And all that yearning went*
> *nowhere and I became a face looking up,*

2. Betty Jean Lifton, *Journey of the Adopted Self* (New York: Basic Books, Harper-Collins, 1994), 116–17.

*waiting to see home and home
never came.*

I'm interested in creating fault lines in
narrative, through unexpected structure, a sometimes long string of
enjambed lines, to give the feeling of a
breathless
falling.

There are many enjambed lines (lines that do not end on a "natural speech pause") in the previous stanza from "Boneshaker." What are the politics of form in a poem about this bonding, written by the adoptee? Is this an accident? I want the story—but I want it fractured, broken, and bleeding. This desire arrives on the page from some subconscious place, some place that defines the "real" as complicated and difficult. And when I revise my work, I often continue this choice in a conscious way—to maintain complications and deliver the reader to a lack of resolution. Not for the cheap drama, but for the sensation of longing, never getting, the dread/anticipation of the ghost story.

As writers, how do we negotiate the wound inside us? Everyone has their sorrows. When I first started to write poetry, I had trouble with the beginnings of poems. I couldn't find a place inside me that seemed like a place to start. The only way I could think of beginning was to stare at a painting until I "got lost," until I forgot my own thoughts. And then I'd begin with whatever came to me, starting maybe with a color, an image, then jumping off into something else, trying not to make sense or even think of sense. The poems that I wrote, in the end, had nothing literally to do with the painting (if there was a boat in the painting, there probably wasn't a boat in the poem)—but perhaps what was translated was some internal logic of the painting, some felt truth. As the adoptee, I looked to the outside, to the image of a stranger to find my world. Many artists, I'm sure, use the art of others as the provocative moment—the moment of conception for a poem. I'm noticing, though, the parallel of the adopted child looking for a place to begin in the eyes of others (her adopted parents)/looking to the physicality of others for some moment of recognition of *something*. I like beginning in the middle. I have an aversion to the happy ending, whether it is written well or not. I have an aversion to the straight narrative, the expected structure of a sentence, a line, a stanza. As the adoptee I'm subconsciously committed to returning to the unreturnable place—the moment of birth. As a writer I'm driven to recreate the movement of rolling and tearing that Sartre referred to—as a way to enact what can't be grasped, but at least to evoke a feeling of continuing—not toward any certain order, but only to more rolling. And yes, of course, other writers could claim the same thing. I'm not interested, though, in theorizing this desire for movement as a commentary on the artificial state of narrative as form (that "story" inserted into a frame of linear telling may be forced and limited, for example) but am invested in this visceral drive to locate myself in the movement of this rolling, the rolling that inhabits the space where the "known" narrative of my birth would be. Is any kind of narrative, then, a "lie" for me as an adoptee? The interruption of story in my writing is not an intellectual gesture that comments on the limitations of story, but an artistic choice that springs from a love of, and belief in, story itself.

Along these same lines, how does the adopted child, with her intimate knowledge of broken bonds, approach connections in thought, or metaphorical associations? As an adoptee, how do I traverse the tracks of connection and disconnection of story in my poetry? What is at stake, then, in the dive into image? When I was growing up, my adoptive father was my lifeline. I loved him and looked to him for many years as my only ally in the world. Even so, the images of connection to him and disconnection exist in matrix in this piece of story:

My father and I are walking by the lake and I can

Ghost Story

hear the terrible lapping of the water against
the docks, the small rocks. I am eight years old
and everything is covered with moss, slimy green,
carpeting the small rocks on either side of the
path we walk. It is early morning, 9 AM, and this
is our daily ritual. We walk from the dock at the
end of the street to the small store at the beach,
where I will get a goody bar or a creamsicle. This
is 1960. This is no convenience store, but a small,
family-owned shop with wooden floors and a stale
smell. I love my father. Every morning I wait for
the walk, the time when it is just him and me.
No world. No one else. We will walk down to the
end of Shady Lane and it is just twenty paces
until I start to feel free of the cottage we share
with my cousins, my mother and sister, my aunts
and uncles. Where we sleep 4 to a bed, all we can
afford for one week a year, it is our vacation,
the best a working-class household can muster. We
hold hands during the one-mile walk and I
hold my breath to escape the stink of rotting
wood, lumps of seaweed, dead fish floating
near the shore. Still, there is the terrible
lapping that never stops. I hold my breath for
as long as I can, trying to look content and
peaceful. Then I turn my head away from
the lake, take in one long gulp of air, and resume
the holding in. I never tell my father I am doing this.
I try to listen well, nod my head, speak in short
phrases, keep my eyes straight ahead, and be with
my father. There is a lot of silence, which I like.
It is absolutely imperative that I don't let my
father know how much I hate the smell of this

Jan Beatty

lake, I am afraid we will never take this walk
again, that our time will be gone forever. This
is my father, my ally, and still the underpinnings
of this fear are tremendous.

I am the adopted child, the ghost in the story. I need to remain visible in an acceptable way, or all bets are off. I need to appear as a biological child might appear, which of course is no one way. This is part of the terror of the child's story: she is trying to build a right way to be—out of nothing—out of watching others, trying to figure out what it is they are doing to try to make themselves acceptable children. Isn't this, in a way, what the writer does? Create a narrative out of fragments, out of watching and weighing? But this is the life of the untold story bearing down on the heart of the child like a Mack truck on a dark interstate—the pressure felt with no explanation, the no belonging, no resembling, the no imprinting of the adopted child living in a dead landscape where no story keeps her alive.

Is it strange that my first book of poems, *Mad River*, begins with "If This Is Sex, It Must Be Tuesday," a poem about my conception? Or is it the only way that makes sense for a writer/adoptee? As far as I know, my birth mother was a poor woman from Garfield. As far as I know, she had a "thing" for hockey players and used to go to hockey games every Tuesday night. As far as I know, my birth father played for the Pittsburgh Hornets.

If This Is Sex, It Must Be Tuesday

*So it was every week, on a Tuesday,
that you and your friend, Ginny,
strayed from the dance at St. Anselm's
to Duquesne Gardens, feigning interest
in hockey, waiting to get laid.
I can picture it—you in fake cashmere*

Ghost Story

> *with pearl buttons, a gabardine skirt*
> *that hit you at midcalf, you and Ginny*
> *shuffling popcorn till last period,*
> *when you'd freshen your lips with* TORRID RED
> *for the after game party at the Webster Hall dorms.*
> *After all, these were the Pittsburgh Hornets,*
> *this was 1951, and you were a poor Irish girl*
> *from Garfield with a hard drive for excitement,*
> *and hockey was it, getting cross-checked by the best,*
> *having stories to tell in your lean, checkered life,*
> *left with no father, a reluctant sister,*
> *and a mother who cleaned houses for the rich.*
> *So when did I happen, this one-night stand*
> *with the MVP after his big, icy win,*
> *the second Tuesday in February, or the third?*
> *Do you remember the feel of his hands on you?*
> *Were they rough, or tender, were they bloody*
> *from fighting? And when your belly grew into*
> *the body you never wanted, did you curse me,*
> *try to cut me? Should I say you did your best,*
> *a spare girl from a broken family,*
> *or should I say it straight—*
> *you wanted it, you took it, like we all do,*
> *you lied to save yourself, you gave away*
> *part of your heart, you couldn't*
> *wish it right.*[3]

What are the politics involved in writing this poem? These images are deliberately created out of a nothingness that is my birth. These concrete details (the cashmere, the gabardine, the blood) are manufactured (not that all "truth" is not), and certainly—poetry is not autobi-

---

3. Jan Beatty, *Mad River* (Pittsburgh: University of Pittsburgh Press, 1995), 5.

ography. I am the ghost writer who makes up the story of my own beginnings—not for a feeling of safety, but as an act of revolution: I am because I say I am. Here is where I come from—if someone knows different, they need to come forward. This is the birth of the author, not the death. Does the hypervigilance of the adopted child who watches patterns and images to survive—does this translate into the ultra awareness of the writer, into a desire to dive into image as a way to get lost, to mirror that original loss? Do these enjambed lines lean over the edge of the stanza's cliff as a metaphor for all this knowing/ not knowing? I don't know. If you are balking at these ideas, recognize that I am not trying to psychoanalyze, but to notice patterns, parallels. And if you continue to leap into the position of, *That happens for everyone . . .* , then I'll ask you: What is embedded in your position of leaping ahead into erasure, of not entertaining this idea? Are you turning your head away from the complications of loss? If so, what *is* this rush toward the happy ending?

During the walks with my father, in that isolated mile of time, I felt as close as I ever did to having a piece of real story:

> *My father has become my ally, my grounding*
> *force. He sees me in a way no one does. He does*
> *not try to change me. As we walk, I know that*
> *the end of this path is coming. I can't accept*
> *its ending. I want the world to be me and my*
> *father, no one else. As we walk past other*
> *cottages, I wonder what the families are*
> *doing inside? Are their children real? Do*
> *they all look alike? We come out into the*
> *open and the terrible lapping stops. But the*
> *terrible openness begins. Who will know that*
> *I am not real? Can they tell with one glance?*
> *Is my father afraid too? I don't think so. Will*

Ghost Story

I do something wrong that will give me away?

The writer is a maker of patterns, a recorder of noticings of sounds, smells, etc. The adopted child monitors these patterns with the hypervigilance of a prisoner, out of a relentless sense of the provisional. The child looks up at the soft red face of the father, it is too dangerous to breathe in and out, the father taking the child's hand by the lake, the incomprehensible importance of the single gesture, the small waves—no, not waves, but rolls of water hitting the sidewall of the path they're on. I'm looking at my father's soft red face. I smile with my breath held. And, returning to the story—is the only redemption for the adopted child buried in the choice to inhabit the position of storyteller? To become the ghost writer? To somehow make it real?

> *We are happy, happy in the terrible passage*
> *of time. How could I freeze this moment—*
> *me and him forever? No one else, no one in.*
> *Fish heads, planks of wood, everything oily*
> *and saturated, things cast off in the hungry*
> *lake. Did he think I was being too quiet?*
> *Give me the terrible water, the gulping*
> *of air—you can keep the world, with its*
> *families, its horribly solid shapes—*
> *I'll be the ghost walking into the woods.*

Jan Beatty's collection of poetry, Mad River, **won the Agnes Lynch Starrett Prize from the University of Pittsburgh Press, and was a finalist in The Great Lakes Colleges Association Award for New Writing in 1995. Other awards include the 1995 State Street Prize for her chapbook,** Ravenous, **the Pablo Neruda Prize for Poetry, and two fellowships from the Pennsylvania Council on the Arts. Her work has appeared in journals such as** Poetry East, Quarterly West, Southern Poetry Review, *and* Witness. *Cur-*

Jan Beatty

rently Beatty teaches writing at the University of Pittsburgh and hosts and produces Prosody, *a public radio show on WYEP-FM, featuring the work of local and national writers.*

CREATIVE NONFICTION

True Stories & Great Writing

equal

CREATIVE NONFICTION

For a subscription and more information, contact us:
Creative Nonfiction
5501 Walnut St., Suite 202
Pittsburgh, PA 15232
Tel: 412 688-0304
Fax: 412 683-9173
E-mail: lgu+@pitt.edu

Begin with 3 Pittsburgh authors
Why these authors?
Why Pittsburgh?

- Industrial Hometown:
  Post World-War II Pittsburgh
- A City to Call Home: Identity
  The Search for Place in
  Post-World War II Pittsburgh.

A Place to Call Home:
City and Identity in Post-WWII
Pittsburgh Novels.